Edexcel GCE History

Britain and the Nationalist Challenge in India 1900–47

Rosemary Rees

Series editors: Martin Collier   Rosemary Rees

Unit 2 Student Book

A PEARSON COMPANY

Published by Pearson Education Limited, a company incorporated in England and Wales, having its registered office at Edinburgh Gate, Harlow, Essex, CM20 2JE. Registered company number: 872828

www.pearsonschoolsandfecolleges.co.uk

Edexcel is a registered trade mark of Edexcel Limited

Text © Pearson Education 2010

First published 2010

12 11 10

10 9 8 7 6 5 4 3 2

British Library Cataloguing in Publication Data

A catalogue record for this book is available from the British Library

ISBN 978 1 846 90504 9

Edited by Karen Hemingway

Typeset by Florence Production Ltd, Stoodleigh, Devon

Original illustrations © Pearson Education Limited 2010

Illustrated by Paul Higgins, part of H2ink

Picture research by Elena Goodinson

Cover photo/illustration © Getty Images: AFP/Dibyangshu Sarkar

Printed in China (GCC/02)

Disclaimer

This material has been published on behalf of Edexcel and offers high-quality support for the delivery of Edexcel qualifications.

This does not mean that the material is essential to achieve any Edexcel qualification, nor does it mean that it is the only suitable material available to support any Edexcel qualification. Edexcel material will not be used verbatim in setting any Edexcel examination or assessment. Any resource lists produced by Edexcel shall include this and other appropriate resources.

Copies of official specifications for all Edexcel qualifications may be found on the Edexcel website: www.edexcel.com

Contents

The Edexcel Specification Unit 2 Option D2 'Britain and the Nationalist Challenge in India 1900–47' does not require any specific knowledge of relationships between India and Britain prior to 1900. Unit 1 is provided as background for this course, and for those undertaking a wider study for coursework or for another Awarding Body.

Acknowledgements

The author and publisher would like to thank the following individuals and organisations for permission to reproduce the following material:

Photographs
pp. 2, 13: Punch Limited; pp. 6, 7: British Library Images Online; p. 8: The Chester Beatty Library; pp. 9, 37: Mary Evans Picture Library; pp. 25, 132: Popperfoto; p. 33: Images of Empire; p. 44: Press Association Images; p. 61: Print Collector / HIP; p. 62: In Flanders Fields Museum; p. 74 (right): Aquarius Collection: Columbia; p. 74 (left): BFI National Archive; pp. 81, 157: National Army Museum; p. 88: British Cartoon Archive, University of Kent www.cartoons.ac.uk: Solo Syndication/ Associated Newspapers Ltd/ David Low; pp. 91, 116, 187: Corbis: Bettmann; p. 95: TopFoto: Dinodia; p. 111: Hulton-Deutsch Collection; p. 117: AFP / Jewel Samad; p. 137: Time & Life Pictures; pp. 138, 151, 179: Getty Images: Hulton Archive; p. 167: The National Library of Wales; p. 179.

Written sources
p. 6: Stephen Ashton, *The British in India: from Trade to Empire*, Batsford, an imprint of Anova Books; p. 11: *A History of India: Volume 2* by Percival Spear (Penguin Books 1965, Revised edition 1970). Copyright © Percival Spear, 1965, 1970. Reproduced by permission of Penguin Books Ltd; pp. 13, 34, 102, 113, 120, 172, 173: *Raj: The Making and Unmaking of British India* by Lawrence James (Little, Brown Book Group 1997); pp. 16, 18, 26, 126, 186, 197: From *Plain Tales from the Raj* by Charles Allen, published by Century. Reprinted by permission of The Random House Group Ltd; pp. 19, 24: From 'Women of the Raj' by Margaret MacMillan. © 1988 Margaret MacMillan. Reprinted by kind permission of Thames & Hudson Ltd, London; p. 21: Ian Copland, *India 1885–1947*, Longman, 2001; p. 22: W. Schlote, *British Overseas Trade from 1700 to the 1930s*, Blackwell 1952. By permission of Wiley-Blackwell; pp. 23, 34, 67, 102, 120, 128, 130, 144, 187: *Modern India: the Origins of an Asian Democracy* by Judith M. Brown (1994) By permission of Oxford University Press, Inc.; pp. 29, 98, 133, 139, 141, 147: Frank Moraes, *Witness to an Era*, Weidenfeld and Nicholson, London; pp. 29, 198: Nirad Chaudhuri, *The Autobiography of an Unknown Indian*, Macmillan 1951; pp. 36, 67: *A History of India* © 2000 John Keay. By permission of HarperCollins Publishers Ltd; pp. 39, 179: *A New History of India* by Stanley Wolpert. By permission of Oxford University Press, Inc.; p. 66: Denis Judd, *Empire*, Harper Collins, 1996; p. 95: Dorothy McLeish (Arvind Nehra), *Letters of a Indian Judge to an English Gentlewoman*, Random House, by permission of David Higham Associates; pp. 105, 111, 116, 169, 198: From *Indian Tales of the Raj* by Zareer Masani, published by BBC Books; p. 129: Tim Leadbeater *Britain and India 1845–1947*, Hodder Education, 2008 © Tim Leadbeater. Reproduced by permission of Hodder & Stoughton Ltd; pp. 130, 132: Ayesha Jalal, *The Sole Spokesman*, Cambridge University Press, 1985; pp. 156, 168: *Liberty or Death* © 1997 Patrick French. By permission of HarperCollins Publishers Ltd; p. 180: © Pamela Mountbatten, *India Remembered* (Pavilion Books, 2007).

Every effort has been made to contact copyright holders of material reproduced in this book. Any omissions will be rectified in subsequent printings if notice is given to the publishers.

The publisher would like to thank Alexander Bristow for his helpful advice.

Introduction

On 14 August 1947, Jawaharlal Nehru, India's first prime minister, addressed the Indian Constituent Assembly. This is part of what he said:

Source A

Long years ago we made a tryst with destiny, and now the time comes when we shall redeem our pledge. At the stroke of the midnight hour, while the world sleeps, India will awake to life and freedom. A moment comes, which comes but rarely in history, when we step out from the old to the new, when an age ends, and when the soul of a nation, long suppressed, finds utterance.

From Jawaharlal Nehru to the Indian Constituent Assembly on 14 August 1947

India had finally won independence from Britain. How had this happened? It happened through vision and planning, intrigue and betrayal, desperation and ambition, violence and bloodshed. India, in 1900, was the land of **maharajahs** with their fabled wealth, glittering palaces, harems and private armies; it was the land where young British officers and civil servants played polo, indulged in tiger hunts and joined gentlemen's clubs, while at the same time subduing rebellions and running a vast country teeming with people, wealth and promise. It was a land of Hindu and Muslim, Jain, Sikh and Christian, with their different belief systems, values and practices. It was a land where Nationalism was becoming a heady idea and a growing force. By 1947, two independent countries, India and Pakistan, stood where once had been Britain's Indian Empire. The story of how this happened is the subject of this book.

Definition

Maharajah
An Indian prince: the ruler of a native state.

Source B

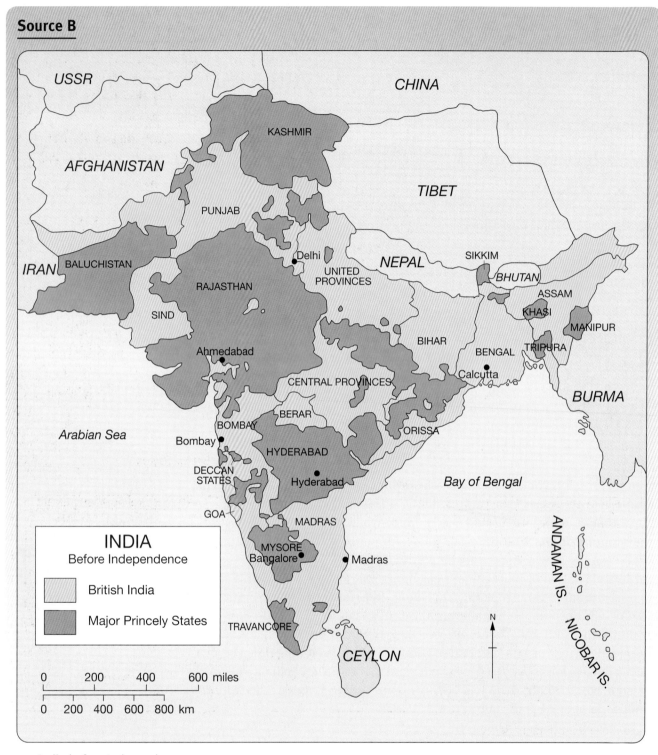

0.1 India before Independence

Source C

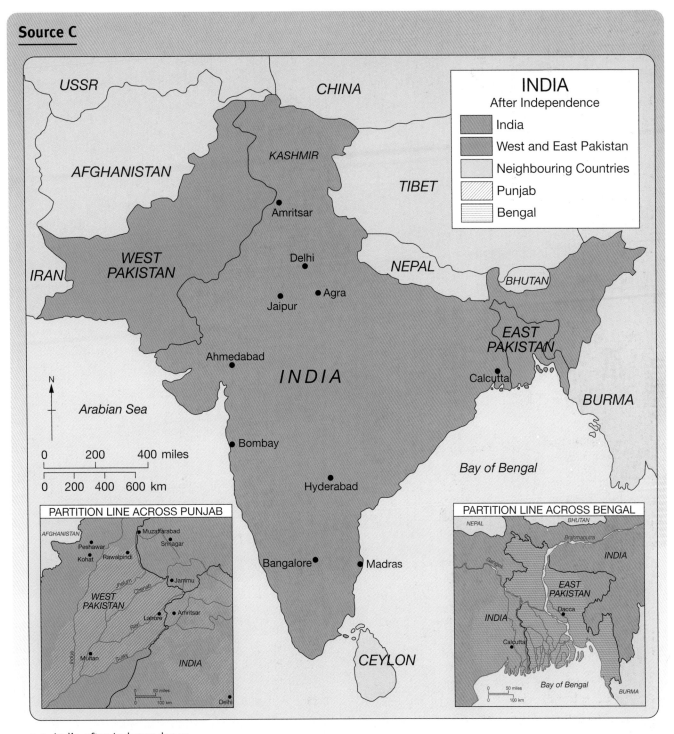

0.2 India after Independence

Discussion point

How useful are maps to an historian?

SKILLS BUILDER

1 Compare Sources B and C. What basic differences in the maps can you spot?

2 What questions would you want to ask about the process whereby the first map changed into the second one?

3 Compare your questions with others in your group and build up a set of questions about India 1900–47. This book should answer them all!

1 From East India Company to Raj

What is this unit about?

This unit focuses on the relationship between Britain and India in the years before 1900. It traces the development of that relationship from one that began with trade and ended with the British government taking responsibility for running almost the whole continent. In it you will:

- find out how the East India Company became a powerful force within India
- learn why the British government took over the running of India from the East India Company
- explore the relationship between British and Indian people before 1900.

In order to understand about the attitudes of individuals and governments after 1900, it is important that you understand how they got to that point and which events and their outcomes coloured how the struggle for Indian independence was to proceed in the twentieth century.

Key questions

- Why did the 'rule' of the East India Company come to an end?
- To what extent was the Indian Mutiny of 1857 a turning point in relationships between the British and Indians?

Timeline

1530	Death of Babur, first Mughal emperor, who controlled most of northern India
1660	Mughal Empire extends over most of India and Afghanistan
1698	Charter granted to the British East India Company giving it a monopoly of trade with India
By 1740	British, Dutch, French and Portuguese establish trading stations in India
1751	Siege of Arcot makes Robert Clive's reputation and marks the beginning of the decline of French power in India
1757	Battle of Plassey leaves Robert Clive in control of Bengal
By 1763	Private involvement in Bengal's trade amounts to over £500,000
1784	British government sets up the Board of Control in London to oversee the activities of the East India Company
1788	Governor-General Warren Hastings impeached
1857	Indian Mutiny
1858	British government passes Government of India Act, transferring all rights and powers of the East India Company directly to the British Crown

| 1876 | Queen Victoria becomes Empress of India |
| 1877 | Most of India's princes accept Queen Victoria as their empress |

Introduction

Source A

"NEW CROWNS FOR OLD ONES!"
(ALADDIN adapted.)

1.1 Cartoon by John Tenniel, *Punch*, 15 April 1876

Caption: 'New Crowns for Old Ones' (Aladdin adapted.)   Credit: ©Punch Limited / TopFoto

SKILLS BUILDER

Discuss these questions in your group.

1 What point is John Tenniel making in Source A?

2 What does the cartoon have to say about Britain's relationship with India?

Before you can begin to answer the Skills Builder questions on this page, you need some background information about the cartoon. The man on the left is the Prime Minister of Great Britain, Benjamin Disraeli. He is dressed up as Aladdin, a storybook character who had a magic lamp in which lived a genie who could do absolutely anything. He is offering a crown labelled 'India' to Queen Victoria. In 1876, Parliament agreed that Queen Victoria should add 'Empress of India' to her many titles.

At the very least, you should have teased out that Great Britain had some form of control over the Indian sub-continent, and that this was probably political control because it is the prime minister who is offering the empress' crown to Queen Victoria. You might also have thought that India must have been important to Great Britain because the Queen is about to become Empress of India.

However, India was half a world away from Great Britain. In the days before air travel, it took as long as six months to reach the ports on India's west coast and even longer to reach the inland towns and cities and the ports on the eastern seaboard. Why would anyone bother? What was the connection between India and Great Britain? In order to discover this, and to understand some of the attitudes and actions of the British and the Indian people, you will need to know something about Britain's involvement in India.

How and why did the British become involved in India?

In the mid-1730s, so the story goes, a schoolboy called Robert Clive truanted from school and climbed to the top of the church steeple in the Shropshire town of Market Drayton. Once there, he sat on the weather vane and shouted down gleefully at the passers-by. Thirty years later, this daredevil younger son of a small landowner was an MP and fabulously rich. In 1772 he was made Lord Lieutenant of Shropshire. How had he managed this? The answer, quite simply, is 'India'.

The British first became seriously involved in India because of trade. They were not the only people, however, to want a share of India's cotton and calico, muslins, chintzes, pepper, indigo and spices. By 1740 the Dutch, French and Portuguese, as well as the British, had established trading stations in India.

The Dutch and English companies depended on private finance; the Portuguese and French companies were funded by their respective governments. The various trading companies regularly shipped gold and silver as well as wool and metals from Europe to their company 'factories' in India, which were really fortified trading stations, and almost always situated on the coast. There they were exchanged for goods the Europeans wanted. In the early days, spices dominated the Indian-European trade; by the end of the eighteenth century, Indian textiles had overtaken spices as the 'must have' commodity back in Europe.

What part did the East India Company play in the British economy?

All British trade with India was run by the East India Company, based in Leadenhall Street in the City of London. Its operations were governed by a charter of 1698, which allowed it to have a **monopoly of trade** with India in return for certain financial restrictions and restrictions on the sort of goods that could be traded. More importantly, the charter allowed for East India Company affairs to be debated in Parliament. So right from the beginning, there was parliamentary interest in what British merchants were doing in India. There was some measure of control, too: Parliament could always refuse to renew the East India Company's charter.

Company shareholders lived mainly in London and the south-east of England, and were an important part of a complex system of international trade, focused on London. The East India Company was a stable, but unspectacular, part of the British economic scene. It handled about

Definition

Monopoly of trade

Only one company or organisation had the right to trade in a certain area or with a specific country or countries. In this case, the only British company allowed to trade in India was the East India Company.

Source B

Your chintz from Ahmedabad, your chintz from Seringapatam and in general all the coloured goods are profitable commodities, whereof send large quantities, taking care the cloth be good.

From a letter written by the directors of the East India Company in London to their merchants in India in 1698

Question

What was the relationship between the British government and the East India Company?

Definition

Mughal Empire

The Mughal Empire covered northern and central India between the sixteenth and eighteenth centuries, during which it became the heart of an Islamic empire and the centre of Islamic culture and learning.

Definitions

Factor

An agent of a company, usually buying and selling on commission for that company.

Writer

A clerk, usually engaged in writing up invoices, checking payments, ordering goods and, in the days before photocopiers, a lot of copying out where duplicates were needed of anything.

13 per cent of British imports and 5 per cent of Britain's exports. It paid its shareholders around 7 per cent annually. However, the East India Company had an importance far beyond that of keeping its shareholders happy. Its importance lay in the way in which the Company conducted, first, its commercial business in India and, later, the development of this commercial business into political power.

How did the East India Company organise its commercial business in India?

Throughout most of the eighteenth century, the British, like other European traders, were more influenced by India than influencing it. It was the Indian people, finance, products and circumstances that dictated how trade and commerce developed. They, and not the Europeans, created the framework within which trade was possible. It had to be like this. India was not a vast continent inhabited by natives anxious to trade precious commodities for a handful of beads. On the contrary, India had a sophisticated and complex system of government, dominated by the **Mughal Empire** (see pages 7–11) but containing some smaller kingdoms, all of which had well-established trading links, routes and patterns within India, Asia and beyond. British merchants had to work with the systems they found in India.

Trading stations

The East India Company's trading stations in Bombay, Calcutta and Madras acted as secure bases from which the Company operated. Each of the Company's trading stations had its own president, or governor. He was advised by his council, made up of senior and very experienced merchants. Beneath this council were other senior merchants who hadn't quite made it to the council, then the junior merchants, then the **factors** and finally the **writers**. It was a hierarchical society where everyone knew his place. Membership of this hierarchy was highly prized within British professional and commercial families. Indeed, to become a writer (the lowliest person within this structure) a young man, who had to be at least 16 years of age, had to be sponsored by one of the directors of the East India Company. So he, or his family, had to be known to them.

The Company's trading stations at Bombay, Calcutta and Madras each had its own army. These armies were intended to protect the interests of the East India Company. So within the trading stations lived soldiers, surgeons and chaplains too. Other Europeans, not working for the East India Company, managed to live under the Company's protection. Shopkeepers, lawyers and jewellers were among those living in Calcutta in the eighteenth century. Life in the trading stations was anything but narrow and strait-laced. Men with a mind for it could spend their spare time at wild parties, dancing, gambling and getting roaring drunk. Indeed, they must have thought, what else was there to do?

Biography

Robert Clive, First Baron Clive of Plassey (1725–74)

The son of a small Shropshire landowner, Robert Clive joined the East India Company in 1742. He spent three periods in India, each time returning with a larger fortune.

From 1746–53 he fought against the French in India and on his return to England, with a fortune, stood as an MP but failed to be elected. He was sent back to India in 1755 and in June 1757 defeated the *Nawab* of Bengal at the Battle of Plassey. He installed a Company supporter as *nawab* and himself became Governor of the Company's Bengal Presidency. On his return to England Clive became MP for Shropshire (1760) and was given an Irish barony. He went back to India as Governor and Commander-in-Chief of Bengal (1765–67) because there was general chaos and financial disorder in Bengal. After reorganising the Company's army and making several administrative reforms to fight corruption, he returned to England for the last time in 1767.

By this time Clive had acquired a fabulous fortune and in 1772 he was made Lord Lieutenant of Shropshire. However, corruption remained in the East India Company and the Directors were forced to ask the British government to save them from bankruptcy. Clive was blamed for the situation. He was forced to defend himself (1772–73) before a parliamentary committee of enquiry and, although he was completely exonerated, he committed suicide in 1774.

Land of opportunity?

Many young men, recruited by the Company to be writers like **Robert Clive**, died on the journey to India. Once there, still more succumbed to malaria, cholera and other tropical diseases against which they had no protection. Others lived out lives of monumental boredom, suffering from the ills of the climate, the distance from home and the tedium of the job. But for some, it was very different. India was the place, and the East India Company the organisation, where young men with daring, bravery, cunning, greed and a great deal of luck, were able to make their fortunes, as the story of Robert Clive shows. In the eighteenth century, a letter from London to India could take as long as six months to arrive. This gave the Company men in India a pretty free hand to make on-the-spot decisions. They had come to India to make their fortune and they acted accordingly.

Private trade and private fortunes

Every single person entering the East India Company as a writer had to sign a covenant with the Company by which they agreed to 'good behaviour' and 'fair dealings'. This must have been very loosely interpreted! Hundreds of men employed by the East India Company as writers, factors and merchants did a lot of work on the side. Using the protection of the Company, they built up complex 'private' trade networks, working in a totally private capacity and for their own, not the Company's, profit. They usually worked with Indians, who were experienced in working with established Indian trading networks, and who supplied local knowledge and considerable capital. These private enterprises extended to having a private merchant fleet based on Calcutta

---

Discussion point

'A corrupt organisation staffed by greedy men.'

How far would you agree with this view of the East India Company and its activities in India? Discuss this in your group. When you have collected evidence on both sides, you could set up a formal debate and reach an argued conclusion. Remember to stick to the values of the time and not twenty-first century ones!

and to private trading, not only within India, but also around the coast and east to China.

As the East India Company's influence expanded, so did the unofficial activities of its members. By 1763, for example, private involvement in Bengal's trade amounted to over £500,000 – more than the East India Company's annual profit! There can be some excuse for what might seem to be something of a racket. Quite simply, the East India Company did not pay its employees enough to live on and they had to make money in other ways. This money wasn't only made through private trade. To be a company employee meant that relationships with the Indians with whom they did business had to be established and had to be positive. The Indians made sure of this (it was in their interests too) and showered East India Company employees with gifts, as was the Mughal custom. A House of Commons select committee worked out that, in the years 1757–69, East India Company employees received, in Bengal alone, over £2 million in presents – and that was only the gifts they had admitted to receiving!

A meeting of cultures?

It seems that, for most of the eighteenth century, Englishmen and Indians mixed together socially as well as professionally without any obvious problems. But, as the nineteenth century progressed, attitudes began to harden.

Source C

1.2 Painting of William Palmer with his two Indian wives, his daughter and two of his sons, together with three other women by Francesco Renaldi, 1786

Source D

In one area of domestic life, relations between the British and Indians were extremely close. British men were in the habit of setting up zenaras [harems] and living with Indian women. These women were known as 'bibis', Indian wives. Formal marriages were rare, but men and women lived together as husband and wife, having children and raising families. They were in fact married in all but name.

Marriage with a young woman from Britain was so expensive that few of the Company [East India Company] servants could afford it. British wives required carriages, dressmakers, hairdressers, ladies' maids and nannies. Any children had to be sent to school in England, the mother often accompanying them.

From S. Ashton, *The British in India: from Trade to Empire*, published in 1987

Source E

1.3 Painting of a British officer enjoying watching a nautch (a dancing display by professional dancing girls) while smoking a **hookah**, c. 1820

SKILLS BUILDER

How far do Sources C, D and E suggest that the British and Indians met on equal terms?

Definition

Hookah
An Asian pipe for smoking tobacco or marijuana, consisting of a flexible tube with a mouthpiece attached to a container of water through which smoke is drawn and cooled.

Why did commercial involvement in India become political?

In 1767, the East India Company's secretary assured the House of Commons that the Company was only interested in trade in India. '[I]t is commercial interest we look for', he told MPs, who were growing worried at the extent of the Company's involvement in the sub-continent. Ten years later, the Secretary to the Treasury noted that the whole idea of the East India Company exercising political power in India was 'absurd and preposterous'. Yet the Company did increasingly exercise political power within India, whether they denied it or not, whether they liked it or not. How did this come about? There was one main reason: the decline of the Mughal Empire. The collapse of this once great empire created a power vacuum and, as power slipped from Mughal hands, Indian claimants warred with each other at the regional level of politics and government. Commerce and trade inevitably suffer when there is political instability and this was the case in India. In attempting to protect their trading interests, the East India Company was drawn into Indian politics and began to exercise political power.

How powerful was the Mughal Empire?

The first Mughal ruler to invade India was Babur, who held Kabul (in Afghanistan) in 1504 and used it as a base from which to direct raids into northern India. By the time of his death in 1530, Babur was in control of a large area of northern India, including Delhi. His descendants continued his policy of conquest until, at its height in about 1660, the Empire extended throughout most of present-day Afghanistan, Pakistan and all but the southernmost part of India.

Under the Mughals, India was not only the heart of a great Islamic empire, but also a centre of Islamic culture and learning. The courts of the five 'Great Mughals' were luxurious places, sparkling with the richness of jewels and precious metals; they were, too, places of patronage for poets and musicians, artists and architects. A Mughal court – particularly under the Emperor Akbar, who ruled from 1562–1605 – was always on the move. This vast, luxurious tented city, accommodating some 250,000 people, with all the 'buildings' of a royal palace including a harem and mosque, moved steadily throughout the Empire, supporting and hunting, conquering and reconquering.

Definitions

Muslim

Muslims believe that there is one true God, Allah, and that Muhammad is his final prophet. There are five pillars of Islam: a declaration of faith in Allah and belief that Muhammad is the messenger of Allah (*Shahadah*); to pray (*Salah*) five times a day; to fast (*Sawm*) during Ramadan from dawn to sunset; to pay a welfare tax (*Zakah*) for distribution to the poor; and to make a pilgrimage (*Hajj*) to Makkah at least once in a lifetime.

Hindu

Hindus believe that all existence comes from an eternal spiritual truth, *Brahman*. The purpose of life is to understand this truth and to understand one's eternal identity as the *atma*, or soul. The soul is eternal and lives many lifetimes in one human body or in many forms of life. The cycle of rebirth is called *samsara* and the soul moves upwards and downwards on the wheel of rebirth. When true understanding is reached, the soul will be released from the cycle of rebirth.

Source F

1.4 This seventeenth-century painting shows the magnificence of the court of the Emperor Akbar. Here, Akbar is receiving a copy of the *Akbarnama*, a history of his reign written on his orders, from his biographer Abdul-azi.

The Mughals were **Muslims** and yet most of the people in their empire were **Hindu**, with completely different beliefs and customs. These differences are explained in detail in Unit 8 pages 123–25, but here it is sufficient just to realise that, in the seventeenth and eighteenth centuries, Hindu and Muslim could and did live peacefully together. The Emperor Akbar was perhaps the foremost of the 'Great Mughals' in making strenuous efforts to prevent religious discord. Perhaps most importantly, one of his many wives was a Hindu princess from Rajputana. She was particularly favoured because it was her son who succeeded Akbar. This marriage was not only a clever move in terms of relationships between Hindus and Muslims, but it bought the loyalty of the fierce Rajput warriors for the next hundred or so years. Akbar encouraged calm and reasoned debate on religious matters; he promoted leading Hindus to high positions in the Mughal civil service; he abolished the *jizya* – a hated poll tax levied only on Hindus, abolished the tax on pilgrimages to Hindu shrines and positively encouraged the building of Hindu temples and the holding of Hindu festivals.

The Mughal emperors used the **mansabdar** system to generate revenue and to help control their vast empire. The emperor would grant land to a *mansabdar* and, with the land, the right to collect revenue. In return, the *mansabdar* had to promise to provide the emperor with soldiers in time of war. The greater the size of the land granted, the greater the number of soldiers the *mansabdar* had to promise. These agreements could be revoked at any time by the emperor and were non-hereditary. This gave the emperor a large degree of control. Strong emperors, like Akbar, were able to move *mansabdars* around the empire every three to four years, promoting the able by making them larger grants of land and demoting the less proficient by granting them smaller areas of land from which to obtain revenue.

This system worked well when an emperor was strong and local officials trustworthy. However, a weak emperor was in trouble. Corrupt village leaders held back revenue for themselves; *mansabdars* retained revenue, refused to provide soldiers for the emperor and sought power for themselves and their followers. This was one of the main reasons for the collapse of the Mughal Empire. In the 12 years after the death of the Emperor Aurangzeb in 1707, there were ten successive emperors, whereas in the previous 181 years there had only been six.

> **Definition**
>
> **Mansabdar**
>
> A person who held a bureaucratic office in the Mughal Empire.

Source G

1.5 This painting shows the Mughal Emperor Farrukhsiyar (1701–19). A few years after this picture was painted, his most senior official, Husain Ali Khan, plotted against the Emperor and had him strangled.

Jat

Peasant farming caste in Hindu society.

Sikh

Learner or disciple of the Guru. Sikhs believe that there is only one God, before whom everyone is equal and to whom everyone has direct access. Sikhs believe that human beings spend their time in a cycle of birth, life and rebirth, and the quality of each life depends on the law of karma and so is determined by behaviour in the previous life. Escape from the cycle is achieved by total knowledge of, and union with, God.

Maratha

A member of the princely and military classes of the kingdom of Maharashtra.

Nawab

A Muslim title; Muslim nobleman.

Discussion point

What were the strengths and the weaknesses of the Mughal Empire? Talk about this in your group. Try to tease out where power lay and where that power was particularly vulnerable.

This weakness at the top led to the rise of faction and the increase in power of local rulers. In the north, the **Jats** and **Sikhs**, and in the west the *Marathas*, firmly resisted Mughal attempts to govern them. In the south, the ruler of Hyderabad ruled over a large, virtually independent state. As the power of the Mughal emperors weakened, more and more small-scale wars were fought throughout the eighteenth century as rival Indian princes battled for supremacy.

What was the reaction of the East India Company to the collapse of the Mughal Empire?

In this complex and complicated situation, the East India Company was another player with a different set of interests. Their main interest was, of course, trade, but there were other imperatives.

A series of European wars between the French and the British spilled over into India, where the French were traders too. Both sides found allies in rival Indian princes and their factions, and so were drawn into India's political struggles.

The first open confrontation occurred in southern India, where General Dupleix and the French East India Company had built up quite a power base. Both the British and French companies wanted their own nominee as *nawab*, or ruler, of Arcot, the area around Madras. At the end of a long struggle, Robert Clive installed the man the British wanted and supported him with arms and cash. Clive had out-manoeuvred the French, leaving them with only a few small enclaves in southern India.

The French and British again backed different factions in the struggle for control of Bengal, which had been a Mughal stronghold. Clive's intervention was again successful and he defeated the *Nawab* Siraj-ud-Daula at the Battle of Plassey in 1757. Here he was helped by a combination of disgruntled soldiers, landholders and influential merchants whose commercial profits were closely linked to those of the East India Company. Commercial interests were, even at this level, involved and no Indian merchant would be likely to support a side that would not deal well with him afterwards.

When Clive returned to India in 1765, the Mughal Emperor, weak and with his forces defeated by the British at Buxar, had conferred on the East India Company administrative rights over Bengal, Bihar and Orissa, a region of roughly 25 million people with an annual revenue of 40 million rupees. The Emperor made the Company his *diwan*, or chief financial manager. With Clive installed as the first British Governor of Bengal, the British were established as a major political force in India. So it seemed that the East India Company had slipped into some of the Mughal Emperors' shoes, taking up the revenue administration for Bengal, the richest province in India.

The British in India continued to gain power and influence over local Indian rulers. The East India Company was immensely wealthy; it could strike hard bargains with local merchants, it loaned money to minor Indian rulers and, when they defaulted on repayments, took over running their states.

How did the British government react?

Back in Britain there was considerable concern about the activities of the East India Company. It was no longer simply a trading company. It had a huge private army and was actively involved in administering a large part of the Indian sub-continent. It was directly answerable to no one but its shareholders.

The British government tried to achieve some sort of control. In 1784, it set up a Board of Control, based in London, to oversee the Company's affairs. The government also created the post of Governor-General for the Company, who was answerable to the Board of Control. To some extent this worked. In 1788, Warren Hastings, who was the first Governor-General of British India from 1773 to 1786, was ordered to appear before the House of Lords, charged with ruthlessness and corruption. After a trial lasting nine years, he was finally acquitted, but that didn't stop concerns about the activities of the East India Company rumbling on. Historian Percival Spear describes the attitude of Governor-General Cornwallis, 1786–93, to the Indians who worked for him:

Source I

Cornwallis had a strong sense of Indian shortcomings. 'Every native of India, I believe,' he wrote, 'is corrupt.' His view of his own countrymen in India was not very different, but whereas he saw a cure for them he could see none at the time for Indians. So all high Indian officials were dismissed and all posts worth more than £500 a year reserved for Europeans. This measure marked the Company's service with an incredibly foreign stamp, and its effects were felt right down to 1947.

From Percival Spear, *A History of India*, published in 1965

Sir Thomas Munro, a British administrator, warned of the dangers of British rule:

Source J

Foreign conquerors have treated the natives with violence, and often with great cruelty, but none has treated them with so much scorn as we; none has unfairly described the whole people as unworthy of trust, as incapable of honesty, and as fit to be employed only where we cannot do without them. It seems to be not only ungenerous, but unwise, to criticise the character of a people fallen under our rule.

From a letter written by Sir Thomas Munro to the Governor-General in 1818

Source H

The government of an exclusive company of merchants is perhaps the worst of all governments for any country whatever.

From Adam Smith, *The Wealth of Nations*, published in 1776

Discussion point

Read Source H. Do you agree with Adam Smith's view of the East India Company's power in India?

SKILLS BUILDER

How far does Source J challenge the attitudes of Governor-General Cornwallis, as described in Source I?

Rebellion! May 1857

Trouble was to hit the East India Company in May 1857. A rising of Indian soldiers within the Company's Bengal army turned into a widespread rebellion involving a number of different grievances.

One of the most significant grievances concerned the conditions of service of the soldiers in the Bengal army. In 1856, the General Enlistment Order imposed the same conditions on **sepoys** serving in the Bengal, Bombay and Madras armies. All *sepoys* were expected to serve wherever the East India Company decided to send them, even abroad. At a stroke, this removed a privilege from the *sepoys* in the Bengal army – the payment of *batta*, an allowance payable if they served 'abroad'.

The trigger for the rebellion appeared to come from the cartridges issued for use with the new Enfield rifle in 1857. The rifles' cartridges were supposedly greased with tallow containing both pork and beef fat. As beef fat was repugnant to the Hindu religion and pork fat offended Muslim beliefs, the *sepoys* refused to use them. The offending cartridges were quickly withdrawn, but the damage had been done. All existing cartridges were suspect as was virtually all official government issue, including such items as flour and cooking oil.

A particularly insensitive handling of the situation in Meerut, an important garrison town about 60 kilometres from Delhi, started the conflagration. There, the garrison commander court-martialled 85 Indians for refusing to use suspect cartridges and publicly humiliated them. The following day, 10 May, the *sepoys* mutinied, began massacring Europeans and marched to Delhi, gathering support as they went. Once in Delhi, they pledged support to the somewhat bemused elderly Mughal emperor who had 'ruled' harmlessly from the Red Fort for over 20 years, with neither subjects nor troops.

Mutiny spread quickly throughout the Bengal army. Within weeks most of the garrisons in the north-west provinces and Oudh were in rebel hands, the British officers, their wives and children slaughtered.

The rebellion wasn't simply a military one. Civilian rebellion spread rapidly across the Gangetic Plain as whole areas of British authority collapsed. There was no carefully planned, orchestrated rebellion. It was more a series of localised responses to separate and different fears of new influences and changing patterns of authority. The revolt spread down the Ganges valley to Agra, Lucknow and Cawnpore. British forces and their families were taken prisoner and murdered. As word of the murders spread, British reprisals were terrible. Entire villages were torched; unarmed Indians and even domestic servants were attacked, mutilated and murdered. Fear and hatred destroyed the bridges that many had so carefully built between Indian and British. Gradually order was restored, but it took until December 1857 before the key strategic points along the Ganges valley were reoccupied and a further five months before all resistance was stamped out.

Definition

Sepoy

A soldier in the Indian army.

It is important to realise that huge areas of India were untouched by this rebellion. Beyond the Gangetic Plain and parts of central India, there were very few disturbances in 1857–58. Bengal, Madras and Bombay were quiet. Even where there were disturbances, there were many instances of Indians loyally defending the British for whom they worked. Indeed, in the Punjab, Sikh princes worked with the British to restore order.

Source K

JUSTICE.

1.6 Cartoon 'Justice', *Punch*, September 1857

Source L

While it is true that large numbers of European men, women and children were murdered with great brutality by the mutineers, it is equally evident that some of the stories of torture, rape ad bestiality were either grossly exaggerated or totally untrue. However, the British relief forces felt that every Indian male capable of carrying arms was guilty of such crimes.

From R. Perkins, *The Kashmir Gate*, published in 1983

Source M

There was a sinister side to the British memory of the Mutiny, and one which would have repercussions in India and in other parts of the empire. Racial arrogance had been on the increase in India for at least a decade before the Mutiny, its spread being reflected in the everyday use of the word 'nigger' for Indian, a term which, during the Mutiny, regularly appeared in print. From what they read in the newspapers, supplemented by the more-or-less instantaneous memoirs and histories of the Mutiny, the British were presented with a story in which a people, hitherto believed capable of improvement, turned against their helpers in the most vicious manner imaginable. It was not just the Raj that had been attacked; the Revolt was an onslaught against everything the mid-Victorians cherished. Firing cannon balls at railway engines symbolised a wilful and irrational rejection of technical progress. The killing of women and children was a calculated assault on national moral values. Both suggested, at least to the cynical, that efforts at uplifting Indians had been misguided and were doomed, if not to failure, then to very limited success.

From Lawrence James, *Raj: The Making and Unmaking of British India*, published in 1997

SKILLS BUILDER

1 Sources K and L are both concerned with the Indian Mutiny. How do you account for the differences between them?

2 Now read Source M. How significant was the Indian Mutiny to (a) the Indians and (b) the British?

The British government spent £36 million restoring order. This was a full year's worth of Indian revenue. It was hardly surprising that, in August 1858, the British Parliament passed the Government of India Act, transferring all rights that the East India Company had enjoyed on Indian soil directly to the British Crown.

The troubles of 1857 demonstrated that Britain was the only power that was capable of maintaining law and order throughout India. British authority could be established, and re-established, by calling on armed forces from Britain to support those stationed in India. However, British authority could only be maintained by relying on a network of Indians who either sympathised with the British or who were willing to co-operate with them until better times came.

The British Raj

The Government of India Act of 1858 meant that Queen Victoria became Queen of India as well as of the United Kingdom, and India's Governor-General became her Viceroy as well as the government's chief executive in India. In the United Kingdom the position of the monarch was buttressed by a hierarchical structure of hereditary nobles and honours, so in India a similar structure was created.

With very few exceptions, the 500 or so Indian princes had remained loyal to the British throughout the Great Rebellion. In British eyes, such loyalty deserved recognition and reward. Existing treaties with India's princes were to be scrupulously maintained and the hated 'doctrine of lapse', whereby princedoms without a direct heir 'lapsed' to British control, was abandoned. A royal order of Indian knights was created; India's princes were grouped and stratified according to status. Status was, of course, dependent upon size of territory, but also on good government and charitable works, and a prince's status was confirmed by minutiae of protocols, among which was the right to insist on a specific number of gun salutes.

In 1876, on the advice of her Prime Minister Benjamin Disraeli, Queen Victoria announced to Parliament that her Indian subjects were 'happy under My rule and loyal to My throne'. Henceforward, she was to adopt the title 'Empress of India' which, for her Indian subjects, translated as 'Kaiser-I-Hind'. In January 1877, in a vast tented assembly outside Delhi, this new imperial role was confirmed by most of India's princes and Indians of importance and influence.

However, the pomp and splendour concealed a number of issues that had to be addressed, as the twentieth century got under way.

The British were beginning to ask some fundamental questions.

- How was India to be administered and financed?
- What was India's worth to Britain?
- What was Britain's duty to India and the Indian people?

Other, equally fundamental questions were being asked by the Indian people.

- What should their attitude be to the new British rulers? Should Indians co-operate with the British **Raj**? Should they oppose it?
- Should Indian people accept or reject the new opportunities offered by the British Raj or stand aloof from them?

There were no right answers to these questions. They were answered in different ways, by different people, at different times.

Definition

Raj
Rule, particularly British rule in India.

Unit summary

What have you learned in this unit?

You have learned how the East India Company started working in India in the seventeenth century as a trading company as one among several European companies. You have found out about the power and extent of the Mughal Empire and how its vulnerability enabled the East India Company to take over most of the land it had once controlled. You have learned how the Indian Mutiny affected relationships between the British and Indians and also enabled the British government to take control of most of India from the East India Company.

What skills have you used in this unit?

You have worked with sources in order to determine the nature of the relationships between the British and Indians in India and have focused on the ways in which the Indian Mutiny changed these. You have used source evaluation to explore the significance of Queen Victoria's acceptance of the title 'Empress of India'.

Exam-style questions

There isn't an exam-style question on this unit because you won't be asked a question on this period in the exam. However, it is essential that you know what was happening, otherwise you won't be able to understand the importance of events after 1900.

RESEARCH TOPIC

Robert Clive (1725–74) played a very large part in the East India Company. A House of Commons committee was set up to enquire into how he had acquired his fabulous wealth. They found it had all been acquired legally. What do you think?

Discussion points

1 The Victorian historian, Sir John Seeley, said that the British 'seem to have conquered and peopled half the world in a fit of absence of mind'. How far do you think he was correct as far as India was concerned?

2 The British call the events of 1857 the 'Indian Mutiny' or the 'Bengal Mutiny'. Indians call it the 'National Uprising' or the 'First War of Independence'. Some historians, believing themselves to be without bias, call what happened 'The Great Rebellion'. What do you think it should be called?

2 Snapshot 1900: living in the Raj

What is this unit about?

This unit focuses on the ways in which Indians and British lived out their lives in the Indian sub-continent at the beginning of the twentieth century. It looks at the societies both created and the ways in which they interacted, including the attitudes each had towards the other. In it you will also:

- find out about the caste system and how this impacted on Indian and British society
- learn about the ways in which the British developed the Indian economy in order to foster Britain's own economic prosperity
- understand the political importance of India to Britain.

Indian society was complicated, complex and of infinite variety. Basic to the way in which it operated was the caste system. Only Hindus lived out their lives within the caste system, but as Hindus made up about 70 per cent of India's population of around 300 million in 1900, obviously it had a tremendous impact on society in the sub-continent. Added to this rich variety was the British Raj. By 1900, around 100,000 British people lived in India. They worked as civil servants, administrators, engineers, policemen and soldiers. Together with their wives and children, they created a separate class that, with few notable exceptions, was determined to remain so.

Key questions

- To what extent did Britain and the British exploit India and the Indians?
- How far was the British Raj a benevolent force in India?

Indian society

Lewis Le Marchand remembers his **ayah** when he was a child in southern India:

Source A

She was very fat and very, very oily about the hair. Her toes were quite enormous and cracked like dry wickets that had had the sun on them for a few days. If the day **chokidar** didn't give me another biscuit with my early morning tea or if there was any sort of trouble, I used to go to her and she usually managed to solve it. I didn't know her name; I called her *ayah*. Sometimes, being a fairly naughty boy, I would anger her, but she'd never show it. She'd turn her back and go and sit down cross-legged on the floor of the **verandah** and take out her knitting, and the more I called her or the more I was naughty or rude, the more she ignored me, until finally I would come along and say, ' *Ayah*, I'm sorry,' and then all would be well.

Ayah looked after me during the day and very often during the evening, but it was mother's privilege – heaven knows why – to bath me and put me to bed. *Ayah* used to wait and, if necessary, sleep outside the door of my room, lying down outside on the mat until such time as my mother would come along and say, 'You can go, *ayah*, little master's asleep.'

From Charles Allen (editor), *Plain Tales from the Raj*, published in 1975

SKILLS BUILDER

Read Source A.

1 Think about the Indians. What attitudes are they showing towards the British?

2 Now think about the British. How are they regarding the Indians?

3 How typical do you think these attitudes were likely to have been?

Indian society: structure and assumptions

The caste system was basic to the Hindus, who made up over two-thirds of Indian society. It spilled over, as you will see, into all aspects of life in India.

How did the caste system operate?

The majority of Indians were born into, and lived out their days within, a hierarchical system of caste. Their place in the social order was determined by the accident of birth – the caste into which they had been born. Caste society ranked groups of people, not individuals, in order from high to low. No one could leave the caste into which they had been born unless they were literally 'out-caste', and then they had no place in society. Marriage took place within the caste and so no one could swap one caste for another. All social relationships, for example those between men and women, relatives, neighbours, employers and employed, were predetermined by caste and learned from childhood. However, as the twentieth century progressed, in some areas and within some societies, the caste system did begin to become flexible.

The assumptions underlying the caste system were those of purity and pollution. Certain substances were considered to be religiously polluting (for example, human and animal waste, dead bodies and anything, such as leather, associated with them) and so the closer whole groups were to such substances, the lower they were in the caste system. Some people, such as women during childbirth, became temporarily polluted and had to be purified. Others, because of their occupation, could never be completely purified and so, in order to protect the purity of the caste above them, the castes had to be kept as separate as possible. There were strict rules, too, about who could touch whom. Those at the bottom of the hierarchy, like scavengers, were literally untouchable.

A basic four-caste system is described in Hindi scriptures. The four castes, called *varnas*, consist of **Brahmins** (priests), *Kshatriyas* (warriors), *Vaishyas* (traders) and *Shudras* (labourers and cultivators). In practice, most Indians experienced caste within the *jati*, which were essentially local groups with a known social order that operated between and within the four main caste groups.

Definitions

Ayah
A children's Indian nanny or nurse employed by British families to look after their children while they were living in India.

Chokidar
Watchman or caretaker.

Verandah
A Hindi word referring to a porch, usually roofed, that runs along the outside wall of a building.

Definition

Brahmin
The highest Hindu caste, consisting originally of priests, then later including educators, law-makers, scholars and preachers.

Although this caste system was one of separation, it was also one of interdependence. Everyone needed the support of those above and below them in the system – even the work of the Untouchables was essential to the smooth running of society. And so a system of patron-client relationships between families was established, often existing over many generations. A blacksmith, for example, needed a landowner to work for, just as the landowner needed someone to make his ploughs, and they both needed someone to take away human waste.

In Source B Marjorie Cashmore, newly arrived in Ranchi, explains how she encountered the intricacies of the caste system when she found a dead bird and asked the gardener to remove it. He refused, saying it was forbidden for him to touch dead birds. Marjorie went on to explain how the large number of servants seemingly required by British households was in part a result of the caste system.

Definition

Masalchee
Kitchen boy.

Source B

So I told the bearer to call the **masalchee**, but the *masalchee* wouldn't touch it. Then I called for the sweeper and he wouldn't touch it, so I asked the bearer who could move it and he told me to send to the bazaar for a dome, a man of very low caste. So we had to pay to get this lad to come and take the bird away.

. . .

The domestics were there, not because you needed them but because they were very strict about their own little trade unions. The man who waited at table might not be prepared to bring your tea in the evening; the cook would perhaps cook but he wouldn't wash up; there would be a special man to dust the floor; another special man to sweep out the verandah and so on. If you had a man to look after the horses he would need to have an assistant who would go and cut the grass.

From Charles Allen (editor), *Plain Tales from the Raj*, published in 1975

In Source C, Joan Allen remembers what happened when she was a child in India and wanted to water her own garden.

Source C

Outside the gardener's hut I saw a nice little earthenware bowl, so I picked it up. The gardener came rushing out of his hut and he was furious. He picked this bowl out of my hands and dashed it to the ground. This was his bowl, and by touching it I had made it untouchable for him, and so he broke it.

From Charles Allen (editor), *Plain Tales from the Raj*, published in 1975

Source D

Wives who knew the customs and languages of India 'would never think of asking a servant to do a thing that was beneath him or against his religion'. The pukka memsahib was never 'tactless enough to bring back bacon from the Club and hand it to a bearer who was a very strict Mohammedan [a Muslim]. One put it upon a table and the sweeper would come and take it away because he was a Hindu and didn't mind touching bacon'.

From Charles Allen (editor), *Plain Tales from the Raj*, published in 1975

Source E

[The British believed] Indians could not be treated as equals as long as they had such extraordinarily backward ways. Take – and the British frequently did – the caste system. What was it but the relic of a primitive form of society, which had all but disappeared centuries ago in Europe? Since all peoples outside the caste system were considered Untouchables, its existence was also galling; the British were the conquerors of India, the representatives of the most advanced society in the world, yet most of their subjects could not bring themselves to eat at the same table with them. New arrivals had to be warned never to shake a *Brahmin* by the hand; the pollution would be so great that the *Brahmin* would have to undergo extensive, and expensive, purification ceremonies.

From Margaret MacMillan, *Women of the Raj*, published in 1988

SKILLS BUILDER

1 How far do Sources B, C and D agree on the impact of the caste system on the British who lived in India?

2 To what extent does Source E challenge the views given in Sources C and D about the impact of the caste system on the British in India?

What was the importance of religion?

Caste, as you have seen, was intimately intertwined with the Hindu religion. But religion, whether it was Hindu or Muslim, Sikh or **Jain**, was a vital bonding force between people and groups. It determined value systems and provided a framework for dress, diet and social customs as well as the rituals associated with a particular form of belief. As well as being a binding force, religion in India, as well as in the rest of the world, was also divisive, setting different groups of people apart from each other, often in mutual misunderstanding and distrust. It is not surprising that such a powerful force played a dominant part in twentieth-century Indian politics, as change inevitably altered the relationships between the different communities.

The majority of Indians in 1900 were Hindu (about 70 per cent), as they were when the first Europeans set foot on Indian soil. Other religions were brought to India with waves of invaders and migrants. Muslims formed the largest minority religion (around 20 per cent) and in some parts of the sub-continent, mostly in the north-west and north-east, they were in the majority. In the north-west, Muslims still tended to hold influential positions, while in the north-east around Bengal, Muslims were more likely to be found forming the peasant class. There were fewer Muslims in southern India, except in Hyderabad, which had been a stronghold of the Mughal Empire.

Definition

Jain

Jainism is an ancient branch of Hinduism. Jains reject the idea of a supreme being and advocate a deep respect for all living things. They are, therefore, strict vegetarians. Jains believe that an immortal and indestructible soul lies within every person and that the soul should seek liberation from the cycle of birth and death. Spiritual advancement will be achieved by following the five vows: *ahimsa* (non-violence), truthfulness, not stealing (including avoiding greed and exploitation), chastity (Jain monks and nuns are greatly respected) and detachment from the pleasures of the world.

Sikhs and **Christians** were the other two sizeable minority groups. Sikhs formed a highly localised group, mainly in the Punjab, and grew out of the interaction between Hindu and Muslim religions in the sixteenth and seventeenth centuries. In the far south of India there was an ancient denomination of Christians who claimed St Thomas as their founder, but most of the Christians in India were those who had been converted by missionaries in the nineteenth century.

You will see, throughout this book, as different groups and communities struggled to adjust identities and imperatives in a changing political framework as they struggled towards independence, just what a powerful force religion was in India. Different caste groups, for example, organised themselves and mobilised their members for political action; Hindu temples became focal points of political activity. To proclaim that certain political policies and plans endangered Islam was a powerful motivating force for Muslims to engage in political action and here the local clerics showed considerable organisational skills.

Discussion point

Was religion likely to be a divisive or unifying factor in India?

You might like to think about the factors that unify and those that divide. For example, would the belief in a divine being tend to unite or divide? Would the existence of a caste system in one religion but not in others tend to unite or divide?

How was India used to serve Britain's interests?

In 1900, the British Empire was at its height. It was the largest and most powerful empire in the world, and this was due in very large part to India – the jewel in the crown of the British Empire. Its sheer size and symbolism made it an indispensable part of British power in the world. Indeed, Lord Curzon, who was **Viceroy** of India from 1898–1905, and Winston Churchill, who was then a prominent Liberal Party politician, agreed that without India Britain would become a second- or even third-rate nation. So how did India provide this power – and glamour – for Britain? How did the British use India to their own advantage? No country acquires an empire out of a sense of altruism – an attitude of unselfish concern for others. Although many individuals, both privately and publicly assured each other and the world that their mission was to 'civilise' the 'native Indians', this was most certainly not the driving force of empire, nor the driving force that kept the British in India. Empires are acquired largely through self-interest and to serve the needs and ambitions of the mother country. True, India was costly to run, but that was nothing, in 1900, compared to the economic benefits India brought to Britain.

Source F

The maintenance of the Indian Empire was always conditional upon it continuing to provide Britain with money, power and influence. Moreover, empires do not come free. There was the matter of costs to be considered: the expenditure of elite manpower, overheads, political effort. So long as the sub-continent remained a hot property, London was prepared to invest heavily to keep it.

From Ian Copland, *India 1885–1947*, published in 2001

Question

What conclusions can you draw from the view given in Source F?

What was the importance of trade?

India's economic role was vital to Britain's position in the world as both a provider of raw materials for British industry and as a market for British manufactured goods. During the nineteenth century, India had become the single largest overseas market for British goods. Initially, these were cotton goods but by 1900 included significant amounts of iron, steel and engineering products, which were very important for the continued prosperity of British staple industries. But trade was not all one way. India supplied Britain with jute, raw cotton, rice, tea, oil-seed, wheat and hides.

Trade between Britain and India was greatly helped by the opening of the Suez Canal in 1869, which, running between the Mediterranean Sea and the Red Sea, drastically reduced travelling time between the countries, and thus reduced the cost of transporting freight. This, in turn, impacted on British foreign policy, where the maintenance of the Suez Canal route to India was always given a high priority.

How were tariffs used to help the British economy?

One way for newly developing countries to protect their own emerging industries was to impose tariffs on goods coming into the country. In this way imported goods became more expensive than home-produced ones, thus allowing domestic industries to grow and develop. Australia and the USA both used this method at the beginning of the twentieth century to encourage their own domestic industries. Nothing of the kind happened in India – quite the reverse: it would hardly be in Britain's interest to have tariffs slapped on goods it wanted to sell in Indian markets. Indeed, towards the end of the nineteenth century, the British government unashamedly made India subordinate to the needs of the Lancashire cotton industry. In 1879, Viceroy Lytton removed all import duties on Lancashire cotton cloth, allowing it to flood the Indian market at a time when the Indian cotton industry desperately needed support and famine stalked the land. Finally, in 1882, tariffs on all British goods imported into India were reduced from 3.5 per cent to nil. Later, Gandhi was to use the position of the Indian cotton industry to great effect. Unsurprisingly, tariff control was one factor fastened on by Indian nationalists as the twentieth century progressed.

Source G

Commodity	1854	1876	1900	1913
Raw cotton	1642	5875	657	1226
Rice	884	2639	1625	1281
Raw jute	510	2799	4101	9182
Tea	24	2429	5576	7839
Leather	18	444	2820	2839
Wheat	0	1647	2	7999
Oil-seeds	0	0	50	398

2.1 UK imports from India, 1854–1913, in £1000s. From W. Schlote, *British Overseas Trade from 1700 to the 1930s*, published in 1952

Source H

Commodity	1854	1876	1900	1913
Manufactured textiles	7191	15,961	19,069	40,729
Iron and steel goods	584	1864	3280	9801
Machinery	101	724	1529	4558
Chemicals	67	232	683	1309
Locomotives, railway carriages	10	155	867	2200
Electrical engineering products	0	145	76	362
Soap	0	22	114	433

2.2 UK exports to India, 1854–1913 in £1000s. From W. Schlote, *British Overseas Trade from 1700 to the 1930s*, published in 1952

SKILLS BUILDER

Study Sources G and H.

1 Which UK import from India increased by the biggest percentage between the years 1854 and 1913?

2 Which UK export to India increased by the biggest percentage between the years 1854 and 1913?

3 What conclusions can you draw from these tables about British and Indian industry, and the relationship between them?

What about investment?

British 'victory' in the Indian Mutiny and subsequent transfer of power from the East India Company to the British Crown resulted in a great increase in British and European capital investment in Indian agriculture and industry. Victory convinced hitherto nervous investors that the British could, and would, continue to control and contain any further rebellion and that the British Empire in India was built on sound foundations. By the beginning of the twentieth century, India received about one-tenth of British overseas investment – about £250 million. By 1910, this had risen to £365 million, nearly half of which was in the form of government loans to subsidise railway development and tea and coffee plantations.

What was the manpower commitment?

Clearly, India provided direct employment for the British people who worked there. Young men went out to work in the government service, as members of the Indian Civil Service (ICS), and other civilian enterprises such as forestry, education, medicine and engineering. As well as receiving salaries while they were working, almost all expatriate employees of government went back to Britain when they retired. There, they received pensions paid for by India and these were one of the main 'home charges' on the Indian revenue. However, it was to the Indian army that the biggest manpower commitment was made and that enabled Britain to have a secure presence in Asia.

Source I

By 1880 there were 66,000 British and 130,000 Indian troops in the Indian army. The army was far more than a career structure or a wage-payer. At no cost to the British tax-payer it was a large force which could be widely deployed to protect Imperial interests over and above its role in India's own defence and internal security; and its presence in the subcontinent helped to safeguard Imperial trade and communications between Europe and Australasia. The value of this 'English barrack in the oriental Seas' (as Lord Salisbury called it in 1882) was indicated by the areas in which India's army was used in the second half of the nineteenth century – China, Persia, Ethiopia, Singapore, Hong Kong, Afghanistan, Egypt, Burma, Nyasa, Sudan and Uganda. Its potential manpower was also great in times of grand emergency; and India made a momentous military contribution in 1914–18 as far west as France, producing for Britain's war effort men, animals, stores and money.

From Judith M. Brown, *Modern India: the Origins of an Asian Democracy*, published in 1994

Discussion point

In 1966 the author Paul Scott wrote a novel about the Raj and called it *The Jewel in the Crown*. What do you think he meant by this? With what justification could India in 1900 be called 'The Jewel in the Crown'?

SKILLS BUILDER

Read Sources G, H and I. What was the value of India to Britain in 1900?

What was life like for the British in India?

It is impossible to under-estimate the impact of the Indian Mutiny of 1857 and the level of racial mistrust it raised between the British in India and the Indians themselves. The bitter legacy of murder and mutilation, of atrocities committed by both sides, poisoned relationships for decades.

Shocked at what they perceived as disloyalty and ingratitude, the British response was to separate themselves from the Indian people. In doing so, they created what was in effect a separate caste, a ruling elite. This separation of rulers from the ruled was to lead to terrible problems as both sides tried to reach new understandings as the twentieth century progressed.

A separate society?

In the great cities of Bombay, Calcutta and Madras, wealthy Raj officials, as well as bankers, lawyers and merchants, along with their families, lived in the great eighteenth-century houses that had once belonged to officials of the East India Company. They were looked after by an army of Indian servants. Those not so well off lived in **bungalows**, though still with Indian servants to do the cleaning and cooking, and single men usually shared a house and servants. In the latter half of the nineteenth century, new towns and suburbs called 'civil lines' and 'camps' were built for British officials and their families. They were deliberately built with wide streets along which a regiment could move swiftly to put down any 'trouble'.

The distrust and suspicion with which most of the British in India viewed the Indians led to the breakdown of the easy, relaxed relationships between the races you read about on page 6. After the Indian Mutiny, far fewer British men took Indian wives or (as far as we can tell) mistresses. They preferred the security of a British wife. Ships travelling from Britain, nicknamed 'fishing fleets', carried considerable numbers of young single women, more hopeful of finding a husband than visiting the faded glories of Mughal India.

Definition

Bungalow

A Hindi word meaning a single storey house.

Source J

Most of the unattached girls who ventured out in the fishing fleet found that their trouble was repaid. The lucky or the cunning got themselves engaged before they landed. In 1922 Kathleen Wilkes was travelling to India to take up a post as a governess. She met a man and 'in a few days under a full moon on the Red Sea we became engaged, much to the delight and interest of many people on board ship'. Not everyone was delighted. 'In my cabin there was a rather senior lady who, rather looking down on me as a governess, said "Oh, I hear you've got engaged to young Griffiths. You've done well for yourself, haven't you. Don't you know? He's one of the heaven born – the Indian Civil Service!"' The ICS were often compared to *Brahmins*, the 'heaven born' at the summit of the caste system.

From Margaret MacMillan, *Women of the Raj*, published in 1988

Children, as you have seen, were looked after by an *ayah*, an Indian nurse, until they were old enough to be packed off to boarding schools in England. The opening of the Suez Canal in 1869, important as it was for political and military reasons, did shorten the journey 'home' and further encouraged the British servants of the Crown to bring their wives out to India and rear their children there. Holidays could now be spent in London and relatives could be visited. To live and work in India was no longer viewed as exile. But for many, separation was a painful experience. Some wives made a different sort of choice and stayed in England with their children, making a home for them there while they went to school. With a husband half a world away, and visits infrequent, there were inevitable strains upon such marriages. So, many wives had to make a choice between their children or their husband.

British life in Calcutta

Calcutta, the administrative capital of British India, was the magnet that drew anyone who wanted to be part of smart society. It was here that the British could live in a more lavish style than they could have afforded in Britain on the same money. When the Viceroy was in residence and the Calcutta season in full swing, there were balls, dances, parties and receptions every night. And always, it was the Indians who prepared the food, waited at table, served the drinks, washed up and swept up afterwards.

Source K

2.3 Photograph of the Calcutta Golf Club, 1910

Discussion point

What can you learn from Source K about British society in India in the early 1900s?

The British formed what to many seemed a separate caste in a society that was divided by caste, but within this British 'caste' there were many hierarchical divisions. Everyone knew exactly where they stood in the social pecking order: with whom they could take tea and with whom they could be the ones to speak first. Indeed, the government published a 'warrant of precedence', with the Viceroy at the top and the sub-deputy opium agent at the bottom. This rigid society continued in India long after education and war had dissolved such barriers in Britain. The privations of war (for example, rationing) did not hit British society in India in the same way it did in the UK and it was perceived, perhaps subconsciously, that the maintenance of barriers would provide continuing security.

British life in Simla

In the hot season, every British person who could afford it (and who hadn't taken advantage of the P&O shipping line and gone back to Britain for a break) moved to the hills where it was cooler and life could be a little more relaxed. The Viceroy and the higher departments of state moved to Simla in the foothills of the Himalayas. With them went the leaders of the business community and everyone whose status made contact with the Viceroy in a social situation acceptable. Simla was cut off from the plains by 58 miles of poor roads and from Calcutta by 1000 miles. Other hill stations, like Poona, were even more remote. Indeed, this remoteness made the hill stations attractive. The British could forget they had to behave like imperialists and begin to enjoy themselves: the men played polo and went hunting, the women played tennis, badminton and croquet. There were balls and picnics. While this might have been fun for the British, it served, in Indian eyes, to separate them even more from the people they governed. And the very business of government tended to be put on hold while the British enjoyed themselves. Vere Birdwood describes her life in India at the time of the Raj:

SKILLS BUILDER

How far do Sources J, K and L suggest that the British in India formed a separate caste?

Source L

We were looked after by Indian servants and we met a great many Indians, and some of us undoubtedly made a very close study of India and Indian customs. But once you stepped inside the home you were back in Cheltenham or Bath. We brought with us in our home lives almost exact replicas of the sort of life that upper-middle-class people lived in England at that time. Nearly everyone in official India sprang from precisely the same educational and cultural background. You went from bungalow to bungalow and you found the same sort of furniture, the same sort of dinner table set, the same kind of conversation. We read the same books, mostly imported by post from England, and I can't really say that we took an awful lot from India.

From Charles Allen (editor), *Plain Tales from the Raj*, published in 1975

However, many Englishwomen despaired of never really being able to recreate their part of England in India and stories abounded of Indian servants using their toes as toast racks and being caught straining soup through their turbans.

Living close to the edge

Not all the British in India, however, were privileged. Those who were not included the missionaries, whose poverty and desire to live among the Indians made them deeply suspect, and businessmen, whose social origins were usually regarded as dubious. Anyone connected with the lower echelons of trade, such as a shopkeeper, was automatically barred from this hierarchical British society that had recreated itself in India.

Anglo-Indians were equally suspect. Numbering about 110,000 at the beginning of the twentieth century, they were accepted by neither the British nor the Indians. The nearest they came to polite British society was in church where they were consigned to the lowliest pews and when they were in receipt of dubious charitable gestures like children's Christmas parties. They themselves identified with Britain, referring to it as 'home' although they had never been there, dressing in European clothes and with the women trying to lighten their complexions with make-up. Yet it was this under-class that formed the backbone of labour on the railways and the postal and telegraph services. The British, who so spurned them, could not administer India without them.

What were the attitudes of the British towards the Indian people?

Lord Curzon, who was Viceroy in the years 1898–1905, had very decided views about the Indian princes and about the role of the British in India:

> **Definition**
>
> **Anglo-Indian**
> Somebody of mixed Indian and British descent.

> **Discussion point**
>
> Why did this essential 'under-class' appear to have no power?

> **Source M**
>
> The Princes are unruly and ignorant and rather undisciplined schoolboys. What they want more than anything else is to be schooled by a firm hand. We sustain the Native States and Princes, not so much in the interests of the Princes themselves, who are often quite undeserving, but in the interests of the people. We are bound to train and discipline and control them and so fit them for the unique position which we have placed within their grasp.
>
> From comments made by Lord Curzon

He was pretty scathing, too, about the handful of Indians who worked in the Indian Civil Service, complaining:

Source N

An increasing number of the higher posts that were meant, and ought to have been exclusively and specially reserved, for Europeans, are being filched away by the superior wits of the native in the English examinations. I believe it to be the greatest peril with which our administration is confronted.

From comments made by Lord Curzon

Discussion point

Just by reading these remarks made by Lord Curzon in Sources M, N and O, what kind of Viceroy do you think he made?

You can check this out when you get to the next unit!

Curzon clearly believed in the British purpose in India and would not be daunted:

Source O

Because I believe in the future of India and the capacity of our own race to guide it to goals that it has never hitherto attained, that I keep courage and press forward.

From comments made by Lord Curzon

Curzon's attitude was reflected by the poet Rudyard Kipling. Born in Bombay in 1865, Kipling worked in India as a journalist when he was a young man before returning to England to live there permanently. Source P contains the first verse of a poem he wrote.

Source P

Take up the White Man's burden –
Send forth the best ye breed –
Go, bind your sons to exile
To serve your captives' need;
To wait, in heavy harness,
On fluttered folk and wild –
Your new-caught sullen peoples,
Half devil and half child.

Kipling also wrote about a *sepoy*, an Indian soldier, called Gunga Din:

Though I've belted you and flayed you,
By the livin' Gawd that made you,
You're a better man than I am, Gunga Din!

From the poem 'Take Up the White Man's Burden' by Rudyard Kipling, written in 1899

SKILLS BUILDER

Read Sources M, N, O and P. How far do they agree on attitudes to the Raj?

What were the attitudes of Indians towards the British Raj?

In many ways this is a very difficult question to answer and it's a question that the rest of this book tries to answer as it records how India moved to independence.

In 1900, when the British Raj was at its height, it was very difficult for ordinary Indian people to be openly critical of those who ruled them. After all, the Raj did employ a great number of Indians, thus providing them with a roof over their heads and food on their tables, an occupation and in some cases the makings of a career structure. But it was an alien rule, not one chosen by the Indian people themselves and not one arising, as the Mughal Empire had, from their own culture. This alien culture brought with it the English language. This language, while providing a unifying element, brought with it words like 'democracy' and 'imperialism' and, more importantly, the concepts behind those words. Indeed, command of English was necessary for Indians, once they were allowed to enter them, to pass examinations that allowed access to the prestigious Indian Civil Service.

Indian children attending British run-schools usually had to wear British-style uniforms, learn British games and work from textbooks produced in England. One Indian man, who went to such a school, remembers his school days:

Source Q

The school textbooks prescribed in British days had a strong imperialist flavour. I remember how many of us squirmed on being called upon to recite a poem about an English hero who was killed in India in a frontier skirmish:

'Let dusky Indians whine and kneel,
An English lad must die.'
I forget who was the author of this 'sensitive' piece.

From **Frank Moraes**, *Witness to an Era*, published in 1973

One wonders, too, at the lack of sensitivity of the teacher who insisted that the pupils recited this poem.

Autobiographer Nirad Chaudhuri recalled his childhood in Calcutta:

Source R

I was influenced by the example of my parents who never went into any kind of society in which they were not treated as equals. I entertained no ambition whatever of hobnobbing with the English in India. As long as I lived in Calcutta I wore no article of English clothing and had none. In general, I disliked and despised the local English.

From Nirad Chaudhuri, *The Autobiography of an Unknown Indian*, published in 1951

Biography

Frank Moraes

An Indian, Moraes was born in 1907 in Mumbai, the son of an Indian official in the days of the Raj. He studied history and law at Oxford University. He worked briefly as a lawyer, but for most of his adult life lived and worked as a journalist and newspaper editor in India, Sri Lanka, Burma and China.

Discussion point

1 How might a teacher at the time have defended getting Indian pupils to read the poem in Source Q?
2 How useful is this source to an historian trying to find out about attitudes of the British to the Indian people?

This attitude to the British was reflected in a leaflet widely circulated in Bengal in 1907:

Source S

Can these thieves really be our rulers? These thieves import a huge number of goods, made in their own country, and sell them in our markets, stealing our wealth and taking life from our people. Can those who steal the harvest from our fields and doom us to hunger, fever and plague really be our rulers? Can foreigners really be our rulers, foreigners who impose on us ever more taxes?

From an anonymous leaflet, published in 1907

Some began to think that the time for change, radical change, had come.

Definition

Indian National Congress
Indian National Congress was founded in 1885 as an all-India, secular political party, but quickly became identified with the majority Hindus.

Source T

At present, we are clerks and willing instruments of our own oppression in the hands of an alien government, and that government is ruling over us not by its innate strength but by keeping us in ignorance and blindness to the perception of this fact. Every Englishman knows that they are a mere handful in this country and it is the business of every one of them to befool you into believing that you are weak and they are strong.

From an address made by Bal Gangadhar Tilak to the **Indian National Congress** *in 1907*

This was a warning indeed that, with the new century, a change in the relationships between the Raj and the Indian people was going to come. By 1900, the British were entrenched in India as a separate, elite class. Most of them regarded it as their right and their duty to rule India. Opinions differed as to whether this was in the interests of the Indians or the British. Among the Indians, many of whom owed their livelihood to the British, there was simmering discontent and growing resentment of what they were coming to regard as an alien rule.

SKILLS BUILDER

1 What is there in Sources S and T to alarm the British imperialist power?
2 How reliable would you consider these sources to be as indicators of unrest in India?

Unit summary

What have you learned in this unit?

You have learned about India in and around 1900. You have found out about the caste system, how it operated and how it impacted on both Indians and British in India. You have learned about the ways in which trade with India contributed to British economic prosperity and how Britain developed Indian agriculture and industry to foster this prosperity. You have understood how India being part of the British Empire was of vital importance to British political prestige and how the Indian army helped maintain this prestige abroad and create security for the development of Britain's worldwide empire.

What skills have you used in this unit?

You have worked with source material, cross-referencing and developing your empathetic understanding regarding the ways in which the British became almost a separate caste within India. You have analysed data presented as tables and related this to the ways in which India was used by Britain to enhance and develop the British economy. Finally, you have worked with source material, cross-referencing and testing for reliability and utility in order to explore the attitudes of the British to Indians and Indians to the British.

Exam tips

This is the sort of question you will find appearing on exam papers as an (a) question.

- Study Sources R, S and T. How far do Sources R, S and T suggest that the days of the Raj were numbered?

Tips for answering (a) questions

- Don't bring in a lot of your own knowledge. All (a) questions focus on the analysis, cross-referencing and evaluation of source material. Your own knowledge won't be credited by the examiner and you will waste valuable time writing it out.
- Do remember that the only knowledge you should introduce will be to put the sources into context. This means, for example, that you might explain that the Indian National Congress was founded in 1885 as an all-India, secular political party, but you should not go on to describe its role in fighting for Indian independence.
- Don't describe (or even re-write) the sources. The examiner will have a copy and to do this will waste your time.
- Do draw inferences from the sources to show how they could be seen to imply that the days of the Raj were numbered.
- Do reach a supported judgement about 'how far' the sources suggest that the days of the Raj were numbered by careful cross-referencing and evaluation.

RESEARCH TOPIC

Rudyard Kipling (1865–1936)

Rudyard Kipling is often portrayed as symbolising British imperialism, particularly with regard to India. Research his life and work to find out whether or not this is true.

3 How was India governed in 1900?

What is this unit about?

This unit focuses on the way in which India was governed in 1900. It looks at the structure of government on the Indian sub-continent and its relationship with the British government in Westminster. You will use a case study of George Nathaniel Curzon, who was Viceroy of India between 1898 and 1905, to deepen your understanding of the governance of India. By 1900, as you have seen, the British Raj was at its height. Not only did most British people agree with their Queen that India was the 'jewel in the crown', but they regarded British rule in India as unassailable. Laws affecting India were made in the British Parliament and implementing these laws in India was managed efficiently. The Indian population were, by and large, co-operative and thousands of Indians worked for and with the British. Most British people, however, failed to realise just how much of their perceived control was an illusion, relying as it did on the lack of systematic opposition from the Indian people and resting on their tacit agreement.

Key questions

- To what extent were the Indian people involved in running their own country?
- How limited was the power of the Raj?

Timeline

1861	India Councils' Act
1883	Lord Ripon's local self-government plan
1885	First Indian National Congress convened
1892	India Councils' Act
1898	Lord Curzon appointed Viceroy of India
1901	North-West Frontier Province created
1904	British takeover of Tibet
1905	Partition of Bengal
1905	Lord Curzon resigns as Viceroy of India

The Raj

The British ruled India from Government House in Calcutta until 1911, when Delhi was made the capital city.

Source A

3.1 View of the Government House in Calcutta, taken from the Ochterlony Monument, c. 1880

SKILLS BUILDER

Look carefully at Source A and use evidence from it in your answers to the following questions.

1 What does this building tell you about British attitudes to governing India?

2 What impression of the British Raj do you think Indian people would get from this building?

3 Do you think this impression was deliberately created by the British?

The Viceroy, the Secretary of State and the Council of India

These three institutions provided the 'top down' structure of the Indian government. No other part of the British Empire had this structure and was paid this level of attention. This was partly because of the size of India, but also because of its importance to Britain. The Viceroy was appointed by the British government in Westminster and so was a political appointment. He was sent out to govern India as the personal representative of the monarch who, in 1900, was Queen Victoria. He was considered to be so important that not only was his salary twice that of the British prime minister, he also had a staff of 700 to make sure his working and living conditions befitted his status.

Back in Westminster, the Secretary of State for India, another political appointment, was responsible for government policy towards the sub-continent. He, too, was answerable to Parliament, where Indian affairs were debated and decisions made.

The Secretary of State was advised, guided and checked by the Council of India. This council consisted of 15 men, none of them Indian, but most of whom had had some experience of living and working in India in their younger days. This meant, of course, that their experience and therefore the advice they gave was sometimes alarmingly out of date. In quiet times this perhaps didn't matter too much. But when affairs in India moved swiftly or threw up hitherto unsuspected challenges, the British response wasn't always appropriate.

Source B

Despite the continuities [with the days of the East India Company] India now lay open to the gaze and greater influence of Parliament. Its people were therefore exposed to the force of British racial and political sentiment to an unprecedented degree. As India's own public became more literate and sensitive, so British parliamentary reactions to Indian affairs could and did become sources of political disquiet in India. Furthermore, all programmes for constitutional reform in India had to go through Parliament where there was often a strategic and vociferous Conservative minority even when a Liberal or (later) Labour government was in power.

Another source of friction built into this system of government was the relationship of Calcutta and Whitehall. The Secretary of State faced a parliamentary audience and a Treasury concerned with balancing Britain's own books, while the Viceroy had to consider Indian opinion and the interests and ideas of his own officials. As the man on the spot, he was often better informed than his London colleague, and on many issues his opinion prevailed though he was technically subordinate to the Secretary of State and the British government. There was constant ebb and flow in the balance of power between Calcutta and Whitehall, depending on the personalities of the two senior officials, on the question at issue, and on the Parliamentary situation.

From Judith M. Brown, *Modern India: the Birth of an Asian Democracy*, published in 1994

SKILLS BUILDER

1 Read Source B. In what ways did the role of the British Parliament in the governance of India lead to friction between Calcutta and Whitehall?

2 How far does Source C support Source B about the Indian Raj?

Source C

In many ways the late-Victorian and Edwardian Raj resembled the spectacles it staged so splendidly. It was stately and moved with the firm, deliberate tread of the principle prop of Indian staged pageantry, the elephant. The direction was always forwards, but the pace was unhurried, which was fortunate, for no one was certain as to the ultimate goal, or when it would be reached. There was also something distinctly elephantine about the government itself. It was a complex and ponderous organism, fundamentally good-natured, but capable of frightening tantrums when its patience was exhausted.

From Lawrence James, *Raj: the Making and Unmaking of British India*, published in 1997

Case study: George Nathaniel Curzon, Viceroy of India, 1898–1905

George Nathaniel Curzon was in many ways the most talented and best-suited man ever to be Viceroy of India. A study of the way in which he interpreted and carried out his role as Viceroy provides us with many insights into the ways in which the Raj operated in India at the turn of the last century.

Early years

George Curzon (1859–1925) was the eldest son and second of 11 children of the fourth Baron Scarsdale and his wife Blanche. He had an education typical of his class: Eton and Balliol College, Oxford. A bullying chant that followed him around school and university was:

Source D

My name is George Nathaniel Curzon
I am a most superior person
My cheeks are pink my hair is sleek
I dine at Blenheim* twice a week.

* Blenheim was the home of the Dukes of Marlborough and the birthplace of Winston Churchill.

Question

What conclusions can you draw from this chant about the attitudes of Curzon's contemporaries to him?

Ambition

While he was still a young man, Curzon set his sights on becoming Viceroy of India and much of what he did was geared to realising this ambition. He travelled extensively in the East in the late 1880s and early 1890s and wrote a great deal, not only about India but also about its land frontiers and the great Asian steppes beyond. He visited Kabul, for example, and made friends with the *amir*, Abdur Rahman; he travelled over the **Pamirs** and through **Chitral** with Major Francis Younghusband as his guide. Throughout these years he developed a passion for Indian archaeology and culture, becoming an expert in both.

But travelling was not enough. Curzon had to get a foothold in politics if he was to fulfil his ambition of becoming Viceroy of India. He worked in Whitehall as under-secretary of state for India (1891–92) and in the Foreign Office (1892–95).

Definitions

Amir

An independent ruler, commander or governor, particularly in Muslim countries.

Pamirs

A high plateau region in Central Asia, located mainly in modern Tajikstan.

Chitral

A princely state, now part of north-west Pakistan.

Ambition achieved!

When, in 1898, Curzon finally achieved his ambition and was appointed Viceroy of India, it might be expected that he would administer the country with a degree of compassion and understanding. However:

Source E

India's history fascinated him, and he was probably better informed about its languages and customs than any other Viceroy. But of its people as other than an administrative commodity and the decadent heirs of an interesting past he knew, and perhaps cared, little. Like the Taj Mahal, to which he devoted much attention, India was a great imperial edifice, which posed a challenge of presentation and preservation. It needed firm direction, not gentle persuasion. History, by whose verdict Curzon set great store, would judge him by how he secured this magnificent construction, both externally against all conceivable threats and internally against all possible decay. To this end he worked heroically and unselfishly; but his example terrorised rather than inspired, his caustic wit devastated rather than delighted. Even the British in India found him quite impossible.

From John Keay, *A History of India*, published in 2000

Curzon was, in fact, an imperialist *par excellence*. He certainly had the traditional British view of India as the 'jewel in the imperial crown', making the following comments to the British Prime Minister, Arthur Balfour:

Source F

For as long as we rule India, we are the greatest power in the world.

. . .

It will be well for England, better for India and best of all for the cause of progressive civilisation if it be clearly understood that we have not the smallest intention of abandoning our Indian possessions and that it is highly improbable that any such intention will be entertained by our posterity.

From comments made by Lord Curzon

Discussion point

What sort of Viceroy was Curzon likely to make?

Efficiency was his watchword

Whatever Curzon's views, his single-mindedness in pursuing his aims cannot be doubted. His compulsive drive, stamina and seemingly inexhaustible capacity for deskwork were obvious to all. His watchword was 'efficiency' and he was determined to lead by example, spending when in India between ten and fourteen hours a day at his desk. While Viceroy he:

- appointed a special commission to study administrative procedures and, as a result of this, proposed office and procedural reforms that helped the administrative machine run more smoothly

- created a new province, the North-West Frontier, in 1901, carving it out of the Punjab and bringing it directly under the control of the Viceroy

- moved control of the Indian railway from the Department of Public Works and brought it under the control of its own board, enabling some 6,000 more miles of track to be laid by 1905
- appointed a director-general of archaeology responsible for unearthing, preserving and conserving India's cultural past. Curzon himself took a personal interest in restoring the Taj Mahal.

In some administrative reforms, however, he failed. He wanted the Governors of Bombay and Madras to send their weekly reports to him instead of to the Secretary of State for India in London and he tried to administer every department and local government from his office.

Foreign policy: a success story?

Remember that, as a young man, Curzon had travelled extensively in the lands along India's land border, and it was here, as Viceroy, that he put his passion for efficiency and order to good use. He was also desperately afraid of Russian expansion into this wild and uncharted area. Curzon:

- created a buffer zone along the Afghan frontier that was patrolled by local militias under British command and funded by British subsidies and in 1901 transferred responsibility for this zone to the new North-West Frontier Province
- directed British troop commanders, operating under the support of the *Maharajah* of Jammu, to push the frontier up to that of the Chinese Sinkiang, thus almost doubling the size of Kashmir
- claimed that the Dalai Lama was seeking Russian aid and convinced Whitehall of the necessity of taking over Tibet. This final 'tidying up' of India's land frontier in 1904 added Tibet to Britain's sphere of influence.

Source G

COLONEL YOUNGHUSBAND'S MISSION TO LASSA: THE PUNISHMENT OF THE RECALCITRANT TIBETANS AT GURU.

3.2 An artist's impression of the British take-over of Tibet in 1904

SKILLS BUILDER

What impression is the artist of Source G trying to convey about the British takeover of Tibet in 1904?

Images of blood-soaked monks fumbling with hoes and flint-lock pistols as they desperately tried to stave off the British invasion were not good advertisements for imperialism and the British Cabinet was beginning to feel a sense of alarm at Curzon's actions and reactions to threats, real and imagined.

The partition of Bengal: Curzon's nemesis?

In 1905, against the advice of all his British and Indian advisors, Curzon announced he was going to divide Bengal into two provinces: Eastern Bengal and Assam, which would have its capital in Dhaka, and Western Bengal, which would include the cities of Bihar and Orissa. Bengal, as it currently stood, was large, unruly and difficult to administer. Efficiency and common sense, so Curzon reasoned, led inevitably to the decision he, and he alone, took to partition the province.

The Hindus immediately opposed this partition because it would create a province, Eastern Bengal, that was dominated by Muslims. Muslims, on the other hand, tended to support partition because it freed them from Hindu control, at least in one of the two new provinces.

Unsurprisingly, partition resulted in rioting and general unrest in Bengal and other parts of India. This unrest ranged from violence to more or less passive resistance. A Bengali terrorist movement carried out a number of murders and a boycott of British goods was started. A massive petition was presented to the Viceroy urging him to bring partition to an end, but to no avail.

At a stroke, Curzon had managed to spark a nationwide protest movement, introduce direct confrontation into British-Indian relationships, provoke sectarian conflict and suggest to the perceptive that partition was a 'solution' the British were not afraid to impose. Gopal Krishna Gokhale put his views to the Indian National Congress in 1905:

Source H

A cruel wrong has been inflicted on our Bengalee brethren and the whole country has been stirred to its deepest depths in sorrow and resentment, as had never been the case before. The scheme of partition, concocted in the dark and carried out in the face of the fiercest opposition that any government measure has encountered during the last half-a-century, will always stand as a complete illustration of the worst features of the present system of bureaucratic rule – its utter contempt for public opinion, its arrogant pretentions to superior wisdom, its reckless disregard of the most cherished feelings of the people, the mockery of an appeal to its sense of justice, its cool preference of [Civil] service interests to those of the governed.

From an address made by Gopal Krishna Gokhale at the
Indian National Congress in 1905

The end game

Curzon resigned as Viceroy within days of the partition of Bengal, but his resignation was not because of the partition. It came as the result of an ongoing row he was having with his military commander-in-chief, Lord Kitchener. On the surface, the row concerned Kitchener's status on the Viceroy's Executive Council. Underlying this was the struggle between military and civil control in India and the personal contest between two arrogant, powerful men. Eventually a compromise situation was arrived at, whereby the commander-in-chief would have a regular council seat with more administrative power, while a second general would have an ordinary seat and would be called a 'military supply member'. Curzon, as agreed, submitted the name of a candidate for the new post – and this was promptly vetoed by Kitchener, who went behind Curzon's back by lobbying against him to Whitehall's army department. The Secretary of State for India asked Curzon to suggest someone else. Angered by this affront, Curzon resigned.

The Indian Civil Service

The Indian Civil Service was an hierarchical structure, ranging from the Crown right down to the humblest local official.

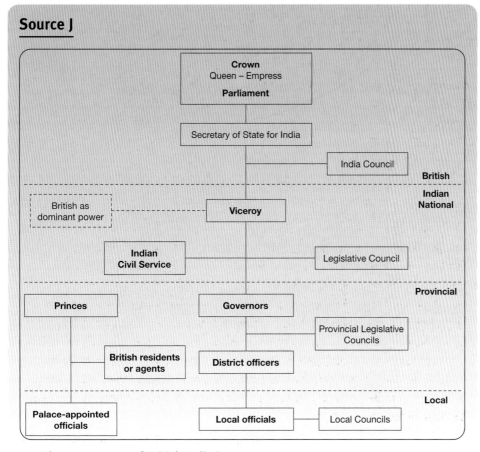

Source J

3.3 The governance of British India in 1900

Question

Now you have read about Curzon's rule as Viceroy of India, use the information, sources and ideas in this case study to answer the following question:

How far would you agree with the view that Curzon made a 'colossal failure' of his job as Viceroy?

Question

What were (a) the strengths and (b) the weaknesses of the Indian Civil Service, set up by the British to enable them to govern India?

Joining the Indian Civil Service

The Indian Civil Service, based in India, was responsible for administering India. In doing so, it became renowned for its efficiency and was the model for administrators throughout the British Empire. Young men wanting a career in the Service had first to pass a competitive exam and then to spend time in India working with a district officer. Leadership and all-round intelligence were prized more than academic achievement because members of the Indian Civil Service had to be able to turn their hands to anything, from tax assessment to school prize-givings, from sorting out local disputes to dealing with rogue elephants.

Working for the Indian Civil Service

When they were still young men, district officers had authority over thousands of Indians. Civil Service district officers developed different attitudes and different sorts of expertise, depending on the districts for which they were responsible. Men administering the Punjab, for example, became expert in agricultural matters, while those in Bengal had to deal with a rapidly rising educated, professional business class of Indian. Some, of course, were not interested in staying too long 'in the field'. Those who did so were suspected of having 'gone native', of developing too much sympathy with the plight of the Indians to the detriment of the ruling British.

Ambitious young men worked for a short time as district officers and then applied for promotion to the government offices in provincial capitals. Here, some of them became overwhelmed by the sheer volume of paperwork. On the one hand, the network of railways and roads, telephone, postal and telegraphic systems built by British engineers helped the efficient administration of India. On the other hand, they meant that letters, instructions, questionnaires and directives could be sent out in their hundreds to all corners of the Indian Empire, and replies analysed and filed for future reference. The system was many times close to grinding to a halt under the sheer weight of bureaucracy. It was systems like this that tended to stifle innovation and block radical thinking.

Lord Curzon had his own view of the Indian Civil Service:

Source K

There are neither originality, nor ideas, nor imagination in the Indian Civil Service; they think the present the best, and improvement or reform sends a cold shiver down their spine. Where would have been any one of the great subjects that I have taken up – Education, Irrigation, Police, Railways – if I had waited for the local governments to give the cue?

From C.H. Philips, *The Evolution of India and Pakistan*, published in 1962

But the one thing nearly all British administrators had in common was their deeply held conviction that the British had a God-given right to be in India and that that right carried with it a responsibility to the Indian people. Members of the Indian Civil Service were well paid. This was because they were expected to be above the sort of bribery the government expected them to be offered by Indians anxious to have their particular project, village or family favoured.

Sir Walter Lawrence joined the Indian Civil Service in 1877, serving mainly in the Punjab and Kashmir. He worked as a private secretary to Viceroy Lord Curzon between 1898 and 1903. Here he reflects on his time in India:

Source L

Our life in India, our very work more or less, rests on illusion. I had the illusion, wherever I was, that I was infallible and invulnerable in my dealing with Indians. How else could I have dealt with angry mobs, with cholera-stricken masses, and with processions of religious fanatics? It was not conceit, heaven knows: it was not the prestige of the British Raj, but it was the illusion which is in the very air of India. They expressed something of the idea when they called us the 'heaven born', and the idea is really make-believe – mutual make-believe. They, the millions, made us believe we had a divine mission. We made them believe we were right. Unconsciously, perhaps, I may have had at the back of my mind that there was a British Battalion and a Battery of Artillery at the Cantonment near Ajmere; but I never thought of this, and I do not think that many of the primitive and simple Mers [tribe living in eastern Rajasthan] had ever heard of or seen English soldiers. But they saw the head of the Queen-Empress on the **rupee** and worshipped it. They had a vague conception of the Raj, which they looked on as a power, omnipotent, all-pervading, benevolent for the most part but capricious, a deity of many shapes and many moods.

From Lewis D. Wurgraft, *The Imperial Imagination: Magic and Myth in Kipling's India*, published in 1983

Definition

Rupee
Indian currency.

Source M

The British in India numbered scarcely 200,000, and of these only a fraction actually ruled, in the sense of administered; at the policy and command level, the Raj was run by about 1,000 members of the Indian Civil Service. Thus it was said that the Service constituted the 'steel frame' of British rule in India. Explicit in this steel frame argument is the Kiplingesque notion that the average British district officer was a pretty capable chap who worked hard, lived clean, and had little regard for personal danger. Implicit is the suggestion that the district officers exercised a kind of sway over the ordinary people they ruled, a sway that was partly rooted in deference for their position as representatives of the government, but was also a function of the sharp physical and social differences that set them apart from their subjects: differences of height, colour, dress and demeanour, that in status-conscious India marked them out as men of high caste.

From Ian Copeland, *India 1885–1947*, published in 2001

Could Indian people work as administrators?

It was possible, but very difficult, for Indians to work in the Indian Civil Service. Stanley Reed, a British journalist working in India in the early years of the twentieth century, explained:

Source N

There was nothing on paper to stop the Indian from competing in the Civil Service examinations, but to do this he had to sit the exams in London and round off his education at a British university. He or his family had to find the ready cash, certainly not less than £1000. The candidate had to face the risks of higher education in a foreign country and a severe test in unfamiliar surroundings. A limited number of Indians won through, and some attained high office. So serious was this handicap that in a personnel of twelve hundred in the early part of this century, not more than fifty were natives.

From S. Reed, *The India I Knew*, published in 1952

Source O

3.4 An Indian Civil Service officer at work in 1925

Question

What can you learn about the administration of India from Source O?

It wasn't until 1919 that Indian Civil Service exams were held in Delhi and Rangoon as well as in Britain.

Although, in 1900, there were few Indians in the Indian Civil Service, Indians did work with the British in other ways. Indians worked as policemen, lawyers and soldiers, for example, but there were always, at least at the beginning of the twentieth century, British officers and officials above them.

How much of India did the British govern?

Source P

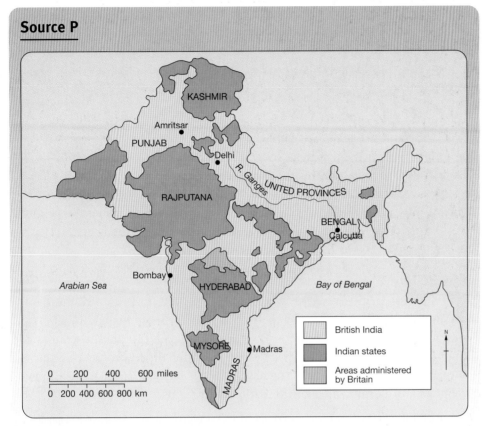

3.5 A map showing the parts of India that were governed directly by the British and those that were governed indirectly through the Indian princes

Discussion point

Would the existence of the Indian states be likely to make the work of the British Raj easier or more difficult?

How were the princely states governed?

The British provinces of India, such as Bombay, Punjab and Madras, were ruled directly by the British government through the Viceroy and the Indian Civil Service. But, as can be seen from Source P (above), there were vast areas of India that did not seem to be subject to the British Raj. About 35 per cent of the country, consisting of 562 separate states, was ruled by their princes. Some of these states were large, about the size of Wales. Hyderabad, for example, covered 77,000 square kilometres and contained around 14 million people. Others were tiny, consisting of a few hundred people. For example, Kathiwar was only a few square kilometres in size and had fewer than 200 inhabitants. How were these states governed?

Treaty arrangements

Rulers of the princely states had, in theory, complete authority over those whom they ruled. Practice, however, was somewhat different. They all had treaty arrangements with Britain. These treaties allowed a degree of local autonomy. Each state could keep its own laws, languages, holidays, ministers and ruler. But each state was under the 'protection' of Britain and

43

so, really, couldn't instigate any action that ran counter to the interests of the British Raj. If, for example, a princely state wanted to set up an industry to manufacture railway carriages or even the upholstery for such carriages, then the Raj would not allow this. The treaties would be scoured, the removal of aid and other support would be threatened and the railways themselves would be forbidden to buy any such products. It simply would not happen.

The Resident

The four largest princely states – Hyderabad, Mysore, Jammu and Kashmir, and Baroda – were under the direct administration of the Viceroy. He was represented in these states by a Resident, whom he appointed. This not only gave these particular princely states status above the others, but in effect created a 'hot line' to the seat of power in India.

The political officer

The remaining princely states, which were deemed by Britain not to be as important as the four largest ones, had political officers instead of a Resident. These political officers were answerable to the administrators of India's provinces. Five princely states were under the authority of Madras, 354 of Bombay, 26 of Bengal, 2 of Assam, 34 of Punjab, 15 of the Central Provinces and Berar, and 2 of the United Provinces.

Source Q

3.6 A British officer rides in state on an elephant to the *maharajah*'s palace during celebrations when a new *maharajah* succeeded to the throne

Discussion point

What does Source Q tell you about the relationship between British India and the princes?

Although the princes were treated with elaborate courtesies, they were never allowed to forget that the British did not regard them as equal allies. Believing it was their duty to guard the princes' subjects as best they could, the British, in the treaties made with the princely states, insisted on the right to intervene and administer a princely state if they felt it was being misgoverned. Thus, while they valued their princely allies, the British never quite believed that they ruled their subjects as well as the Raj could, if only it was given the opportunity to do so.

Was power-sharing a possibility?

What was the impact of the Indian Mutiny?

During the final years of the nineteenth century, there was a slow but steady growth within India of western-educated Indians. The British administration in India became gradually aware that they should make some sort of accommodation with these highly educated and influential Indians. The Indian Mutiny of 1857 (see page 12) had given the British a fright; it had shown the more perceptive among them just what could happen if the rulers became seriously out of touch with the ruled. What, many British were beginning to argue, could be more sensible than using these educated Indians to alert the Raj to potential problems and advise as to possible strategies? Furthermore, although Indians such as these could not claim to represent Indian society, they were a legitimate interest group which, the British argued, should be taken seriously.

In the immediate aftermath of the Indian Mutiny, the British set up a number of consultative councils that were intended to give them 'ears to the ground'. But the British were careful not to give these councils any real power – they were, after all, to operate in an advisory capacity only. The British made sure, too, that the councillors were their nominees and, later, that they were elected on a franchise that was biased in favour of the educated and wealthy Indian.

What did the 1861 Indian Councils' Act permit?

The 1861 Indian Councils' Act reorganised the Viceroy's Legislative Council, which advised the Viceroy and his provincial governors, and allowed for provincial legislative councils to be set up. Members of these councils, however, were chosen by government, not elected, and, as they were only permitted to discuss legislation not enact it, their role was somewhat limited. Even so, the Secretary of State for India, Sir Charles Wood, clearly believed that this Act was of immense importance: 'The Act is a great experiment. That everything is changing in India is obvious enough, and that the old autocratic government cannot stand unmodified is indisputable.'

What was Lord Ripon's Plan?

In 1883, Lord Ripon (Viceroy 1880–84) introduced a local self-government plan. Most Indian towns already had municipal corporations or councils, and some districts had local rural boards as well. Indians usually formed a majority on these bodies. From 1883, they were given extra powers to raise money for local works. This had the advantage of reducing the financial cost to the Raj and of making local bodies responsible to their electorate. Municipal corporations and rural boards would soon be voted out of power if they tried to raise and spend too much of their electorate's money. This was regarded by the Raj more as a cost-cutting exercise than a move toward local self-government. 'We shall not subvert the British Empire by allowing the Bengali Baboo to discuss his own schools and drains', commented Sir Evelyn Baring, secretary to the Viceroy. Indeed, since the 1860s, the British Raj had suffered a series of budgetary crises due, among other things, to the increasing cost of defending the Empire. The Ripon reforms offered an ideal way of saving money.

The First Indian National Congress

Two years later, in 1885, the first Indian National Congress was convened (see pages 50–53) and met in Bombay. At first, it was just that – a congress, a discussion forum. It certainly wasn't a political party and couldn't, at this stage, even be described as a movement. It wasn't unique, either: a similar convention was held at the same time in Bombay, although they were to merge the following year. And it wasn't exclusively Indian: its founder was a white British man, a former Secretary for Agriculture in the Calcutta government. What does seem to have been happening at this point was that Indian opinion was beginning to be articulated in a far more formal context than ever before.

Question

How much power had been devolved to Indians by 1900?

Discussion point

Why do you think the British were unwilling to allow Indians to enter the Indian Civil Service yet were more prepared to allow them a voice in provincial assemblies?

How progressive was the 1892 Indian Councils' Act?

The 1892 Indian Councils' Act allowed municipalities and district boards to 'recommend' additional members to the provincial legislative councils. This gave the first real opportunity for educated Indians to take part in a formal consultative process that was part of the structure of the Raj. As well as discussing legislation (allowed under the 1861 Act), in future, councils could discuss finance as well and ask questions of the executive and expect them to be answered. Even so, the majority of people sitting on provincial councils were still officials of the Raj.

How limited was the Raj?

The British Raj might seem to have been all-powerful in India and the Indian Empire a kind of model super-state, an example to which the rest of the British Empire should aspire. But was this, in reality, the case? Just how much control did the British have in India?

The British had an army in India and could, if necessary, call upon regiments stationed elsewhere in the Empire and in Britain. But an army was a blunt instrument when it came to every-day crowd control and the management of demonstrations. For this, the British had to rely on the police and they were stretched very thinly indeed. Large towns like Madras had one policeman to every 2000 inhabitants and in the countryside the police were almost non-existent. So, while India was spared invasion and inter-state conflict, murders, muggings and riots were commonplace.

There were only a few personnel available in the Indian Civil Service for district administration. This meant that most of the day-to-day work had to be undertaken by low-paid Indians. Many of these Indian officials were corrupt. They took bribes, falsified records and found employment for their friends and relatives. In 1884 in the Tanjore District, for example, over 800,000 rupees, which should have gone into the district revenue, ended up in the pockets of a group of Madrasi *Brahmins* led by the collector's chief native assistant. Thus British authority was often severely compromised by local people who were working to different agendas. Much depended on deals struck and favours that could be bought.

The value of the support given to the British by the Indian princes was often doubtful. Several times toward the end of the nineteenth century, the British had intervened in the internal affairs of a state to correct gross injustices and mismanagements, and in some cases deposed the sitting ruler before reforms could be instituted.

The administrative structure set up by the British in India provided an effective framework within which the power of the British Raj could be exercised. However, this was a framework only. What became known in the twentieth century as the Raj's 'steel frame' was still made predominantly of British manpower. The British were unable to rule simply by force. They were reliant on thousands of Indians, whom they kept as subordinates and whose loyalty they perceived as doubtful, to keep the wheels of administration turning. The exercise of British power depended very much on the co-operation of the Indian people.

Questions

1 List the ways in which the Raj could be thought of as being vulnerable.
2 How could the Raj be removed?

Unit summary

What have you learned in this unit?

You have learned about the structure of government in British India and about the ways in which it operated at local and national level, as well as about the overall control of the British Parliament in Westminster. A case study of George Curzon, who was Viceroy between 1898 and 1905, has shed light on the role of Viceroy at the beginning of the twentieth century. You have learned about the extent of British rule in the Indian sub-continent and the relationship of British India with the princely states. Finally, you have considered the limitations of the power of the Raj and whether power-sharing with the Indian community was a possibility.

What skills have you used in this unit?

You have worked with source material to enhance your understanding of the stresses and strains that existed within the administration of British India. You have analysed sources in order to understand the level of support and challenge they provide when related to a range of ideas and opinions about the nature of British rule in India, cross-referencing between them as appropriate. In particular, you have used the source material to detect the weaknesses of the Raj and potential unrest in the Indian community.

Exam tips

This is the sort of question you will find appearing on exam papers as a (b) question.

- Study Sources K, L and M, and use your own knowledge. How far do you agree with the view, expressed in Source M, that the Indian Civil Service constituted the 'steel frame' for British rule in India?

Tips for answering (b) questions

- Do be clear about the question focus. What is being claimed? In this case, what is being claimed is that the Indian Civil Service created a 'steel frame' for British rule in India. You will need to define what you understand by 'steel frame' so that the examiner can see how you use this criterion when you test it against the sources and your own knowledge.
- What does a 'steel frame' mean? You could define it as a 'firm structure' or a 'rigid framework'. Both would be acceptable – or you could use both and point out the ambiguity of the phrase. It could be used negatively or positively.
- Analyse the sources to establish points that support and points that challenge the view given in the question.
- Develop each point by reference to your own wider knowledge, using it to reinforce and/or develop the points derived from the sources.
- Combine the points into arguments for and against the stated view.
- Evaluate the conflicting arguments.
- Present a judgement as to the validity of the stated view.
- And, above all, plan your answer.

RESEARCH TOPIC

Many fictional books have been written about India, and films made from some of them. Find a fictional book, film or DVD about India and assess how close it comes to reality. Here are some ideas:

- Forster, E.M. *Passage to India*
- Roy, A. *The God of Small Things*
- Rushdie, S. *Midnight's Children*
- Scott, P. *The Raj Quartet*
- Seth, V. *A Suitable Boy*

4 Change and continuity, 1900–19

What is this unit about?

As you have seen, in the years to 1900, the British Raj had developed strategies for ensuring that it was never again caught unawares by a rising as devastating as the Indian Mutiny. A major strategy was to embark on a process whereby a small number of carefully selected Indians were enabled to participate, albeit marginally, in the Raj's decision-making process. A second, no less important, strategy was to devolve some financial management to Indians to enable them to manage their own affairs at a local level. Thus the need for some sort of rapprochement with the Indian people was not really questioned by any of the British in positions of authority. The problem was to decide how much to give and when to give it.

This unit focuses on the ways in which this problem was addressed in the years to 1919. Twice during the early twentieth century the British were forced by pressure of events to face this dilemma: between 1906 and 1909 and again between 1916 and 1919. How the imperial authorities reacted and what the impact of this was on India and Indian affairs was to have a profound impact on the direction Indian politics were to take. This somewhat careful and almost unwilling rapprochement was running in tandem with a growing sense of national consciousness among the Indian people.

Key questions

- How far did the British Raj make concessions to Indian demands for involvement in the governance of India?
- To what extent, and why, did Indian nationalism develop in the years to 1919?

Timeline

1885	First meeting of the Indian National Congress
1905	Lord Minto replaces Lord Curzon as Viceroy of India
	John Morley becomes Secretary of State at the India Office in London
1906	Simla Deputation of Muslims to Lord Minto
1908	Morley–Minto Reforms announced
1909	India Councils Act
1910	Lord Hardinge becomes Viceroy of India
1911	*Durbar* to celebrate the coronation of King George V and Queen Mary held in Delhi
	Capital of British India moved from Calcutta to Delhi
	Reunification of Bengal

1914	Outbreak of the First World War
1916	Lord Chelmsford becomes Viceroy of India
	Lucknow Pact
1917	Edwin Montagu becomes Secretary of State at the India Office in London
	Montagu Declaration
1919	Rowlatt Acts
	Montagu-Chelmsford Report
	Government of India Act

Indian Nationalism

In 1883, Allan Octavian Hume, a former member of the Indian Civil Service, an outspoken critic of the Raj who rose to be Secretary of the Revenue and Agriculture Department, wrote an open letter to Calcutta University graduates. This is part of what he wrote.

Source A

If only fifty men can be found with sufficient power of self-sacrifice, sufficient love for and pride in their country, sufficient genuine and unselfish heartfelt patriotism to take the initiative, India can be reborn.

From a letter written by Allan Octavian Hume in 1883

SKILLS BUILDER

- What sort of person is Allan Hume trying to reach? Why?
- From what you know of India so far, what would you expect the response to have been to a letter like this?
- Should the Raj have felt threatened by what Allan Hume wrote?

Two years later, in 1885, 73 representatives from every province of British India met in Bombay at the first annual meeting of the Indian National Congress, presided over by Womesh C. Bonnerjee, a barrister of the Calcutta High Court. Simultaneously, a national conference of the Indian Association, an organisation started by the Bengali politician and editor Surendranath Banerjea, was held in Calcutta. The Bombay meeting, however, was more prestigious and more broadly based, and the following year the two were to merge. The holding of these two conferences were indicative of the need felt by the movers and shakers of Indian opinion for a more formal forum in which to discuss, form and direct Indian national sentiment.

Who attended the first meeting of the Indian National Congress?

Most of the delegates at the Congress were high-caste Hindus, all of whom spoke English and most of whom were lawyers, although there was a smattering of teachers, journalists and businessmen among them, along with some wealthy landowners and merchants. The delegates were not exclusively Indian. Allan Hume, for example, who had been instrumental in calling the Congress in the first place and a close friend of the Liberal politician Lord Ripon (Viceroy 1880–84), attended and played a key advisory role. It is important to emphasise that in these early days, the Congress was simply a forum for discussion. It was not a political party and could not even, in any sense, be called a movement. Later, however, it was to become the organisational vehicle for Indian's first great Nationalist Movement (see pages 89–103).

What did the first meeting of the Indian National Congress want?

The delegates met for three days and everyone proclaimed their loyalty to the British Crown and, by extension, to the Raj. However, all the people who spoke expressed some level of dissatisfaction with the ways in which the Raj was governing India. Delegates wanted:

- the basis of the Indian government to be widened so that the 'people should have their proper and legitimate share in it'
- the opening of the Indian Civil Service to Indians
- opportunities for Indians to serve on various government councils
- more of India's wealth to be spent on internal improvements and less on the military
- the abolition of the Secretary of State's council in Whitehall, viewing it as a waste of India's resources and a block to radical progress within India.

Initially, these resolutions were framed within the spirit of co-operation with the Raj, but, as you will see later, they formed the platform from which more radical demands were made, culminating in the demand for independence. However, not everyone agreed about the nature and purpose of the Congress. **Annie Besant** (see page 52) was instrumental in setting up the Congress and here recounts part of an address made by its president at the first meeting:

Definition

Swaraj
Self rule.

Source B

'Indians are British citizens and claim all British citizens' rights. The first of these is freedom.' He then claimed for Indians in India all the control that Englishmen had in England. This was a necessity, in order to remedy the great economic evil which was at the root of Indian poverty. It was 'absolutely necessary' for the progress and welfare of the Indian people. 'The whole matter can be comprised in one word, Self-government, or *Swaraj*.' When should a beginning be made which should automatically develop into full Self-Government? At once. 'Not only has the time fully arrived, but had arrived long past.'

From Annie Besant, *How India Wrought for Freedom*, published in 1915

Source C

The people of India are not the 7000 students at universities, but the millions with whom neither education nor the influence of European ideas have transformed. We are under the shadow of an enormous danger – the overpopulation of the country. Where is there a more crying need for sanitary reform than amongst those who insist on bathing in their tanks of drinking water and where millions die of disease? What misery is spread amongst millions of women by the immoral custom of child marriage! Yet where have any of these been the subject of serious enquiry [by Congress]? The fact is that Congress is the product of a tiny section of the Indian community touched by European education, ideas and literature. They neither represent the aristocratic section of Indian society, nor are they in contact with the great mass of the population: they do not understand their wants or necessities. They are very imperfectly fitted to grasp any of the larger questions which affect the stability or safety of the Empire as a whole.

To hand over, therefore, the government of India, either partially or otherwise to such a body as this, would simply be to place millions of men, dozens of nationalities, and hundreds of the most stupendous interests under the domination of a microscopic minority, possessing neither experience, administrative ability, nor any adequate conception of the nature of the tasks before them.

From a Minute on British policy in India written by Viceroy Lord Dufferin in November 1888

SKILLS BUILDER

Read Sources B and C.

1 What, according to Annie Besant's report, were the reasons why India should have independence?

2 What reasons does Viceroy Dufferin give for opposing Indian involvement in governance?

3 Set up a debate between 'Annie Besant' and 'Viceroy Dufferin', with individuals or groups of two or three students taking on the role of each person. Try to convince the rest of the group that your view about Indian independence is correct.

Biography

Annie Besant (1847–1933)

In England, Annie Besant was a social reformer, Vice-President of the National Secular Society and a free thinker. She formed a close relationship with Charles Bradlaugh, with whom she co-edited *The National Reformer* and with whom in 1875 she was prosecuted for spreading information about birth-control. She became a Socialist, joined the Fabian Society and worked to publicise trade union issues, being instrumental in organising the Bryant and May's match girls' strike.

In 1889, Annie converted to theosophy, a philosophy based on an understanding of the nature of God, seeing this as a link between Socialism and spirituality. She visited India in 1893, where the headquarters of the Theosophical Society were located. Deciding India was her one true home, she settled there for the rest of her life.

Annie learned Sanskrit, studied Hindu religious books and was determined to raise Hindu self-esteem in the face of the imperialism of the British Raj. She founded the Central Hindu College in 1898 and a network of schools throughout India that were administered by the Theosophical Society. After 1913, Annie turned her attention to Indian Independence and, in 1917, was appointed President of Congress, a post she held until 1923. Gradually, however, she lost nationalist support and was eclipsed by the campaigns of Gandhi.

Hindu or Muslim?

Congress was, at the start, dominated by Hindus, most of whom were high-caste. Although a substantial number of **Parsis** and Jains attended the first meeting, there were, significantly, only two Muslims. This situation had changed by the time of the third annual meeting of Congress, held in Madras, where 83 of the 600 delegates were Muslim. However, this domination of Congress by Hindus was to continue and India's largest minority community never felt easy under its umbrella. This led them (see pages 122–135) to turn to and create alternative political organisations, which were themselves to pursue a different sort of nationalist agenda.

Source D

Year	Place	Number of delegates	Brahmin	Non-Brahmin Hindu	Muslim	Parsi	Christian	Other
1892	Allahabad	625	261	254	91	1	10	8
1893	Lahore	867	207	523	65	20	12	40
1894	Madras	1163	744	371	23	6	12	7
1895	Poona	1584	996	494	25	16	10	43
1896	Calcutta	784	282	427	54	4	15	2
1897	Amraoti	692	287	327	57	8	8	5
1898	Madras	614	401	192	10	2	7	2
1899	Lucknow	739	135	280	313	2	6	3
1900	Lahore	567	65	400	56	4	4	38
1901	Calcutta	896	268	533	74	2	7	12
1902	Ahmedabad	471	115	306	20	22	6	2
1903	Madras	538	336	180	9	5	2	6
1904	Bombay	1010	189	715	35	65	1	5
1905	Benares	757	268	437	20	6	2	24
1906	Calcutta	1663	523	1046	45	25	8	16
1907	No data							
1908	Madras	626	383	206	10	20	5	2
1909	Lahore	243	63	169	5	2	2	2

4.1 The religious make-up of the Indian National Congress meetings from 1892 to 1909. From P. Gosh, *The Development of the Indian National Congress 1892–1909,* published in 1960

Definition

Parsi

Parsis believe in a good and just God – Ahura Mazda – who created the world to be a battleground between himself and the evil spirit, Angra Mainyu, in which evil would be defeated. The role of mankind is to serve the creator and honour his seven creations: sky, water, earth, plant, animal, human and fire. Although Ahura Mazda is wise, he is vulnerable and humans must be his assistants in order to help restore harmony in a world stricken by evil.

SKILLS BUILDER

Work in pairs or small groups.

1 What conclusions can you draw from Source D about the religious make-up of the Indian National Congress meetings from 1892 to 1909?

2 In your judgement, did the city in which Congress met have an impact on its religious make-up? (An atlas may be helpful here.)

Was Congress the only way Indians were making their views heard?

Something as organised as Congress doesn't come out of nowhere. All kinds of threads, all kinds of different initiatives, led to the 1885 meeting. Here are some examples.

In 1870, the *Brahmin* Mahadev Govind Ranade founded the 'Sarvajanik Sabha' (All People's Association) in Poona. Its aim was to help all Indians realise their potential by making full and effective use of the existing political institutions. Although prevented by his position on the Indian bench from formally joining the Indian National Congress, he founded India's National Social Conference in 1887, which considered social issues, particularly the plight of Hindu widows.

Gopal Krishna Gokhale was a follower of Ranade, who developed the idea of nationalism by insisting on the need for Indians to reform their own social and religious ideas and resolve their own internal conflicts before they could begin to consider anything as radical as political independence.

In 1879, Vasudeo Balwant Phadke, a petty clerk in the government's Military Accounts Department suddenly got the bit between his teeth, named himself 'Minister to Shivaji II' and rode off into the hills of Maharashtra to raise an army against the Crown. This wasn't, perhaps, as crazy as it may sound. Shivaji (1627–80) was the founder of the Maratha kingdom. Inspired by the heroes of Hindu mythologies, he considered it his mission to liberate India from the Islamic Mughals. Phadke was following this example and, in his view, living out Hindu mythology and history. It took the British four years to catch him!

Biography

Gopal Krishna Gokhale (1866–1915)

A member of the Indian National Congress from 1889, Gokhale became its joint secretary six years later, sharing the office with the extremist, Bal Tilak.

Gopal was a moderate and a reformer. He deprecated the caste system and untouchability, and supported the emancipation of women. He believed that the introduction of Western education into India was a positive and liberalising influence, and advocated free primary school education for all children. He wanted greater autonomy for Indians, but only for those who would co-operate with the Raj. In doing this, he argued, India stood the best chance of becoming a self-governing dominion within the British Empire.

While supporting the Raj in general terms, he wasn't afraid to criticise it. He believed, for example, that Britain's economic policy in India was disastrous, leading to considerable poverty and suffering. He was constantly arguing for increased industrialisation and for the mechanisation of agriculture.

Gopal visited England many times and was involved in discussions with John Morley that led directly to the Morley–Minto Reforms and the Indian Councils Act of 1909.

Another nationalist, Vihnu Hari Chiplunkar, was so inspired by Phadke that he, too, left his government post. Instead of taking to the hills, he opened a private school in Poona. Chiplunkar's poetry and political essays inspired many young people, including **Bal Gangadhar Tilak**.

By the beginning of the twentieth century, Indian nationalism was well established in a far more formal setting than ever before. It did not simply have a voice, it had the organisational basis from which to grow and develop as a political force.

Biography

Bal Gangadhar Tilak (1856–1920)

Indian nationalist, social reformer and the first popular leader of an Indian independence movement, Tilak was born into a middle-class Hindu family. After a modern, college education he first taught mathematics and then became a journalist.

Tilak founded the Marathi daily newspaper *Kesari*, in which he strongly criticised the Raj for its suppression of freedom of expression, especially after the partition of Bengal. Tilak joined the Indian National Congress in the 1890s where he opposed the moderate approach of Gokhale. When the Congress party split into two factions, Tilak led the extremists *(Garam Dal)*. Arrested on charges of sedition in 1906, and defended by Muhammad Ali Jinnah, Tilak was convicted and imprisoned in Mandalay, Burma, until 1914. On his release, he rejoined the Indian National Congress.

Tilak criticised Gandhi's strategy of non-violent, civil disobedience as a way of gaining independence for India. Mellowing in later life, Tilak favoured political dialogue as a way of moving forward. Although he wanted independence for India, he wanted this independence to be exercised within the British Empire.

The Morley–Minto reforms, 1909

In 1909, Viceroy Lord Minto and Lord **John Morley** (see page 56), the Secretary of State for India introduced a whole raft of reforms.

Why were reforms necessary?

Backlash against Lord Curzon's partition of Bengal (see pages 38–39) had spread far beyond Bengal. When Minto arrived in India to take over as Viceroy from Lord Curzon, agitation against partition was at its height. Minto was himself threatened with assassination.

Towards the end of 1906, the Lieutenant-General of the Punjab, Denzil Ibbetson, faced such unrest that he feared an uprising similar to the Indian Mutiny 50 years earlier. Beginning as a protest against proposals for higher

Biography

John Morley (1838–1923)

The British general election of 1906 swept the Liberal Party to power and John Morley into the Indian Office as Secretary of State and a peerage two years later.

Morley was a liberal reformer and a follower of the philosopher J.S. Mill. In Gladstone's administration, Morley had supported Home Rule for Ireland and, in the early years of the twentieth century, was a strong supporter of female suffrage. In 1914, he resigned from the government because of his opposition to the First World War and later failed to persuade the coalition government to work for a negotiated peace.

As Secretary of State for India, Morley saw it as his duty to spread throughout India the ideals of justice, law and humanity that he saw as being fundamental to civilisation. He wanted Indian people to become more involved in governing India in order to eliminate that sense of inferiority that had been impressed upon them by the Raj and to enable India to make progress towards achieving his ideals for the country. He most definitely did not see Indian participation in government as one of the steps towards independence for India, neither was he in favour of universal suffrage in the Indian context. This was because he believed it was dangerous to apply democratic principles to people so fragmented by religion, race and caste. It would then be too easy, he maintained, for one faction to override the needs of another. Checks and balances were what were required to enable all 'voices' to be heard.

charges and stricter regulations for settlers in areas irrigated by government-funded waterways, the situation escalated at such a rate that Ibbetson feared a conspiracy. Riots and murders were commonplace and there were rumours that the Punjabi army was on the point of mutiny. However, the whole affair turned out to be something of a damp squib. While Minto, based in India, suspected a conspiracy, Morley, the Secretary of State for India based in London, did not. An enquiry into the loyalty of the Punjabi soldiers revealed that they had been considerably swayed by agitators, who had urged them to strike in order to gain redress of grievances such as pay and promotion prospects. At this critical point, Ibbetson left India for medical treatment in England. The potential threat to the loyalty of the whole Punjabi army and the devastating consequences this would have on the Raj convinced Minto that the proposed charges and regulations should be withdrawn, and they were. The Punjabis went wild with delight and made their continuing loyalty to the Crown abundantly clear.

The Indian National Congress was growing increasingly concerned about the extremists in its midst and by the power struggle that was going on within Congress between the extremists and the moderates. Morley, in particular, was influenced by Gopal Krishna Gokhale (see page 54), a highly educated, moderate Indian who visited England many times and with whom Morley had many frank discussions about the difficulties faced by Indians in positions of influence in maintaining a moderate stance.

Morley, back in England, and Lord Minto, on the spot in India, together became convinced that more concessions had to be made to the Indian people. Indians had to be drawn in still further to the process of government. It had become clear that politically active Indians could, in certain circumstances, sway the masses behind them. It was thus obvious, at least to Morley, that loyalty to the British Raj had to be both encouraged and rewarded.

What was the significance of the Simla Deputation?

Agitation by the Indian National Congress against the partition of Bengal was mainly a protest against the 'divide and rule' policy that Viceroy Curzon and the Governor of Bengal were attempting to carry out. Many Muslims, however, believed that the Indian National Congress' agitation showed that they would not be fairly treated by any organisation with a Hindu majority. To safeguard their interests, Muslim leaders drew up a plan for separate electorates and presented it to the Viceroy, Lord Minto, at Simla in 1906.

The Simla Deputation consisted of some 70 delegates representing all shades of Muslim opinion. The deputation stressed that the Muslim community should not be judged by its numerical strength alone but by its political importance and the service it had rendered to the Empire. The deputation further pointed out that western ideas of democracy were not appropriate for India and stressed the need for care when introducing or extending the electoral system in whatever sphere – local or national.

Minto replied by assuring the Simla Deputation that their political rights and interests as a community would be safeguarded in any administrative reorganisation in which he was involved.

Lady Minto wrote her diary entry for 1 October 1906 in Simla:

Source E

This has been a very eventful day: as someone said to me, an epoch in Indian history. We are aware of the feeling of unrest that exists throughout India, and the dissatisfaction that prevails amongst people of all classes and creeds. The Mahommedan population, which numbers sixty-two millions, who have always been intensely loyal, resent not having proper representation, and consider themselves slighted in many ways, preference having been given to the Hindus. The agitators have been most anxious to foster this feeling and have naturally done their utmost to secure the co-operation of this vast community. The younger generation were wavering, inclined to throw in their lot with the advanced agitators of the Congress. The Mahommedans decided, before taking action, that they would bring an Address to the Viceroy, mentioning their grievances. Minto then read his answer, which he had thought out most carefully: 'Your Address, as I understand it, is a claim that, in any system of representation, whether it affects a Municipality, a District Board, or a Legislative Council, in which it is proposed to introduce or increase an electoral organisation, the Mahommedan community should be represented as a community. I am entirely in accord with you.'

A journal entry written by Lady Minto on 1 October 1906

Questions

1 What is Lady Minto's attitude to the Hindus?
2 Why do you think Lord Minto was prepared to move away from the 'one man, one vote' principle to community representation when he was administering India?

This assurance was to have long-term significance as the Raj struggled to give Indians a greater say in their own affairs.

What were the reforms proposed by Morley and Minto?

Morley seems to have been the driving force behind the reforms that were finally agreed. It was Lord Minto who proposed a series of moderate reforms that he said would 'satisfy the legitimate aspirations of all but the most advanced Indians' and John Morley who came back with much more radical proposals. Minto, for example, envisaged a modest increase in the number of Indians nominated by the Raj to serve on the various councils, while Morley proposed a larger number of Indian representatives and wanted them to be elected. Morley was determined to reduce the number of officials (invariably white and invariably British) serving on provincial councils and on the Viceroy's Executive Council.

The reforms that were finally agreed between Lord John Morley and Lord Minto were announced in November 1908 and enshrined in the Indian Councils Act of 1909:

- Sixty Indian representatives were to be elected to serve on the Viceroy's Executive Council; 27 of these were to be elected from territorial constituencies and special interest groups. However, officials remained in the majority.
- The provincial councils were to be enlarged sufficiently to create non-official majorities.
- Separate electorates were provided for Muslims and Hindus in order to allow the minority Muslims to have a voice in the various councils.

Additionally, Morley appointed two Indians to his London-based group of advisers. Minto, responding to Morley's urging to act in a similar way, appointed Satyendra Sinha, the advocate-general of Bengal, to be his law member. However, Minto and his officials in Calcutta, although believing the reforms to be essential, thought of them as a defensive action. Morley, on the other hand, regarded them as a significant step toward colonial self-government.

Question

What did Lord Morley hope the effects of the reforms would be?

Source F

There are three classes of people whom we have to consider in dealing with a scheme of this kind. There are the extremists, who nurse fanatic dreams that someday they will drive us out of India. The second group nourishes no hopes of this sort, but hope for autonomy or self-government of the colonial species and pattern. And then the third section of this classification asks for no more than to be admitted to co-operation in our administration. I believe the effect of the Reforms has been, is being, and will be to draw the second class, who hope for autonomy, into the third class, who will be content with being admitted to a fair and full co-operation.

From a speech by Lord Morley to the House of Lords in 1909

What were the effects of the Morley–Minto Reforms?

By far the most important effect of the Morley–Minto Reforms was that from 1909 onwards, Indians were involved in policy making both in India and, because of Morley's nominations, in Britain too. Their voice, at this stage, may not have been loud, but it was a voice, and it was a voice that was legally entitled to be heard.

However, there were those for whom the reforms were either too much or too little.

The 'extremists'

The right to vote was restricted to the rich and privileged. Indian vested interests were protected because seats were reserved for landowners and members of chambers of commerce. These were exactly the sorts of moderate men who could be expected to support the Raj. Thousands of politically minded Indians expected more; the extremists were isolated and regarded the reforms as nothing more than cynical window-dressing on the part of the Raj. They continued their fight for full Indian self-government, and terrorism in all its forms continued.

Administrators

Many British administrators were disappointed and disheartened by the changes, which diluted their power. They were no longer in the majority on provincial councils and had to contend with a substantial Indian minority on the Viceroy's Executive Council. Many British administrators genuinely believed that they governed India in the best interests of the Indians. They believed that, divided by faction, caste and religion, Indian people could not be expected to govern India impartially. Dispassionate judgement, they maintained, was beyond the mentality of the Indians.

The Indian Civil Service had for years maintained that they spoke for the vast mass of Indian people. They couldn't maintain this stance any longer and so believed their influence had been diminished. They feared for their future.

Congress

Congress, dominated by Hindus, while generally supporting the reforms, bitterly regretted that electoral procedures were designed to achieve a balance of minority interests. Muslim interests were protected by creating a separate electorate for them and by imposing lower property and educational qualifications for Muslim voters than for Hindus. Congress would have had it otherwise.

Question

Was the Indian National Congress loyal to the Raj, or not, at this time?

SKILLS BUILDER

How far do Sources E, F and G suggest that the Morley–Minto Reforms only benefited the Muslims?

Definition

Durbar

In Mughal India, *durbars* were open ceremonial gatherings to receive subjects and visitors in audience, conduct official business and confer honours. The British Raj adopted the idea of a *durbar* and held great ceremonial events that they called *durbars*. Lord Lytton held a *durbar*, for example, when Queen Victoria was proclaimed Empress of India in 1876. The great Delhi *durbars* of 1903 and 1911 were staged to celebrate the coronations of the British kings Edward VII and George V. These were fantastic ceremonial displays, involving hundreds of *maharajahs*, bejewelled elephants, music and dancing.

Source G

That this Congress, whilst gratefully appreciating the earnest and arduous endeavours of Lord Morley and Lord Minto in extending to the people of this country a fairly liberal measure of constitutional reforms as now embodied in the Indian Councils Act, deems it is its duty to place on record its strong sense of disapproval of the creation of separate electorates on the basis of religion and regrets that the Regulations framed under the Act have not been framed in the same liberal spirit in which Lord Morley's despatch of last year was conceived.

From the Indian National Congress Resolution at its Lahore session in 1909

Source H

The 1909 Indian Councils Act modestly extended the franchise, but quite substantially increased the numbers of elected and nominated Indians on the provincial and central legislative councils of the Raj. The British, by holding out the prospect of progress towards responsible government, were undoubtedly hoping to contain and defuse the forces of Indian Nationalism. Thus the extension of democratic institutions was used as a means of shoring up the fundamentally autocratic British Raj.

From Denis Judd, Empire, published in 1996

Reasserting the Raj?

The Indian Councils Act of 1909 ended over 100 years of all-white, colonial rule. Colonial rule itself, on the other hand, most definitely had not come to an end. The British Raj asserted itself both symbolically and literally, culminating in the 1911 **durbar** to celebrate the coronation of King George V and Queen Mary.

The Morley–Minto Reforms were announced in November 1908, the 50th anniversary of the British take-over of the administration of India from the East India Company. The Reforms had placated the Muslims by agreeing to the principle of separate Muslim and Hindu electorates. The British now felt able to move to balance this with the reunification of Bengal, which had been summarily divided by Viceroy Curzon in 1905 (see pages 38–39) This decision was announced at the 1911 *durbar*. In time for the 1911 *durbar*, the capital of India was moved from Calcutta to Delhi, the powerbase of the old Mughal Empire, pleasing the Muslims. Nearly every ruling prince and person of note in India attended the 1911 *durbar* to pay homage to their king-emperor. The sovereigns then appeared on a balcony built on the Red Fort in Delhi, where below more than half a million ordinary Indians had gathered to greet them. The sovereigns, as you can see from Source I, appeared in their coronation robes. King George wore the imperial crown, containing 6170 diamonds as well as sapphires, emeralds and rubies.

Source I

4.2 King George V and Queen Mary at the Delhi *durbar*, held in December 1911 to celebrate their coronation

Question

How far would you agree that the 1911 Delhi *durbar* was nothing more than a public reminder that the future of India was still determined by the British Crown and Parliament?

What was the impact of the First World War on India (1914–18)?

Involvement in the war

The outbreak of war in Europe was met with instant loyalty and declarations of support across all sections of Indian society. Offers of support poured in from the princely states, from Congress and from the **Muslim League**. Even Bal Tilak, leader of the extremist faction in Congress, declared 'our sense of loyalty is inherent and unswerving'. Twenty-seven of the largest princely states immediately put their imperial service troops at the Viceroy's disposal. A hospital ship, the *Loyalty* was commissioned, fully fitted and provisioned by the princes. Recruitment exceeded all expectations and Indian troops were soon sailing for Flanders, Gallipoli and Mesopotamia, serving overseas as combatants and support staff, dwarfing all other imperial contributions to the war effort. By November 1918, some 827,000 Indians had enlisted as combatants, in addition to those already serving in 1914. It seems from official figures that around 64,449 Indian soldiers died in the war.

Definition

Muslim League
The All-Indian Muslim League was founded at the annual Muhammadan Educational Conference held in Dhaka in December 1906. About 3000 delegates attended and supported *Nawab Salim Ullah Khan's* proposal that a political party be established to look after the interests of Muslims: the All-Indian Muslim League.

Source J

Gentlemen of India marching to chasten German hooligans. Les troupes indiennes viennent châtier les brigands allemands.

4.3 A postcard showing Sikh troops disembarking at Marseilles, France, en route for the trenches of the Western Front

Question

Why do you think a photograph of Indian soldiers would have been sold as a postcard? Who would have bought it? To whom would they have sent it?

The Western Front

In August and September 1914, as German troops swept through Belgium into France, decimating the British expeditionary force, fresh new troops were desperately needed. The Indian army, with 161,000 trained soldiers, seemed the obvious choice. The first Indian expeditionary force, made up of 16,000 British and 28,500 Indian troops of the Lahore and Meerut divisions and the Secunderabad cavalry brigade embarked from Karachi on 24 August 1914, reaching Marseilles on 26 September. They got to the Western Front just in time for the first battle of Ypres. There, their losses were heavy: the average Indian battalion had 764 fighting men and by early November the 47th Sikhs, for example, were down to 385 fit soldiers. In early 1915, the Indian regiments were rested, but were soon back in the trenches. They provided half the Allied fighting force at Neuve Chapelle and the Lahore division was thrown into the counter-attack at the second battle of Ypres in April 1915.

In December 1915, the two infantry divisions were withdrawn from France and sent to the Middle East. Some historians argue that this was because of their low morale and War Office fears that the Indians could not survive another winter on the Western Front. On the other hand, it made perfect sense to concentrate the Indian army in the Middle East, where it was easier to send supplies and reinforcements from India. Two Indian cavalry divisions remained on the Western Front until March 1918, when they were transferred to Palestine to take part in operations against the Turks.

The problem of religion

Religion only became a problem after Turkey entered the war because, in the eyes of Muslims, the British Empire was now at war with a Muslim power. Muslims in the Indian army faced a huge dilemma. Most Muslim soldiers agreed that the war was still lawful, although there were desertions from Muslim units on the Western Front and elsewhere. There were, too, at least three mutinies of Muslim troops, usually when they thought they were going to be sent to fight against Turks.

Attitudes to fighting

For most Indian soldiers, going to war was part of their well-established ancestral tradition of obligation to whomsoever was their emperor. Interestingly, few claimed to be fighting for India. Most cited the King or the Empire as legitimate causes for which they were fighting. In the case of the 1914–18 war, their king-emperor was George V and so they loyally enlisted under his colours. This attitude was reflected in their letters home from the Front.

- Havildar [equivalent to Sergeant] Singh wrote from the western front in September 1915 'If I die I go to Paradise. It is a fine thing to die in battle. We must honour him who feeds us. Our dear government's rule is very good and gracious.'

- Pirhan Dyal, also serving in France, wrote: 'We must be true to our salt and he who is faithful will go to paradise.'

- A *Jat* Havildar, recovering from his wounds, wrote home: 'Who remembers a man who dies in his bed? But it is our duty as Khastris to kill the enemy and then a man becomes a hero.'

- The sister of three brothers stationed in Egypt wrote: 'War is the task of young men, to sport with death upon the field of battle, to be as a tiger and to draw the sword of honour and daring.'

Compromising internal control?

Thousands upon thousands of Indians left India to fight in the imperial cause. Thousands of British troops stationed in India left too, withdrawn to support allied troops in France and Mesopotamia. Along with them went many Indian Civil Service men and expatriate civilians, who volunteered to fight in the armed forces. By March 1915, there was not a single regular British battalion left in India. Any sort of uprising in this situation would be very difficult to contain.

Great expectations?

The presence of so many Indian soldiers fighting alongside British and white colonial battalions not only increased the self-esteem of the Indians but also strengthened the arguments of Indian politicians that Indians should be given a greater say in Indian affairs. The Allies, in rallying support for their cause, frequently referred to the war as one being fought to defend the rights of nations and the sanctity of treaties. They spoke, too,

Definition

Self-determination

The right of nations to determine their own future.

Question

What is the implication embedded in Gandhi's statement?

of the importance of democracy and of **self-determination** – the freedom for countries to determine their own affairs. As the Indians listened and assimilated these values, they began to apply them to their own situation back in India.

Source K

[We must give] such humble assistance as we may be considered capable of performing, as an earnest declaration of our desire to share the responsibilities of membership of a great Empire, just as we would share its privileges.

From a statement made by a then little-known lawyer Mohandas Gandhi in 1914

What was the economic impact of the First World War?

Economics and politics frequently go hand in hand. A prosperous economy tends to make individuals and whole nations more self-confident and more inclined to pursue their objectives in national and international contexts. Similarly, economic problems involving unemployment, crop failures and the like can make people turn on those who govern them and demand change. The outcomes look very similar although the causes are different. Such was the case with India.

Winners and losers

India had poured men and materials into the war effort and in doing so had become a crucial source of supply for the Allied cause. By the end of December 1919, some 1.5 million Indians had been recruited into combatant and non-combatant roles, and nearly all of them had been sent overseas – including 184,350 animals.

By the end of the First World War, Indian revenues had contributed over £146 million to the Allied war effort. About half of this amount was made up of war loans, which in 1917 raised £35.5 million and in 1918 a further £38 million. Military expenditure had risen dramatically, too, and revenue demands in India were raised by 16 per cent in 1916–17, 14 per cent in 1917–18 and 10 per cent in 1918–19. Thus most ordinary people felt the effects of the war through increased taxation. They were also bothered by shortages of fuel and by rising prices. During the war, prices of food grains rose by 93 per cent, of Indian-made goods by 60 per cent and imported goods by 190 per cent. These rises were brought about by the disruption war brought to normal trading patterns, exchange rate problems and the demands of the military. The government tried to control prices, but was too often frustrated by profiteers and speculators. The situation was exacerbated by the failure of the monsoons to arrive in 1918–19 and consequent grain shortages and famine. Life for many was hard, just as it was on the home front in western European countries. Yet the war did benefit some, and not just the speculators and profiteers. Indian manufacturing industries, particularly cotton, iron and steel, sugar, engineering and chemicals, expanded in order to replace goods normally imported. Shareholders saw their dividends rocket. In Bombay, dividends from cloth mills jumped from 6 per cent in 1914 to over 30 per cent in 1917. In Ahmedabad, the cotton manufacturing centre of India, one mill owner reported a trebling of profits.

It was against this background that the Viceroy had to juggle the demands of London for India's resources and the concerns of his district officers at localised distress and disturbances as they watched prices spiralling out of control. In some areas, groups of local government officials went on strike and there were serious concerns by some provincial governments that local support for the Raj was crumbling. By 1918, the Viceroy's office in Delhi was receiving regular reports from provincial legislatures of food riots, petty violence and looting. It was fortunate for British rule in India that these outbreaks were sporadic and never coalesced into a general campaign against increased taxation. If it had done, the withdrawal of so many troops to Europe and the departure of hundreds of Indian Civil Service men and expatriate civilians, would have made the domestic Indian situation very tricky, to say the least. Indeed, as early as 1914 Viceroy Hardinge had warned about 'the risks involved in denuding India of troops: there is no disguising the fact that our position in India is a bit of a gamble at the present time.'

It was hardly surprising that the economic effects of war very rapidly had political repercussions.

What were the political effects of the First World War?

The political problems posed by the war were infinitely more complicated than attempting to deal with local protests against intolerable localised conditions. Issues were created that could only be dealt with in India because they focused on the nature of Britain's relationship with India and the Indian people. Broad national shifts in the political spectrum had been created and were to present serious challenges to the Raj. Indian soldiers had fought alongside white British and colonial forces, strengthening their self-esteem. Indian political arguments that the war should be a turning point in Indian–Raj relationships were also strengthened as a consequence. Indians were beginning to apply to their own situation the concepts of democracy and freedom that their European and, later, US Allies said they were fighting for.

Congress and the Muslim League

As early as 1915, Congress was speaking openly about self-government and about the changes in attitude that the war was bringing. Early that year, Congress president, Banerjea made a speech:

Source L

Brother delegates, the idea of re-adjustment is in the air, not only here in India but all the world over. The heart of the Empire is set upon it: it is the problem of problems upon which humanity is engaged. What is this war for? Why are these enormous sufferings endured? Because it is a war of re-adjustment, a war that will set right the claims of minor nationalities, uphold and vindicate the sanctity of treaties, proclamations – ours is one – charters and similar 'scraps of paper'. They are talking about what will happen after the war in Canada, in Australia; they are talking about it from the floor of the House of Commons and in the gatherings of public men and ministers of the state. May we not also talk about it a little from our stand-point? Are we to be charged with embarrassing the government when we follow the examples of illustrious public men, men weighted with a sense of responsibility at least as onerous as that felt by our critics and our candid friends?

From a speech made by Surendranath Banerjea to Congress in 1915

By 1916, the political situation in India had hardened, largely because the Muslim League and Congress had buried their differences. How had this happened? The annulment of the partition of Bengal had alarmed the Muslim League. Believing this meant that the British would no longer regard them as a separate community deserving of separate electoral treatment, they had tried to find some sort of accommodation with the Hindus. In this, they had been successful, helped in no small part by the efforts of the Englishwoman Annie Besant and her All-Indian Home Rule League, the Muslim leader **Muhammad Ali Jinnah** and the Hindu extremist Bal Tilak.

Biography

Muhammad Ali Jinnah (1876–1948)

Born on 25 December 1976, Jinnah's family was part of the prosperous business community of Karachi. Educated there, Jinnah went to England for further studies in 1892 and in 1896 was called to the English Bar.

He started his political career by attending the National Congress in 1906. He was a member of the Imperial Legislative Council in 1909, until he resigned in protest ten years later. He joined the Muslim League in 1913 and the Home Rule Movement under Annie Besant in 1917.

Jinnah worked hard to create a situation in which Hindu and Muslim could create a united, independent India together. However, a widening gulf opened up between Jinnah and Gandhi on the subject of protecting the Muslim position and on Gandhi's civil disobedience programme. Resigning from Congress in 1920, Jinnah became the main spokesman for the Muslim cause within India.

When compromise failed, Jinnah pursued the separatist line on his return from England in 1935. In 1940, the League passed the Lahore Resolution, calling for a separate Muslim state somewhere in India. With Indian independence in 1947 came partition.

Jinnah became the first Governor-General of Pakistan in 1947, dying from a combination of lung cancer and tuberculosis a year later.

The Lucknow Pact of 1916 was an agreement between Congress and the Muslim League whereby it was agreed that Muslims would have a fixed proportion of seats in an Indian parliament and extra seats in areas where they were in a minority. Thus the Muslims believed they had been given assurances by the Hindus that were similar to those obtained earlier from the British government and felt themselves able to work with the Hindu-dominated Congress. In a similar way, the deaths of the moderates Gopal Krishna Gokhale and Pherozeshah Mehta enabled Congress to find a formula whereby the extremist Bal Tilak could re-enter Congress. It was hardly surprising that one of the first resolutions passed in 1916 by the newly united Congress was to urge the British to 'issue a proclamation stating it is the aim and intention of British policy to confer self-government on India at an early date'.

SKILLS BUILDER

1 How far do Sources M and N disagree about the Lucknow Pact of 1916?

2 The authors of Sources L and O were anticipating reform of some kind. To what extent are their reasons the same?

Source M

The 1916 Lucknow Pact, by which Congress and the League agreed a joint programme, would see the League accept Muslim under-representation in Muslim majority areas (like east Bengal) in return for Congress' acceptance of Hindu under-representation in Hindu majority areas (like the United Provinces). Here was precisely the political horse-trading essential to the working of a plural society. Both sides embraced it; so even did an 'extremist' like the lately returned Tilak. At this stage, with one partition having just failed, another was unthinkable; it was eminently avoidable.

From John Keay, *A History of India*, published in 2000

Source N

The Congress-League pact was emphatically not an agreement between Congress and the whole Muslim community, any more than the foundation of the League had signified the emergence of a unified Muslim community with a single political voice. At the time of the pact the League probably had between 500 and 800 members, and the Lucknow agreement did not even represent all of them because the negotiations were carried on by a clique led by UP [United Provinces] 'Young Party' Muslims.

From Judith M. Brown, *Modern India: the Origins of an Asian Democracy*, published in 1994

The Imperial Legislative Council

The attitude of Congress was reflected in the Viceroy's Imperial Legislative Council. Madan Mohan Malaviya was Congress President in 1909 and 1918 and a member of the Imperial Legislative Council from 1910 to 1920:

Source O

I need hardly say that the question of reform is a much larger one now than it was before the war. As Mr Lloyd George [the British Prime Minister] said the other day, the war has changed us very much. It has changed the angle of vision in India as well as in England. I venture to say that the war has put the clock fifty years forward, and I hope that India will achieve in the next few years what she might not have done in fifty years. Some persons are frightened at the use of the term 'Home Rule'; some cannot bear to hear even 'Self-Government on Colonial lines.' But all will have to recognise that the reforms after the war will have to be such as will meet the requirements of India today and of tomorrow, such as will satisfy the aspirations of her people to take their legitimate part in the administration of their own country.

From a speech made by Madan Mohan Malaviya in 1917

Home Rule leagues

The claims made by Congress and by the Imperial Legislative Council were backed by two totally new and innovative organisations that were set up in 1916: Home Rule leagues. Their aim was to stimulate public opinion and organise public pressure for Home Rule for India. One was started by Bal Tilak and operated mainly in western India; the other was founded by Annie Besant and spread throughout the rest of the country. Both organisations used newspapers, rallies, vernacular pamphlets, preachers and songs in an attempt to reach the masses, which hitherto had been disinterested in the doings of Congress, the Muslim League and the Imperial Legislative Council. It worked. After one year, over 60,000 Indians had joined the Home Rule leagues. The conventional assemblies were alarmed by the outspoken demands of these leagues; the British Raj even more so. The two leaders were banned from several provinces, students were forbidden to attend their meetings and Annie Besant was interned in June 1917.

How would the British government react to these demands for self-government?

Edwin Montagu, Lord Chelmsford and the Government of India Act 1919

The British government faced a huge dilemma. They could not ignore the enormous sacrifices made by the Indian people and the steadfast loyalty they had shown to the British Crown. They were aware that the Indian people and their politicians were looking for a reward for this loyalty. They could not ignore, either, their own belief in the rights of people to democracy and self-determination. On the other hand, they faced the spectacle of the **overthrow of tsardom in Russia**, seen by many Indian politicians as a sign that a new day was dawning and by the British establishment as a sign that anarchy was just around the corner. Could British rule in India be overthrown, too?

What was the Montagu Declaration?

July 1917 saw Edwin Montagu as Secretary of State at the India Office. A passionate Liberal, who had worked under John Morley at the India Office before the war, Montagu was clear that a straightforward statement of British policy toward India was essential. Working closely with the Viceroy Lord Chelmsford, the Montagu Declaration was formulated and agreed by the British government:

Definition

Overthrow of tsardom in Russia

In the 1917 revolution in Russia, the ruler of Russia, the Tsar Nicholas, was overthrown and his family murdered. They were replaced first, by a provisional government and then by a Bolshevik one.

Source P

The policy of His Majesty's Government, with which the Government of India are in complete accord, is that of the increasing association of Indians in every branch of the administration and the gradual development of self-governing institutions with a view to the progressive realisation of responsible government in India as part of the British Empire.

From the Montagu Declaration in 1917

Britain was now implicitly committed to allowing Indians to govern themselves, but within the context of the British Empire. Although no timescale was given, the declaration ended by saying that Montagu would visit India to 'consider with the Viceroy the views of local governments, and to receive with him the suggestions of representative bodies and others'.

Montagu's travels

Edwin Montagu travelled extensively in India between November 1917 and May 1918, listening to all kinds of opinion from all sorts of different people. A keen ornithologist and game hunter, he found much to amaze and delight him in the activities arranged for him by the Indian princes. However, he found little to amaze and delight in what he saw as the 'dead hand' of British administration. Very little, he believed, had changed since the days of Curzon (see pages 35–39), where slow and complex bureaucracy could, even after Curzon's administrative reforms, stifle radical ideas and reform. He was very much afraid the Viceroy would succumb to the reactionaries among his administration and was particularly critical of a Colonel O'Dwyer, who was adamantly opposed to any more Indian participation in government.

The Montagu-Chelmsford Report and the Government of India Act 1919

The proposals decided upon by Secretary of State Montagu and Viceroy Chelmsford were published in July 1918 and became law as the Government of India Act in December 1919.

- The Viceroy was to be advised by a council of six civilians, three of whom had to be Indians, and the Commander-in-Chief of the British Army in India. The Viceroy could enforce laws even if the legislative councils rejected them and he could choose his own officials.

- The provincial and central legislative councils were enlarged.

- The provincial councils were given control over Indian education, agriculture, health, local self-government and public works.

- The British retained control of military matters, foreign affairs, currency, communications and criminal law.

- The franchise was extended, although it was still linked to the amount and type of tax men paid. After 1919, about 10 per cent of the adult male population were enfranchised. All former soldiers were automatically given the vote.

- Provincial legislatures could give the vote to women if they wished to, and some did. Even so, the number of women voters was less than 1 per cent of the provincial adult female population.

- There were 'reserved' seats in all provincial legislatures for different religious groups (for example, Sikhs, Muslims, Indian Christians) and special interest groups like landowners and university graduates.

This system was called **dyarchy** because it divided power in the provinces (albeit unequally) between the Indians and the British.

Definition

Dyarchy
Government by two independent authorities, in India this system divided power in the provinces between the Indians and the British from 1919 to 1935.

Question

What were (a) the strengths and (b) the weaknesses of dyarchy?

How did people react to the Government of India Act?

In many ways, the dyarchy system was an extension of the Minto-Morley reforms ten years earlier. Like them, it tried to enlist the co-operation of India's educated middle class in governing India. However, it took the Morley–Minto Reforms further by shifting more and more decision-making from the centre to the provinces and by involving more Indians in the governing of their own country. There were, however, problems.

- Montagu saw the Act as a welcome further step towards Indian self-government, and so did his horrified critics.

- In the House of Commons, India became a contentious issue. On the Right, MPs were convinced the government was losing its nerve and would soon lose India; on the Left, there were protests that the reforms hadn't gone far enough.

- The Indian Civil Service felt its strength and influence was slipping away.

- Many Indians welcomed the Act, even though it didn't offer immediate self-government.

- Many people, British and Indian, hated the idea of 'reserved seats' with specific electorates, considering them divisive and anti-democratic. Indeed, Montagu and Chelmsford themselves disliked the idea, but felt bound to respect the Lucknow Pact of 1916.

- Those Indians hoping for Home Rule were bitterly disappointed. As details of the reforms became known, unrest and violence increased, especially in the Punjab.

- The Indian National Congress rejected the Montagu-Chelmsford reforms and boycotted the first elections held under the 1919 Act.

The situation in India was exacerbated by the recession that set in when the war ended. There were layoffs and unemployment as the demand for war materials, particularly textiles, collapsed. Added to this, the Spanish flu epidemic that hit Europe affected India too, killing more than 13 million people. And in India the situation was exacerbated by the failure of the monsoon to deliver and the consequent crop failure and regional famine. Add to this the British government's very real fear of Bolshevism taking hold in post-war India (the Russian revolutions of 1917 had established a Bolshevik regime there), and it is understandable that an unstable situation was created in the sub-continent, leading to further unrest, disturbances and riots. The British Raj responded in the only way it knew how – by repression to be enforced by the Rowlatt Acts.

What were the effects of the Rowlatt Acts?

In a word: disastrous!

What did the Rowlatt Commission propose?

As early as 1917, the Indian government, afraid that the situation was slipping away from them, appointed a Scottish judge, Mr S.A.T. Rowlatt to 'investigate revolutionary conspiracies'. The Rowlatt Commission reported in July 1918. It isolated Bengal, Bombay and Punjab as centres of revolutionary activity and recommended that the old wartime controls should be used there to contain the situation. These included imprisonment without trial, trial by judges sitting without a jury, censorship and house arrest of suspects. These proposals were incorporated into the Rowlatt Acts, passed in March 1919, and sanctioned by Montagu with extreme reluctance. He told the Viceroy that they were 'extremely repugnant', although he conceded he appreciated the need to stamp out rebellion and riot. However, Viceroy Chelmsford went ahead and the measure was pushed through the Imperial Legislative Council in the face of opposition from every single Indian member.

The Muslim leader Muhammad Ali Jinnah and several of his colleagues resigned in protest when the Rowlatt Acts were pushed through the Indian Legislative Council (see Source Q).

What damage did the Acts do?

In reality, the new powers were found to be unnecessary and were soon repealed. But the damage had been done. All Indian members of the Imperial Legislative Council were opposed to the Rowlatt Acts. The impression was created – loud and clear – that the promises made by the Montagu-Chelmsford reforms were meaningless. In the end, when the chips were down, it seemed that the British government was prepared to use force to crush Indian opposition. The Acts suggested, furthermore, that the British had no intention of relaxing their grip on India. Thus the Rowlatt Acts alienated a wide range of public opinion in India and came close to wrecking the 1919 Government of India Act.

Unit Summary

What have you learned in this unit?

The period 1900–19 was marked by both change and continuity. The British made concessions to Indian opinion in that they invited Indian participation in the decision-making process by way of the Morley–Minto Reforms and the Indian Councils Act of 1909, the Montagu-Chelmsford Report and the Government of India Act 1919. Yet these concessions can be seen as a way of strengthening the Raj and their control within India, as exemplified by the Rowlatt Acts. For Indians, the period saw a growing awareness of their desire for self-government, heightened by their experience of the First World War. While many were satisfied with the concessions made by the British, there was a steady growth of groundswell opinion that Indians should be in complete control of their own affairs.

> **Source Q**
>
> The fundamental principles of justice have been uprooted and the constitutional rights of the people have been violated, at a time when there is no real danger to the state, by an overfretful and incompetent bureaucracy which is neither responsible to the people nor in touch with real public opinion.
>
> From a letter written by Muhammad Ali Jinnah to Viceroy Chelmsford on 28 March 1919

What skills have you learned in this unit?

You have used your skills of comprehension, inference-making and cross-referencing to explore the way in which the Indian National Congress was founded and disagreements about its nature and purpose. You have interpreted data regarding the religious composition of the early meetings of Congress and, in analysing a variety of source material and relating its analysis to the appropriate historical context, have begun to understand the basis of what was later to become an insurmountable Hindu-Muslim divide. Finally, your analysis of source material will have led you to an understanding of the complexity of British motives in making concessions to Indian demands for a share in the government of their country.

Exam tips

This is the sort of question you will find appearing on the exam paper as a (b) question.

- Read Sources H, P and Q. Do you agree with the view, expressed in Source H, that the concessions made to Indian democracy by 1919 were given simply to shore up the British Raj?

You tackled a (b) question at the end of Unit 3. Look back at the exam tips you were given there (see page 48) before developing and building on them here. Follow these tips to write a successful answer to a (b) question.

- Check on the view expressed in Source H. Read Source H carefully and write the 'view' in the middle of what will be a spider diagram.
- Read Sources P and Q carefully. Establish points that support and points that challenge the view and set those as the spider's 'legs', using knowledge to reinforce and challenge.
- Cross-reference between the different 'legs' for similarities and differences.

You are now ready to write up your answer. Remember to:

- combine the different points into arguments for and against the stated view
- evaluate the conflicting arguments by reference to the quality of the evidence used
- reach a supported judgement.

RESEARCH TOPIC

You will have seen that Indian involvement in the First World War had a profound effect upon Indian thinking about such concepts as freedom, independence and democracy.

Either research the Indian contribution in one of the theatres of war from 1914 to 1918, or choose one Indian soldier (for example, *Sepoy* Khudadad Khan, VC) and research his contribution to the war.

5 Flashpoint! The Amritsar Massacre

What is this unit about?

This unit focuses on one incident, the massacre at Amritsar in 1919, which was to have a profound effect on Anglo-Indian relationships for many years afterwards. In focusing on just one incident in a case study, it will be possible to examine this relationship in considerable detail and, in doing so, come to an understanding of the dynamics of that relationship.

Key questions

- Who or what was to blame for the Amritsar Massacre?
- What does the Amritsar Massacre reveal about Anglo-Indian relationships?

Timeline

1919	30 March	*Hartals* organised
	6 April	More *hartals* organised
	10 April	Rioting in Amritsar
		Marcia Sherwood brutally assaulted
	11 April	British women and children take refuge in Gobindgarh Fort
	12 April	Dyer heads up a show of force in Amritsar
	13 April	Proclamations are read throughout Amritsar
		Massacre at Jallianwala *Bagh*
	14 April	Martial law imposed in Amritsar
		Dyer invents the Crawling Order
	11 November	Lord Hunter and colleagues arrive in Lahore
		Hunter Committee sets to work hearing evidence
		Indian National Congress Punjab Sub-Committee hears evidence
1920	20 February	Report of the Indian National Congress Punjab Sub-Committee published
	3 May	Dyer arrives back in Britain
	26 May	Hunter Report published
	8 July	Commons debate the Amritsar Massacre
	19 July	Lords debate the Amritsar Massacre

Case study: the Amritsar Massacre – tensions revealed?

Opposition to the Rowlatt Acts flared up throughout India, but nowhere more fiercely than in the Punjab and nowhere more frighteningly than in the town of Amritsar, the administrative capital.

Source A

5.1 Two stills from the film *Gandhi* made by Richard Attenborough in the mid-1980s, a section of which dealt with the massacre at Amritsar in 1919

SKILLS BUILDER

1 What is happening in Source A? What immediate impression do these images give you?

2 What conclusions can you draw, just from these images, about the relationship between the Indian people and the British Raj?

3 These images were taken from a film made nearly 70 years after the incident. What use are they (i) to the general public and (ii) to historians?

Why did the rioting in Amritsar begin?

Two leading nationalists, Dr Saifuddin Kitchlew, a young Cambridge-educated barrister, and Dr Satya Pal, a medical doctor, organised a series of *hartals* (workplace lockouts) on 30 March and 6 April as a protest against the Rowlatt Acts (see pages 70–71). There was no serious unrest as a result and the days were marked by an impressive display of Hindu-Muslim solidarity. However, the authorities decided to arrest the two men and then trouble broke out on a large scale. Rioting began on 10 April, originally in support of the two detained men, but quickly turned into a general anti-European attack. Banks were stormed, buildings fired and three Europeans killed. A mission doctor, Marcia Sherwood, was brutally beaten by Indian youths and only saved from certain death by Hindus who found and treated her. By 11 April, over 100 terrified and exhausted European women and children had taken refuge in the Gobindgarh Fort, trying to find a place of safety in a city where the British had lost control to the mob.

Source B

During the first night, three survivors who had escaped into the police station were brought out of the city in Indian clothes. They told us of the infuriated crowds that had swept through the city on that terrible afternoon, drunk with their victory over unarmed men and calling for 'white blood'. The booty from the National Bank had been carried out into the district as proof that the British rule was over, and all the riff-raff for miles around hurried in to be early on the spot if looting began again.

Every hour brought in some news from outside: of firing at Lahore, of murders at Kasur, of trains derailed and lines torn up, of telegraph wires cut and government buildings and railway stations burnt; and we were very anxious about Europeans in the neighbourhood. The news was often vague, but with the breakdown in communications and our own experience, we were left to imagine the worst, and the native population had some excuse for their belief that the British Raj was over.

From an account given by an anonymous Englishwomen who had taken refuge in the Gobindgarh Fort, quoted in Robert Furneaux, *Massacre at Amritsar*, published in 1963

Biography

Michael O'Dwyer (1864–1940)

The sixth child in a large Irish family, Michael O'Dwyer passed the examinations for the Indian Civil Service and went out to India in 1885.

His first posting was to Shahpur in the Punjab where he undertook land settlement work and was made Director of Land Records and Agriculture. He was selected by Viceroy Curzon to help sort out the new North-West Frontier Province and its separation from the Punjab. He was promoted up through the Indian Civil Service and finally became Lieutenant Governor of the Punjab in 1912.

During his time as Governor (1912–19), he gained a reputation for firmness and some regarded him as little less than a dictator. It was during his time as Governor of the Punjab that the Amritsar Massacre occurred. Some Indian historians believe that the massacre was planned beforehand by O'Dwyer and top British bureaucrats, but there is, as yet, little hard evidence to support this theory.

O'Dwyer was assassinated in London by Udham Singh, a Punjabi, on 13 March 1940 in revenge for the Amritsar Massacre.

What was the British reaction?

The Governor of the Punjab, **Michael O'Dwyer** was convinced that the riots were part of a carefully planned uprising, luring Indian soldiers into a mutiny. So his reaction to the situation in Amritsar was to treat it as the first stage in a general insurrection aimed at overthrowing the Raj. He

SKILLS BUILDER

Using Source B as evidence, how justified was the British reaction to the rioting?

ordered Brigadier-General **Rex Dyer**, a tough career soldier who had been born in India and who commanded the 45th Brigade based at Jalandhar, to go with his men to Amritsar and sort the situation out. As Dyer left, he said to his son 'Mussulmans and Hindus are united. I have been expecting this, there is a very big show coming.' Ironically, it was Dyer himself who turned the situation into a 'big show'.

Biography

Reginald 'Rex' Edward Harry Dyer (1864–1927)

Reginald Dyer was born in Murree, then in India but now in Pakistan, and grew up in Simla and attended the British school there. He joined the army as an officer in 1885 and served in riot control duties in Belfast (1886) and the Third Burma War (1886–87). He then transferred to the Indian army, where he commanded the 25th Punjabis in India and Hong Kong.

He showed such bravery during the First World War that he was mentioned in dispatches and was made a Companion of the Bath. However, it is for the Amritsar Massacre that he will be remembered. Heavily censured by both the Hunter Commission and the Indian National Congress, he was relieved of his post and recalled to England. Parliament debated his case twice, with the Lords supporting him and the Commons censuring him.

Dyer resigned his commission in 1920 and died of natural causes seven years later.

Dyer arrives at Amritsar

Dyer had under his command about 1000 troops, roughly one-third of whom were British, and two armoured cars equipped with machine guns. They stationed themselves in the Ram **Bagh**, a parkland area laid out as gardens with running water and plenty of space for the men to pitch their tents. On 12 April, Dyer led 400 troops and the armoured cars through the streets of Amritsar. This was intended as a show of force, but one that didn't really work. The Indians lining the streets jeered at the troops and shouted threatening slogans such as 'The British Raj is at an end.' Back in the Ram *Bagh*, Dyer was told of similar disturbances in the Punjab cities of Lahore and Kasur. He became even more convinced that a general uprising was imminent.

The following day, 13 April, was Baisakhi Day. It marked the beginning of one of the most important religious festivals in the Punjab, which lasted for several days. Thousands of pilgrims began flocking into Amritsar to worship in the Golden Temple; still more thousands came for the horse and cattle fairs that were part of the festivities. Hundreds of these people and their families converged on the Jallianwala *Bagh*, a large open space of about eight acres of beaten earth. They intended staying there for the duration of the festival, talking, resting and meeting with the residents of

Definition

Bagh
A garden.

Amritsar. Arrangements were also made for a political meeting to be held in part of the Jallianwala *Bagh* so that people could voice their opinions and make their feelings felt about the Rowlatt Acts.

It was at 10.30 a.m. on 13 April that Dyer and a detachment of troops re-entered Amritsar. At various points in the city, accompanied by drumbeats to catch the crowd's attention, two separate proclamations were read out.

Source C

(i) The inhabitants of Amritsar are warned by means of this proclamation that if they damage any property or commit any act of violence in the neighbourhood of Amritsar, such acts will be considered to have been instigated from the city of Amritsar, and we shall arrange to punish the inhabitants of Amritsar in accordance with military law. All meetings and assemblies are prohibited by this proclamation, and we shall act in accordance with military law in order to disperse all such assemblies forthwith.

(ii) 1. It is hereby notified that no inhabitant of Amritsar is permitted to go out of the city in his own or in a hired conveyance or on foot without obtaining a pass from the under-mentioned officers [nine listed].

2. No inhabitant of the city is permitted to go out of his house after 8 p.m. Persons going out into the street after 8 p.m. will be liable to be shot.

3. No procession is permitted at any time in the bazaars or in any part of the city or at any place outside the city. Any such procession or gathering will be considered illegal, and will be dealt with accordingly, and, if necessary, will be dispersed by means of arms.

The proclamation that was read out at 19 places in Amritsar on 13 April 1919

Source D

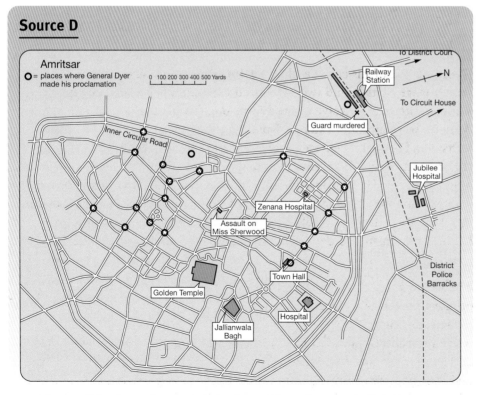

5.2 A map of Amritsar, showing where the proclamations were read out

SKILLS BUILDER

1 Read Source C.

a) How sensible were these orders?

b) Do you think that making the proclamations was the best way to bring calm to Amritsar?

2 Study Source D. Are you surprised that no proclamations were made anywhere near to the Jallianwala *Bagh*?

The massacre

On the afternoon of 13 April, a meeting started in the Jallianwala *Bagh* as planned. Estimates as to the number of people in the *Bagh* vary from 15,000 to 50,000, but there were certainly a lot and they were certainly unarmed. Some of them were playing cards, throwing dice, gossiping and generally relaxing in the warm sun; most, however, had come for the meeting. This began by passing two resolutions. One called for the repeal of the Rowlatt Acts; the other expressed sympathy with the dead and bereaved in the previous days' riots. Speeches were made and poems recited. Then the unimaginable happened.

The sound of heavy boots, marching at the double, was heard. Dyer, with Gurkha and Sikh infantrymen, appeared through the narrow passageway at one end of the *Bagh*. Without a word of warning, they knelt and, at a word of command from their British subaltern, fired repeatedly into the crowd. There was absolute chaos as thousands of people tried firstly to escape and, when they couldn't, protect themselves and their families and friends. Altogether Dyer's men fired 1650 rounds of ammunition in ten to fifteen minutes, killing nearly 400 people and leaving a further 1500 wounded. Then, just as suddenly, Dyer and his men wheeled round and departed. They left the injured to fend for themselves or wait for help from family and friends brave enough to risk the curfew.

SKILLS BUILDER

1 What information do Sources E and F provide about what happened at the Jallianwala *Bagh*?

2 What problems would historians face when using Sources E and F as evidence of what happened at the Jallianwala *Bagh*?

Source E

For many trapped in the garden, the deadly fire meant the slaughter of the totally innocent, for they had arrived in Amritsar to celebrate Baisakhi and had made their way to the Jallianwala *Bagh*, totally ignorant of Dyer's proclamation or the protest meeting.

Daulat Ram Bhatia had gone with his school friend Ram Nath to listen to the speeches. As he sat on the ground, he heard shouts of 'Army here; army here'. Immediately the rifles opened fire and he heard someone shout out that the soldiers were only firing blanks. Seconds later a bullet ploughed through his leg and another went through the upper jaw of his classmate, killing him instantly. He found shelter behind the peepul tree and stayed there, drenched with blood, until the firing ceased and the soldiers departed. It was his fifteenth birthday.

From Alfred Draper, *The Amritsar Massacre*, published in 1985

Source F

I did not enter the *Bagh* from the side where the soldiers had come out because I was afraid, but went round and entered by jumping over a wall. A dying man asked for water. When I tried to take water from a pit, I saw many dead bodies floating in it. Some living men had also hidden themselves in the same pit. I went to find my son. There were 800 or 1000 wounded and dead lying near the walls and there were others who ran away wounded and died either in their own houses or in the surrounding lanes. I could not find my son. I heard wailing from those who had been shot and who were crying for water. Then I ran back home and heard my son was safe. I did not hear any proclamation forbidding people to attend public meetings.

From the evidence given by Sadar Partap Singh to the Indian National Congress enquiry in September 1919

Source G

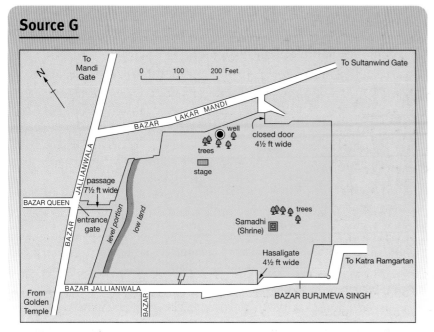

5.3 Plan of the Jallianwala *Bagh* in 1919

Question

How does Source G help explain why so many people were killed and injured in the Jallianwala *Bagh* on 13 April 1919?

SKILLS BUILDER

Read Sources B, H and I. How far would you agree with the view that General Dyer was justified in the actions he took?

Source H

I fired and continued to fire until the crowd dispersed, and I consider this is the least amount of firing which would produce the necessary moral and widespread effect it was my duty to produce if I was to justify my action. If more troops had been at hand the casualties would have been greater in proportion. It was no longer a question of simply dispersing the crowd, but one of producing a sufficient moral effect from a military point of view not only on those who were present, but more especially throughout the Punjab. There could be no question of undue severity.

From the report on the Amritsar Massacre written by General Dyer for his superior officers on 25 August 1919

Source I

He could not remain on the defensive. His forces were not only small; part of them was wanted elsewhere, and the rebellion was spreading. On the 10th the mob had struck a blow that was reverberating over India. It had given heart to their cause. They had tasted blood, they had not been punished, they began to feel themselves masters of the situation. Therefore, with a wasting force he opposed a growing force. His best hope lay in immediate action.

So much was clear. But how to strike? In the narrow streets, among the high houses and mazy lanes and courtyards of the city the rebels had the advantage of position. They could harass him and avoid his blow. Street fighting he knew to be a bloody, precarious, inconclusive business, in which, besides, the innocent were likely to suffer more than the guilty. Moreover, if the rebels chose their ground cunningly, and made their stand in the neighbourhood of the Golden Temple, there was the added risk of kindling the fanaticism of the Sikhs. Thus he was in this desperate situation; he could not wait and he could not fight.

But this unexpected gift of fortune, this unhoped for defiance, this concentration of rebels in an open space – it gave him such an opportunity as he could not have devised. It separated the guilty from the innocent; it placed them where he would have wished them to be – within reach of his sword.

From Ian Colvin, *The Life of General Dyer*, published in 1929

Martial law

Later on 13 April, Dyer wrote a report of what had happened and sent it to his superior officer, General William Beynon:

Source J

I entered the Jallianwala *Bagh* by a very narrow lane, which necessitated leaving my armoured cars behind.

On entering I saw a dense crowd, estimated at about 5000, a man on a raised platform addressing the audience and making gesticulations with his hands.

I realised that my force was small and to hesitate might induce attack. I immediately opened fire and dispersed the mob. I estimated that between 200 and 300 of the crowd were killed. My party fired 1620 rounds.

I returned to my headquarters about 18.00 hours. At 22.00 hours, accompanied by a force, I visited all my pickets and marched through the city in order to make sure that my order as to inhabitants not being out of their homes after 20.00 hours had been obeyed. The city was absolutely quiet and not a soul was to be seen. I returned to Headquarters at midnight. The inhabitants have asked permission to bury the dead in accordance with my orders. This I am allowing.

From General Dyer's report to General William Beynon, received on 14 April 1919

Question

In the context of Indian and British politics at the time, are you surprised by Dyer's report and the reply?

Definition

Salaam

A greeting accompanied by a low bow.

Beynon's reply simply stated: 'Your action correct and the Lieutenant-Governor [O'Dwyer] agrees.'

Secure in his superiors' approval, Dyer felt able to push forward with further harsh actions. Using threats of further violence, he forced a stunned and grieving town to return to a semblance of normality. Shops and businesses opened and gradually people began to go about their daily affairs. Then Dyer declared martial law. But it was martial law that was aimed at humiliating the Indians who lived in Amritsar.

- Any Indian who passed Dyer or any other European had to **salaam**. If they did not, they were flogged, arrested or made to suffer indignities that were of immense significance to people locked into a system where caste, religion and social status were so important.

- In order to enable troops to move around the city, every means of transport was commandeered from the Indian population, including bicycles.

- All the Indian lawyers in Amritsar were forced to work as special constables and, in particular, witness floggings.

- All third-class railway tickets were withdrawn, making it virtually impossible for ordinary Indians to travel anywhere outside Amritsar.

- No more than two Indians were allowed to walk abreast on the pavements of Amritsar.

- The city's water and electricity supplies were cut off in the Indian quarters, causing great hardship to thousands of Indians.

Possibly the worse punishment of all, and which probably roused the Indians to even greater anger than the killings in the Jallianwala *Bagh*, was the Crawling Order. Dyer decided that the Kucha Tawarian, the narrow lane where Marcia Sherwood was assaulted and left for dead, should become hallowed ground. He ordered that any Indians who wanted to pass along the narrow street had to crawl along it on all fours, in the muck, filth and general detritus that had collected there. He explained his reasons for making the order to his superior officers:

Source K

A helpless woman had been mercilessly beaten in a most cruel manner by a lot of cowards. She was beaten with sticks and shoes and knocked down six times. It seemed intolerable to me that some suitable punishment could not be meted out. Civil law is at an end and I searched my brain for some punishment to meet the case.

From a report written by General Dyer on 25 August 1919

Source L

5.4 British soldiers enforcing the Crawling Order

Dyer himself presided over a court in the Ram *Bagh*, where he meted out floggings and other forms of humiliating punishment to Indians found to be in breach of some element of martial law. He was not too particular as to whether the punishments went to the guilty or the innocent. What mattered was that the British Raj had to be seen to be in charge.

Repercussions

Details of what was happening in Amritsar began arriving in Britain. The Secretary of State for India, Edwin Montagu, was growing increasingly angry at the way in which martial law was being applied. The vast distance between London and Delhi, let alone Amritsar, meant that he never felt he had command of the whole picture. News could take weeks to reach him and, when it did, the situation on the ground had changed, rendering inappropriate any decision he was likely to make. Nevertheless, he was horrified when details of the Crawling Order emerged.

Source M

When you pass an order that all Indians must crawl past a particular place, when you pass an order to say that all Indians must *salaam* any officer of His Majesty the King, you are enforcing racial humiliation. When you take selected schoolboys from a school, guilty or innocent, and whip them publicly, when you whip people before they have been convicted, when you flog a wedding party, you are indulging in frightfulness. Are you going to keep your hold on India by terrorism, racial humiliation, and subordination, and frightfulness, or are you going to rest it upon the growing goodwill of the people of the Indian Empire?

From Edwin Montagu, Secretary of State for India in a
House of Commons debate on 8 July 1919

SKILLS BUILDER

Study Sources K, L and M.

1 What differences can be seen in the attitude of Dyer and Montagu to the Crawling Order?

2 How do these sources highlight problems for the effective governing of India?

The Hunter Committee

Pressed by MPs in the House of Commons and growing increasingly alarmed at the information filtering through from India, Edwin Montagu pushed ahead with his plans for an enquiry into the Amritsar Massacre. In a letter to the newly appointed Chairman of the Committee, Lord Hunter (former Solicitor-General for Scotland), Montagu urged that the inquiry should be utterly fearless in its search for the truth.

On 11 November 1919, Hunter and his colleagues arrived in Lahore. Their job was to listen to evidence, ask questions and reach a conclusion about the events of 13 April. But nothing is that simple. As the witnesses arrived, they were alternately booed or cheered by the crowd; journalists, now that martial law and with it censorship had been lifted, had a field day. The trained lawyers on the Committee tied many of the witnesses, including Dyer, in knots. Dyer admitted that he would have used the machine guns if he could have got the armoured cars into the Jallianwala *Bagh*; that he had not issued a warning to the crowd before opening fire; that he had continued firing until his ammunition was exhausted, regardless of the effect on the crowd; that he wanted to punish the Punjabis because they had been 'naughty boys'; that he had considered razing Amritsar to the ground. Dyer believed he had given his evidence truthfully. He had, and it was damning. In their report, the Hunter Committee roundly censured Dyer.

Source N

The action taken by General Dyer has been described by others as having saved the situation in the Punjab and having averted a rebellion on a scale similar to the Mutiny. It does not, however, appear to us possible to draw this conclusion, particularly in view of the fact that it is not proved that a conspiracy to overthrow the British power had been formed prior to the outbreak.

After carefully weighing all the factors, we can arrive at no other conclusion than that, at Jallianwala *Bagh*, General Dyer acted beyond the necessity of the case, beyond what any reasonable man would have thought to be necessary, and that he did not act with as much humanity as the case permitted.

From the Hunter Committee Report, published in May 1920

The report gently reprimanded O'Dwyer. The three Indian members of the Hunter Committee condemned Dyer and O'Dwyer.

The Indian view

The Punjab Sub-Committee of the Indian National Congress set up its own enquiry. It heard evidence in advance of the Hunter Committee and completed its report earlier. The Punjab Sub-Committee examined 1700 witnesses and published 650 verified statements. Their final report, including graphic photographs, amounted to a savage indictment of the way in which India was governed and was calculated to arouse deep feelings of anger and resentment among the Indian subjects of the British Raj. Their findings were unsurprising:

Source O

The people of the Punjab were incensed against Sir Michael O'Dwyer's administration by reason of his studied contempt and distrust of the educated classes, and by reason of the cruel and compulsory methods adopted during the war, for obtaining recruits and monetary contributions and his suppression of public opinion by gagging the local press and shutting out nationalist newspapers from outside the Punjab.

The Rowlatt agitation disturbed the public mind and should be repealed.

The Jallianwala *Bagh* massacre was a calculated piece of inhumanity towards utterly innocent and unarmed men, including children, and unparalleled for its ferocity in the history of modern British administration.

From the Indian National Congress Punjab Sub-Committee's Report, published in February 1920

SKILLS BUILDER

Read Sources N and O.

1 What similarities and differences are there between the reports of the Hunter Committee and of the Punjab Committee?

2 Does this make one of the reports more reliable than the other? Explain your answer.

Discharge – but disgrace?

It was over. Dyer was summoned to Delhi and informed that the Hunter Committee had censured him, that the Viceroy's Council and the

Commander-in-Chief agreed with them and that he had no choice but to resign. This he did.

As Dyer and his wife were supervising the crating up of their belongings for the long sea journey back to Britain, a deputation of British women presented him with an illuminated address 'on behalf of the ladies of the Punjab':

Source P

We, the undersigned, desire to express our heartfelt gratitude for the firmness you displayed in the crisis which arose in this Province last April. We deplore the loss of life which occurred, but we believe it was your action which saved the Punjab and thereby preserved the honour and lives of hundreds of women and children. We trust, sir, that you will understand that we who would have suffered most had the outbreak spread, are not unmindful of what we owe to you.

From the illuminated address made 'on behalf of the ladies of the Punjab' to General Dyer

This view was supported by Miles Irving, a British official in the Punjab at the time of the massacre:

SKILLS BUILDER

Is it surprising that the views expressed in Source Q seem to be at odds with those of the Hunter Committee and Congress? Why do you think this is?

Source Q

The whole rebellion collapsed. Not only the mob that was fired upon dispersed and all trouble ceased in the city of Amritsar, but also it was felt throughout the district. One of the reasons why there had been a danger was that the people not in the district thought for some reason or other that the Arm of Government was paralysed. The inaction of the police when the National Bank was burned lent some colour to that belief and there was an idea that the government could do nothing, and this came as disillusionment.

From R.E.H. Dyer, *Army Disturbances in the Punjab*, published in 1920

The entire garrison, officers and their wives, NCOs and *sepoys* turned out to cheer Dyer and his wife and to sing 'For he's a jolly good fellow' as they boarded the train for Bombay. Large crowds also gathered on the quayside at Bombay to wish them well.

Controversy in the press

The Dyers' ship berthed at Southampton on 3 May 1920. Immediately he was embroiled in controversy. Speaking to a *Daily Mail* reporter, Dyer insisted 'It was my duty – my horrible, dirty duty'. He reminded people that civil control of Amritsar had been handed over to him; no one in authority had condemned him for the massacre – on the contrary, he said, he had been congratulated by his superiors. If he had done wrong, he insisted, as a soldier he should have been tried by a court martial, not asked to resign because a civilian committee censured him. The press and public opinion in both India and in Britain took up entrenched positions. For some, Dyer was the man who had saved India; the *Morning Post* opened a fund for him, rapidly amassed £26,000 and presented him with a sword of honour and some much needed cash. For others, he was the man who had brought disgrace to the Raj.

Arguments in Parliament

The controversy spilled over into Parliament, where a heated Commons debate on 8 July turned into more of a censure on Edwin Montagu, the Secretary of State for India (see Source M). Montagu argued that if Britain chose to rule India by the sword alone, it would be driven out by the united opinion of the civilised world. From the government benches, Churchill defended Montagu, stoutly denouncing the 'frightfulness' of the massacre, while the Ulsterman Sir Edward Carson argued that Dyer had stopped a revolution that was part of a global plot to overthrow the British Empire. Accusations and counter-accusations flew across the chamber and in the end the government, with their motion to censure Dyer, held the day.

In the Lords, 11 days later, the debate went quite the other way. The motion 'That this House deplores the conduct of the case of General Dyer as unjust to that officer, and as establishing a precedent dangerous to the preservation of law and order in the face of rebellion' was carried by a majority of 43 votes. Of course, the Lords' decision couldn't reverse that of the Commons, but many people saw it as a vindication of Dyer and his actions at Amritsar. Still others feared for its impact on Anglo-Indian relations.

The eminent Indian, Rabindranath Tagore was in London at the time of the parliamentary debates:

Source R

The result of the Dyer debates in both Houses of Parliament makes painfully evident the attitude of mind of the ruling classes of the country towards India. It shows that no outrage, however monstrous, committed against us by the agents of their government, can arouse feelings of indignation in the hearts of those from whom our governors are chosen. The unashamed condoning of brutality expressed in their speeches and echoed in their newspapers is ugly in its frightfulness. The late events have conclusively proved that our true salvation lies in our own hands.

From a letter written by Rabindranath Tagore to his family in July 1920

Tagore then returned the knighthood that had been conferred on him after he won the Nobel Prize for literature in 1913.

SKILLS BUILDER

To what extent can the views expressed in Tagore's letter be supported by the evidence in this unit?

Epilogue

Amritsar and its aftermath turned millions of loyal Indians against the Raj. They believed that Amritsar had revealed the true face of British rule and that any British reform that tended toward Indian independence was a sham. When **Motilal Nehru** presided over the Amritsar Congress in 1919, he warned delegates: 'If our lives and honour are to remain at the mercy of an irresponsible executive and military, if the ordinary rights of human beings are denied to us, then all talk of reform is a mockery'.

Ironically, a few days earlier, King George V had, by royal proclamation, enacted the Montagu-Chelmsford reforms. They would, he maintained, usher in a new era in Anglo-Indian relations.

Biography

Motilal Nehru (1861–1931)

Born in Delhi to a Kashmiri *Brahmin* family, Nehru was one of the first generation of young Indians to have a western-style college education in India. He became a barrister and settled in Allahabad in the province of Uttar Pradesh.

Nehru's legal practice flourished and by 1910 he was leading a wealthy, westernised lifestyle and had emerged as one of the moderate leaders of Congress.

Gandhi and his philosophy had a tremendous impact on him, and Motilal Nehru became one of the first Congress members to abandon western dress and to try to limit his consumption of imported goods. Although initially close to Gandhi, and arrested several times for his participation in non-violent protests, he openly criticised Gandhi's suspension of non-violent protests in 1922. He briefly joined the Swaraj Party, which aimed to put Indians in British-sponsored councils in order to wreck them, but this failed and he rejoined the Congress Party. Nehru chaired the Nehru Commission of 1928, which was intended to counter the Simon Commission and proposed dominion status for India.

Unit summary

What have you learned in this unit?

You have learned how and why one man, General Dyer, commanded his soldiers to put down what he judged to be a riot in the Jallianwala *Bagh*, Amritsar. You have found out how this action, and the martial law that followed it, had tremendous repercussions in India and in Britain. Formal enquirics were held, press campaigns were run and the whole issue debated by both Houses of Parliament. You have seen how the massacre generated questions about the nature of the Raj and how it served to harden Indian opinion against British rule.

What skills have you used in this unit?

You have used your skills of comprehension, inference-making, cross-referencing and analysis in order to consider the use of film, understand what happened at the Jallianwala *Bagh*, evaluate motive, compare and contrast two reports on the massacre and explore the reaction to the massacre in India and in Britain. Overall, you have used your skills at source evaluation, combined with your own knowledge, to reach a judgement on where to place responsibility for the massacre.

Exam tips

This is the sort of question you will find appearing on the exam paper as an (a) question.

- Study sources M, P and R. How far does Source M challenge the view of the Raj given in Sources P and R?

You tackled an (a) type question at the end of Unit 2. Look back at the exam tips you were given there (see page 31) before developing and building on them here. Follow these tips to write a successful answer to an (a) question.

- Get underneath the sources and make inferences from them.
- Compare the sources by analysing their similarities ad differences.
- Contextualise the sources, giving weight to the significance of their origin, nature and purpose.
- Reach a judgement on 'how far' by using the sources as a set.

Remember, there is an Exam Zone section at the end of the book (see pages 194–200) to help you further.

Now plan an answer to the question above and write a response.

RESEARCH TOPIC

Source S was published in two British newspapers, *The Daily News* and *The Star* on 16 December 1919. It was drawn by the left-wing cartoonist, David Low.

What point is Low making in Source S? You will need to research the relationship between Britain and Ireland at the time in order fully to understand the point Low is making and which the British public in 1919 would have understood.

Source S

5.5 Cartoon by David Low, printed in *The Daily News* and *The Star*, 16 December 1919

6 Gandhi, *swaraj* and the Congress Party

What is this unit about?

This unit focuses on Mohandas Karamchand Gandhi and his early years as a lawyer and politician. It explores his impact on Congress and the philosophy that led him to develop a policy of non-cooperation with the British Raj.

In the years to 1914, Congress was a political party for the privileged few, supported by wealthy Indians. It most certainly did not have anything like a mass following throughout India. Congress debated issues, was consulted by various agencies of the Raj and its members fell out among themselves. The most notable tensions were those between Gopal Krishna Gokhale, who believed Indians should respect the Raj and move slowly toward the distant goal of self-government, and Bal Gangadhar Tilak, who was prepared to use force to reach the same end (see pages 54–55).

Yet by the early 1920s, Congress had become a political party with a mass appeal and a following of millions throughout India. It had sharpened its ideals and its force, and the Raj could not afford to ignore it. How had this happened? It had demands and was tightly focused on independence. The fact that it was a force in the land had happened because of the hard work, vision and charisma of one man: Mohandas Karamchand Gandhi.

Key questions

- How did Gandhi turn Congress into a political party with mass appeal?
- In what ways was Gandhi's philosophy expressed in action?

Timeline

1869	Birth of Gandhi
1882	Gandhi marries Kasturba Makharji
1888	Gandhi studies law in England
1893	Gandhi works in South Africa as a lawyer
1907	Gandhi begins developing his ideas about non-violent protest
1914	Gandhi leaves South Africa for India
1915	Gandhi abandons western-style dress and begins his daily routine of spinning
1917	Gandhi intervenes in local situations, giving legal advice and resolving disputes
1917–18	Gandhi forges links with local leaders
1919	First *hartal* (*satyagraha*) in response to the Rowlatt Acts

1920	Gandhi emerges as the leader of Congress
1920–22	Second *satyagraha*; civil disobedience campaign
1922	Gandhi turns from political agitation to social welfare work in villages

Unpromising beginnings

There was absolutely nothing in Gandhi's early years to make him stand out as a potential leader. He was born in 1869 into a family which had for generations worked as minor administrators in the princely states. He married **Kasturba Makhanji** in 1882 when he was 13 years old and as a young man he was shy, awkward and had a poor command of English. On the death of his father in 1888, his family decided to send the young Gandhi to England to train as a lawyer. He returned to India as a qualified barrister, but failed to win cases as he was frequently too shy and embarrassed to speak out in defence of his clients. The offer of a years' contract with an Indian legal firm in South Africa must have come as a welcome relief.

Biography

Kasturba (Makhanji) Gandhi (1869–1944)

Kasturba was the daughter of a wealthy businessman, Gokuladas Makhanji of Porbandar. She married Mohandas Gandhi in May 1882 when they were both 13 years old. When Gandhi left to study law in England in 1888, she stayed behind in India with their newborn son, Harilal. They were to have three more sons: Manilal (1892), Ramdas (1897) and Devdas (1900).

In 1906, Gandhi decided to observe celibacy and he says Kasturba eagerly agreed to this. We do not know what she really thought, nor do we know what she thought about the women followers who lived in *ashrams* (see page 95) with Gandhi and saw to his daily needs. We do know that, although she always stood by her husband, she found it difficult to accept all his ideas.

In 1897, Kasturba travelled to South Africa to be with her husband and from 1904 to 1914 was active in the Phoenix Settlement near Durban. In 1913, she was arrested and spent three months in prison because of her protest against Indians' working conditions.

Kasturba travelled back to India with her husband. Once in India, her main role was to teach hygiene, discipline, reading and writing to women and children. She lived in *ashrams* with Gandhi. His autobiography records her refusal to join in all communal activities, like cleaning the lavatories, and there were also disagreements between them about what she saw as his neglect of their sons.

Kasturba died in 1944 from a severe heart attack following complications arising from *ashram* living, stress, pneumonia and bronchitis.

How important was Gandhi's South African experience?

The time Gandhi spent in South Africa was of immense importance in both practical and philosophical ways. He went to South Africa in 1893 and stayed until 1914. He worked there with the Indian community, gradually building up his skills and experience until he was their main spokesman in their struggles with the racial policies of the South African government.

Source A

6.1 Gandhi, seated in the centre, with his colleagues at his law office in South Africa, 1913

Gandhi's work meant that he gradually built up experience and expertise through:

- working with a wide range of Indians from all castes, backgrounds and religions
- learning to co-operate and confront individuals in positions of authority in South Africa and in London
- learning about publicity by launching his first journal *Indian Opinion*, in which he wrote about issues, rallied support and suggested coping strategies
- beginning to experiment with a variety of ways of protesting, including marches, rallies and press campaigns
- experimenting with direct, but non-violent opposition, such as burning registration documents.

It was this wide range of practical experiences that was to serve Gandhi, and the Congress Party, well on his return to India at the beginning of the First World War.

Definition

Satyagraha

A word made up by Gandhi to mean 'life-force' or 'soul-force' and which he and his followers applied to non-cooperation with the British authorities. It is important to note that Gandhi hated the term 'passive resistance' and never wanted it applied to his methods. Passive resistance means just that – resisting authority by doing nothing. So sitting down in the street or tying yourself to railings would probably, depending on the context, be classed as passive resistance. But removing your children from school and refusing to attend government parties would be an active way of resisting the Raj – by non-violent non-cooperation.

In philosophical terms, it was in South Africa that Gandhi began to develop his concept of **satyagraha**, which permeated his philosophical and political writings, thoughts and actions from about 1907 until his death 40 years later.

Source B

Mr Gandhi is a man of great saintliness of character, an ascetic, but hopelessly unpractical and unversed in everyday affairs. Your Majesty may remember that he was responsible for the Passive Resistance movement amongst the Indians in South Africa some ten years ago, and that it was with the very greatest difficulty that the South African government of the time found themselves able to cope with him. Indeed, they were only able to do so by persuading him to leave South Africa. As a proof of the esteem in which Mr Gandhi is held by even those who most strongly opposed his action, I may say that rumour has it that when he was imprisoned in South Africa, General Smuts [general in the Anglo-Boer War, South African politician and Prime Minister of South Africa 1919–24 and 1933–48] used to visit him in prison to discuss philosophy with him. This is a digression, but it has this importance, that it shows the estimation in which Mr Gandhi is held by everyone who comes across him, and this fact renders the task of dealing with him much more difficult than if he were a mere agitating politician.

From a letter written by Viceroy Chelmsford to King George V on 21 May 1919

SKILLS BUILDER

Read Source B.

1 What was Viceroy Chelmsford's attitude to Gandhi?
2 Why did he think the Raj could have problems in dealing with Gandhi?

What was Gandhi's philosophy?

Gandhi's philosophy was underpinned by his concept of *satyagraha*, a word he made up and which he used to mean 'truth-force' or 'soul-force' and to describe non-violent resistance to injustice or evil. It worked like this. Every single individual, Gandhi believed, was created to search for the truth. This truth permeates the universe and is present in the deepest part of everyone's being. In order to be fully human, each person has to reach that truth within themselves. Because every individual is at different points on their own personal journey to this truth, non-violence in relationships between individuals and groups of individuals is essential. This is because the weaker must not be forced to accept the views of the stronger against their own truth, no matter how weakly that truth is being held and sought. No one should be inhibited in his or her quest, and violence inhibits that search for inner meaning.

Source C

Satyagraha is not physical force. A **satyagrahi** does not inflict pain on the adversary; he does not seek his destruction. A *satyagrahi* never resorts to firearms. In the use of *satyagraha*, there is no ill-will whatever.

Satyagraha is a pure soul-force. Truth is the very substance of the soul. That is why this force is called *satyagraha*. The soul is informed with knowledge. In it burns the flame of love. If someone gives us pain through ignorance, we shall win him through love. Ruled by love, the world goes on. In English there is a saying 'Might is right'. Then there is the doctrine of the survival of the fittest. Both these ideas are contradictory to the above principle. Neither is wholly true. If ill-will were the chief motive force, the world would have been destroyed long ago; and neither would I have had the opportunity to write this article nor would the hopes of the readers be fulfilled. We are alive solely because of love. We are all ourselves the proof of this. Deluded by modern western civilisation, we have forgotten our ancient civilisation and worship the might of arms.

From M.K. Gandhi, *The Collected Works of Mahatma Gandhi*, published 1960–94

Definition

Satyagrahi

A person who follows Gandhi's teachings with regard to *satyagraha*.

SKILLS BUILDER

How far might the concerns of Viceroy Chelmsford, as expressed in Source B, be confirmed by Gandhi's views about *satyagraha*, expressed in Source C?

Were Gandhi's ideas in line with traditional Hindu philosophy?

It was the concept of *satyagraha* that set Gandhi's philosophy apart from traditional Hindu thought. Forms of self-suffering in order to change an opponent's mind were well known in Gujarat, just as passive resistance was well known to Western thought. But for Gandhi and his followers, *satyagraha* was only for those strong enough in their commitment to truth to undergo suffering in its cause. It solved the eternal dilemma between means and ends, because *satyagraha* was both the means and the end. Those who carried it out became even stronger followers of truth; those against whom it operated were converted to a deeper vision of the truth. In all situations of conflict, Gandhi believed *satyagraha* could only generate truth and never falsehood.

How did Gandhi become the leader of Congress?

Gandhi formed a strong friendship with Gokhale, who visited him in South Africa and admired his work there. However, Gokhale was well aware of just how out of touch Gandhi was with India and Indian affairs. He advised Gandhi to keep out of public life for at least a year while he found his feet and developed an understanding of the political dynamics in the country. Gandhi took this advice to heart when he arrived back in India in 1915.

Winning hearts and minds

He may have been out of touch with the complexity of current events in India, but this didn't stop Gandhi from having a very clear vision of the sort of society he wanted India to become or from creating a plan to achieve this. He started from the premise that western technology had failed. It had not added to the sum total of human happiness and, indeed, had made man a slave to machines.

Source D

Formerly, people worked in the open air only as much as they liked. Now, thousands of workmen meet together and for the sake of their own maintenance, they work in factories or mines. Their condition is worse than that of beasts. They are obliged to work, at the risk of their lives, at most dangerous occupations, for the sake of millionaires.

Formerly, men were made slaves under physical compulsion. Now, they are enslaved by temptation of money and of the luxuries that money can buy. There are now diseases of which people never dreamt before, and an army of doctors is engaged in finding out their cures, and so hospitals have increased. This is a test of civilisation.

Formerly, special messengers were required and much expense was incurred in order to send letters; today, anyone can abuse his fellow by means of a letter for one penny.

From M.K. Gandhi, 'Hind Swaraj', in R. Iyer (editor) *The Moral and Political Writings of Mahatma Gandhi Volume 1 Civilisation, Politics and Religion*, published in 1986

Gandhi believed that people were much happier when they lived in small, self-sufficient communities. These communities would grow their own food, spin their own thread and weave their own cloth for their own garments. Freedom for India, he hoped, would be accompanied by the dismantling of the state and the return to small, simple communities of the past. Of course, the idea was completely unworkable. Bombay, Madras, Delhi and Calcutta were bustling modern cities, teeming with millions of people who couldn't possibly return to their rural origins. But the idea of self-sufficient rural communities caught on and the Indian peasant masses began to take notice of Gandhi and to see in him someone with whose ideas they could identify.

Gandhi increasingly adopted a peasant lifestyle. He discarded the western clothes of an English-educated lawyer and began wearing the Indian *dhoti*. This was a full-flowing cloth which men wore, covering the legs and which could be hitched up to look like a loincloth. Always a vegetarian, he began eating more and more frugally, again, as the Indian peasants did. And, as the peasants did, he walked everywhere whenever he could. No other Indian politician behaved like this. The Indian masses now began to identify not only with his ideas but also with Gandhi himself. He looked and behaved like one of them. In about 1915, Gandhi began a routine of daily spinning, believing it would bring him into closer contact with the millions of Indian peasants for whom spinning with a *charka*, or spinning wheel, was a daily task.

Definitions

Dhoti

Long, flowing piece of cloth worn by men, which could be hitched up to look like a loincloth.

Charka

The spinning wheel became the symbol of the Congress Party. Gandhi believed that daily spinning would bring India's leaders into closer contact with peasant life and enhance the dignity of labour in the minds of India's intellectuals who had never had to do hard physical work.

Source E

6.2 Gandhi spinning thread. The spinning wheel – a *charka* – became the symbol of the Congress Party

There were those who realised how ridiculously impractical Gandhi's ideas were. Arvind Nehra, a Cambridge university-educated lawyer like Gandhi, became a judge under the Raj. He corresponded for many years with the wife of an English colonel.

Source F

In India we have a new prophet, this Mr Gandhi. I know little of him save that my family in India write that he is a sincere man and believes implicitly in his own heart that he is acting for the good of the country. The mistakes of the really sincere do so much more harm than the follies of the mischievous and the wilful, that I am a little anxious for Mr Gandhi. His ideals are about as unattainable as those with which I left Cambridge. I also was going to make a new heaven and a new earth and bring about a better understanding between black men and white men, and it all seemed so very easy.

Gandhi preaches that everyone must do without foreign goods and wear only the native manufactured **kaddar**. So for interest's sake I sat down and worked this out the other night, only to discover that there would be something like three inches of *kaddar* per head of the population, and since even the loin cloth of my people requires more than this, lo, another distant Utopia!

From Arvind Nehra, *Letters of a Indian Judge to an English Gentlewoman*, published in 1934

Gandhi rejected the lifestyle of Indians of his caste and profession, preferring instead to live in **ashrams**, austere communities of fellow believers and followers. This involved renouncing all sexual relationships as part of an individual's move towards purification. Gandhi had now identified himself with those traditional Indian beliefs that regarded the emission of semen as a loss of strength; therefore, not to indulge in the sexual act was a sign of power.

In these ways, Gandhi associated himself with the mass of Indian people and acquired a vast following. His renunciation of contemporary values and society, and his search for the truth, led to people calling him *Mahatma*.

Source G

Then when he [Gandhi] came into the political field in a big way and made – well, rather astounding proposals asking, for instance, lawyers to give up their practice, and live simply and on next to nothing; everybody to wear hand spun clothes made in the villages; and the whole atmosphere changed, and many of our older leaders, who wanted to co-operate with him, nevertheless were not quite clear what all this meant, because they'd been thinking differently. But he caught on so well with the Indian people, the masses, that that brought some conviction to older leaders, who were pulled then towards him. The fact that stood out about Gandhi was how he attracted people of different kinds and thereby he became a link between different groups from the poorest peasant, whom he always sought to represent, to princes and rich industrialists.

Comments from Jawaharlal Nehru in conversation originally broadcast on radio, in Francis Watson and Hallam Tennyson (editors) *Talking of Gandhi*, published in 1969

SKILLS BUILDER

Read Source G. What did Nehru believe were Gandhi's strengths as a politician?

Question

Gandhi's vision of an Indian society consisting of self-sufficient rural communities was clearly unworkable in the twentieth-century world. Why, then, did so many Indian politicians and people support him?

Political manoeuvrings

Gandhi's outward humility convinced the leading Congress politicians that he was no threat to them. But Gandhi's moral values and vision for India's future meant that, in his view, he had to take part in the political process. He bided his time and, when he did move, did so cautiously.

In 1917, he intervened in local situations: for example, where the peasant farmers of Champaran in north Bihar were forced by white planters to grow indigo on disadvantageous terms and in Ahmedabad in Gujarat where cotton mill-workers were earning a pittance. In Bihar, *satyagraha* took the form of his refusal to leave the district and, in Gujarat, he fasted until the situation was resolved. In both these cases, the positive outcome was probably due more to other political re-alignments than to Gandhi's *satyagraha,* but nevertheless his was an impressive performance.

In the years 1917–18, Gandhi embarked on forging relationships with up-and-coming regional leaders, such as the Mayor of Ahmedabad, Vallabhbhai Patel, the Bihari lawyer Rajendra Prasad and the young **Jawaharlal Nehru**. Gandhi was obviously developing an astute political awareness as to which people were likely to be of use to him in future struggles.

Biography

Jawaharlal Nehru (1889–1964)

Jawaharlal was born and brought up in a wealthy Kashmiri household, the son of Motilal Nehru, who was an important Indian barrister and leading Congress politician.

Jawaharlal had an English education: Harrow School and Cambridge University, where he read law. He returned to India, where the Amritsar Massacre and the impact of Gandhi on Congress changed his life.

A popular orator and deeply involved in the Non-Cooperation Movement, he was in and out of prison in the 1920s and 1930s. He refused to compromise with the Muslim League and, through his negotiations with the British during the Second World War, was held by many to be largely responsible for the intransigence of Jinnah, which led to Partition.

He became head of the interim government in 1946 and helped Louis Mountbatten (see pages 177–78) negotiate the final stages of independence. He remained Prime Minister of India until his death in 1964.

He developed connections with two important communities that had largely been neglected by Congress politicians: Muslims and businessmen. This paid off hugely: the Muslims by supporting his take-over of Congress in 1920 and the business community by pay-rolling his non-cooperation campaign (see page 99).

But not all the *satyagraha* campaigns went well. Horrified by the repressive nature of the Rowlatt Acts (see pages 70–71), which ordinary political protest and a unanimous vote in the Imperial Legislative Council had failed to stop, Gandhi called for a *satyagraha* in April 1919. His idea was to hold a series of **hartals** throughout India, using this form of direct, non-violent action to break the impasse between politicians. It failed. *Hartals* were held, to a greater or lesser extent, in most of India's provinces. However, the degree to which they were observed varied from region to region within and between provinces. More seriously, the stoppages erupted into violence in Gujarat and the Punjab. Gandhi immediately called a stop to the Rowlatt *satyagraha,* but even so that failed to stop the violence. It was a dreadful lesson. *Satyagraha* would only work if everyone involved understood its basic tenets and were not using it as a pretext to follow other agendas.

Definition

Hartal

A stoppage of work, usually occasioned by a lockout, and used as a protest.

SKILLS BUILDER

How far does Source H make you change your mind about what you wrote about Viceroy Chelmsford in answer to the questions relating to Source B on page 92?

Source H

What a damned nuisance these saintly fanatics are! Incapable of hurting a fly, honest, but he enters light-heartedly on a course of action which is the negation of all government and may lead to much hardship to people who are ignorant and easily led astray.

From a telegram written by Viceroy Chelmsford to Secretary of State Montagu

Question

'Gandhi's emergence as leader of Congress was carefully calculated.' How far does the evidence support this judgement?

SKILLS BUILDER

How far does Source H challenge Sources I and J about Gandhi's leadership qualities?

What about the Raj?

When Gandhi left South Africa, he was not vehemently anti-Raj. Indeed, many of his speeches in the years from 1915 to 1918 were in support of British involvement in the First World War and of India's contribution to that involvement. But three things led Gandhi to change his mind and to develop the idea of *swaraj*, or self-rule:

- the Rowlatt Acts, which aimed at continuing indefinitely the repressive war-time restrictions

- the Amritsar Massacre of April 1919 and its tacit endorsement by large sections of the British community in India

- one of the outcomes of the **Paris Peace Conference** that ended the First World War was that Turkey had to pay a huge indemnity and lose its colonial territories. This confirmed the worst fears of Indian Muslims – that white Europeans (and Americans) had little concern for Islamic nations. It made Gandhi realise that this could increase the idea of separateness among Muslims.

By 1920, Gandhi had emerged as the leading Indian politician. There was no other all-Indian political leader or group who could organise opposition to him. Gokhale died in 1915, Annie Besant was seen as a woman of little consequence and Tilak died in 1920. Members of Congress were so divided about which path was the best way forward that they couldn't unite to oppose Gandhi. Members of social and religious groups, who had previously exercised little influence at meetings of Congress, now appeared as delegates supporting Gandhi. In addition, there was wide geographical support for Gandhi because of the many local disputes with which he had been involved.

So it was that members of Congress had little alternative but to ally with Gandhi. They were prepared, provided they could influence its pattern and timing, to support Gandhi, *satyagraha* and *swaraj*.

Source I

[Gandhi said] It's up to you to choose me as your leader or not. It's up to you to throw me out when you want to. It's up to you to cut off my head when you want to, but so long as I am your leader, I am the leader and there's martial law. So this curious mixture of extreme modesty and simplicity, with an iron will, an iron command always put across in a soft way.

Comments from Jawaharlal Nehru in conversation originally broadcast on radio, in Francis Watson and Hallam Tennyson (editors) *Talking of Gandhi*, published in 1969

Source J

Gandhi, with his emaciated shrunken figure and his gnome-like face behind metal-rimmed glasses, was not impressive at first sight. He had, however, a magnificent head, and his bare chest was nobly proportioned, his voice low, and his manner in an odd but striking way somewhat kingly. Years later I was to describe it dramatically but mistakenly as the majesty of the meek. Gandhi was often mild but he was never really meek. His eyes, as I noticed later, could sometimes be stony.

From Frank Moraes, *Witness to an Era*, published in 1973

How effective was Gandhi's civil disobedience campaign of 1920–22?

Congress' annual meeting, which in 1920 was held at Nagpur, was of immense significance. Gandhi dominated the proceedings and, by the force of his arguments, his ability to bind together Hindus and Muslims, and his sheer charisma, he persuaded the delegates to vote for his policy of non-cooperation with the British Raj. They did so by a majority of just over two to one. Gandhi's aim was, quite simply, to make the Raj ungovernable. If this happened, Gandhi predicted that the Raj would wither and die within a year and *swaraj* would follow. It all seemed so simple.

What did non-cooperation entail?

Gandhi and through him, Congress, urged all Indians to:

- boycott elections to the new legislative assemblies
- hand back all titles and decorations awarded by the Raj
- remove their children from government schools
- refuse invitations to social events put on by the Raj
- boycott the law courts
- withhold taxes
- refuse to buy imported goods
- leave all government posts.

Some of this was completely unrealistic. Lawyers, for example, were unlikely to want to abandon their lucrative practices and parents would not want to deny their children an education for an indefinite period of time. But many areas of non-cooperation were realistic and could quite easily cause the machinery of government to grind to a halt. Mass refusal to pay taxes, for example, would stop most government departments functioning.

In support of the 'Swaraj Resolution', Gandhi proposed:

Source K

The Resolution which I have the honour to move is as follows:

'The object of the Indian National Congress is the attainment of *Swaraj* by the people of India by all legitimate and peaceful means.'

I want you to accompany the carrying out of this Resolution with a faith and a determination which nothing on earth can move, that you are intent on getting *swaraj* at the earliest possible moment, and that you are intent on getting *swaraj* by means that is legitimate, that is honourable, and by means that is non-violent, that is peaceful.

From a speech made by M.K. Gandhi, *Report of the 35th Indian National Congress* 1920

From triumph to disaster

Gandhi, mindful of what happened to his earlier *satyagraha* campaign against the Rowlatt Acts, was terrified that the movement would again fall into the hands of the mob. Accordingly, he targeted those areas of government where Indian non-cooperation was unlikely to bring them into open conflict with the police. These, too, happened to be those areas, such as taxation and administration, which were vital to the functioning of the Raj. Here there were some initial successes. For example, students boycotted their examinations, taxes were not paid, a large number of qualified voters (up to 90 per cent in some areas) stayed away from the 1920 elections, around 200 lawyers stopped work and, during the visit of the Duke of Connaught to Calcutta in 1921, shops were closed throughout the city and very few Indians were present at official ceremonies of welcome.

Source L

Although in their opinion, the movement is unconstitutional in that it has as its object the paralysis and subversion of the existing administration of the country, Government has hitherto refrained from instituting criminal proceedings against those of its promoters who have advocated simultaneously with non-cooperation abstention from violence, and they have instructed local governments only to take action against those persons who have gone beyond the limits originally set by the organisers and have by speech or writing openly incited the public to violence or have attempted to tamper with the loyalty of the army or of the police. In adopting this policy, Government has been influenced by several considerations:

They have been reluctant to interfere with liberty of speech and the freedom of the press

Government is at all times reluctant to embark on a campaign against individuals some of whom may be motivated by honest, if misguided, motives

The third, and chief consideration, is Government's trust in the common sense of India, their belief that the sanity of the classes and the masses alike would reject non-cooperation as a visionary and unrealistic scheme, which if successful could only result in widespread disorder, political chaos, and the ruin of all those who have any real stake in the country. The appeal of non-cooperation is to prejudice and ignorance.

From the Government of India's Resolution on the Non-Cooperation Movement, *Gazette of India*, 6 November 1920

Definition

Jihad

Struggle (or war) in defence of Islam. This is the definition of Lesser *Jihad*. Greater *Jihad* is the personal struggle for spiritual self-perfection.

Millions of Indians, however, were unable or unwilling to understand the morality of *satyagraha*, and followed their own agendas, mostly paying off old scores and attempting to drive forward new initiatives. Violence broke out at different times and in different provinces. The Bombay *hartal*, for example, scheduled to coincide with the arrival of the Prince of Wales, turned into four days of looting and burning in which 53 demonstrators were killed and hundreds injured. In Rangpur, the mob attacked moneylenders. The Muslim Moplahs of Malaba declared a **jihad**, killing British people and wealthy Hindu and Muslim landlords and moneylenders, as well as forcing Hindu peasants and labourers to convert to Islam. In the Punjab and later in the Gangetic Plain, Deccan and other parts of India, Hindus forced Muslims to 'wash away their pollution' by total immersion in water tanks and rivers. Many drowned amid communal rioting and the always fragile Hindu-Muslim alliance was in serious jeopardy. *Satyagraha* was spiralling out of control and turning into Gandhi's worst nightmare.

Matters came to a head in February 1922, when Congress supporters in Chauri Chaura, a village in Gorakhpur, torched a police station and burned to death the 22 Indian policemen inside. Gandhi immediately withdrew to his *ashram* to fast and meditate, emerging some days later to call an immediate end to the *satyagraha*. His supporters were horrified. So much that was positive had been gained – why throw it all away because of a few outbreaks of violence?

Question

Did this serious outbreak of communal violence mean that the Indian Government was correct in its views, as expressed in Source L, about *satyagraha*?

Source M

I must tell you that this was the last straw. I was much disturbed by the Madras doings, but I drowned the warning voice. I received letters both from Hindus and Mohammedans from Calcutta, Allahabad and the Punjab, all these before the Gorakhpur incident, telling me that the wrong was not all on the government side, that our people were becoming aggressive, defiant and threatening, that they were getting out-of-hand and were not non-violent in demeanour. I assure you that if the thing had not been suspended we would have been leading not a non-violent struggle but essentially a violent struggle. It is undoubtedly true that non-violence is spreading like the scent of attar of roses throughout the length and breadth of this land, but the foetid smell of violence is still powerful and it would be unwise to ignore or underrate it. The cause will prosper by this retreat. The movement has drifted from the right path. We have come back to our moorings and we can again go straight ahead.

Explanation by M.K. Gandhi to Jawaharlal Nehru as to why he called off the *satyagraha*

Gandhi was adamant. He turned away from political agitation and work on his 'constructive programme', which emphasised social welfare work in the villages along with, of course, hand spinning and weaving. This was back to basics indeed. Less than a month later, at the end of February 1922, Gandhi was arrested by the British authorities and charged with 'promoting disaffection towards the government established by law', to which he pleaded guilty and was sentenced to six years imprisonment. Was it all over?

Something lost and something gained?

Gandhi's idea that *satyagraha* could, of itself, bring about *swaraj* had been discredited, but Gandhi himself was clear that the concept wasn't wrong – what was wrong was that the Indian people were not yet ready for the sort of self-discipline that was necessary to make it effective.

One outstanding feature of Congress' commitment to *satyagraha* was the way in which members had involved themselves in peasant communities and had acquired a deeper understanding of peasants' needs. Peasants had hitherto been more or less ignored by members of Congress. For example, Jawaharlal Nehru was a member of Congress who was educated at an

English public school (Harrow) and at Cambridge University where he read law and became a barrister, like his father Motilal Nehru (see page 86). He led a pretty privileged life. In the summer of 1920, Jawaharlal made the decision to travel extensively in Adawh, in the heart of the province in which he had been born. This is part of his reaction to what he saw and heard there:

Question

What impact did Jawaharlal Nerhu's travels in Adawh have on him?

Source N

They were in miserable rags, men and women, but their faces were full of excitement. . . Looking at them and their misery and overflowing gratitude, I was filled with shame, shame at my own easy-going and comfortable life and our own petty politics of the city which ignored this vast multitude of semi-naked sons and daughters of India. A new picture of India seemed to rise before me, naked, starving, crushed and utterly miserable. And their faith in us, casual visitors from the distant city, embarrassed me and filled me with a new responsibility that frightened me.

From Jawaharlal Nehru, *Autobiography*, published in 1942

Allied to this was Congress' growing ability to understand and exploit local grievances and to link these, albeit not always successfully, with the broader campaign for *swaraj*. What seems to have impressed Congress more than anything was the sense of excitement, of dynamism and the feeling that India was on the move – but to which destination?

Source O

The first national episode in Gandhi's presentation of a radical alternative for India was of considerable significance. Most obviously it demonstrated that Gandhi was now a national figure. British and Indians alike could no longer ignore or ridicule him: his saintly politics were proved to have powerful repercussions. Non-cooperation also elicited from the British a changed attitude to political agitation which posed them a new problem because it was non-violent and so wide-scale, and because it erupted just when they were playing for wider political co-operation in the reformed constitution.

From Judith M. Brown, *Modern India: the Origins of an Asian Democracy*, published in 1994

Source P

For all his humility, Gandhi was at heart a vain man who wanted Indian freedom on his own terms and through his own methods. When both had failed, he stepped down and turned his attention to spinning and Hindu education, giving the impression that he considered these equally important as the achievement of Indian nationhood.

From Lawrence James, *Raj: the Making and Unmaking of British India*, published in 1997

Unit summary

What have you learned in this unit?

You have learned that by 1922, Gandhi had become the undisputed leader of Congress, and about how he came to power. You have seen how he galvanised Congress members into setting the goal of *swaraj* and had given them *satyagraha* as the means whereby self-rule could be achieved. You have seen that Gandhi himself was something of an enigma. Obsessed with the totally impractical idea of an India composed of rural communities devoted to spinning and weaving their own cloth, he nevertheless inspired millions of Indians at all levels of sophistication to follow him and adopt his methods. However, his 1920–22 *satyagraha* spiralled out of his control and he was imprisoned by the authorities. Nevertheless, the British Raj, acknowledging it was dependent on the goodwill of the Indian people, had to take notice of him and his methods, and, if it was to survive, to respond appropriately.

What skills have you learned in this unit?

You have used your skills of source analysis to develop an understanding of the philosophy of *satyagraha* and how Gandhi believed it would lead to *swaraj*, and you have worked with sources generated by the Raj in order to demonstrate their range of reactions to Gandhi and *satyagraha*. Your evaluation of a range of sources has enabled you to understand how Gandhi rose to be leader of Congress and you have considered how such an apparently impractical political programme could attract such a large following. Finally, you have used your skills at source evaluation and combined them with your own knowledge to reach a judgement about the significance of the 1920–22 *satyagraha*.

Exam tips

This is the sort of question you will find appearing on the exam paper as a (b) question.

- Study Sources L, M and O, and use your own knowledge. Do you agree with the view, expressed in Source O, that the *satyagraha* of 1920–22 was 'of considerable significance'?

You tackled (b) style questions at the end of Units 3 and 4. Look back to the exam tips you were given there because you will need them to answer this question. At the end of Unit 4 you created a spider diagram as a plan. This time, use whichever sort of plan you like best and which works for you. But be sure to plan!

- Be very sure you know what view is being expressed in Source O.
- Analyse and interpret Sources L and M so as to establish points that support and points that challenge the view given in Source O.
- Cross-reference between the sources by focusing on support and challenge.
- Use your wider knowledge both to reinforce and to challenge the points derived from the sources.
- Combine the points into arguments for and against the view given in Source O.
- Evaluate the conflicting arguments by considering the quality of the evidence used, involving a consideration of provenance (where appropriate) and the weight of evidence and range of knowledge you can find in support.
- Present a supported judgement as to the validity of the stated view and/or any alternatives.

7 Retrenchment in the 1920s

What is this unit about?

Following the collapse of Gandhi's civil disobedience campaign of 1920–22, the 1920s were largely a time of regrouping and consolidation on the part of both the British Raj and Congress. This regrouping and consolidation, however, was for a purpose. The end of the 1920s saw a British government desperately striving to keep the Empire and the British Raj intact while at the same time conciliating Indian opinion. It also saw Gandhi attempting his most ambitious *satyagraha* yet and, alarmingly for the future, one from which the Muslims withdrew.

Key questions

- What was the impact of the Simon Commission?
- How successful was Gandhi's salt *satyagraha*?

Timeline

1922		Gandhi is in prison
1920s		Congress reorganises and increases its membership
1923		Members of Congress are allowed to stand for election to councils set up by the Raj
1924		Gandhi is released from prison
1926		Irwin appointed Viceroy of India
1928		'Young hooligans' enter the political arena
		Simon Commission disembarks at Bombay
		Nehru Report sets out a basic constitution for an independent India
1929	October	Irwin Declaration asserts India should aim for dominion status
	December	Lahore Congress decides on *purna swaraj* (complete independence)
1930	January 26	designated Independence Day
	March	Start of the Salt March
	April	Jawaharal Nehru imprisoned for six months
	June	Civil disobedience campaign reaches its height
	November	First Round Table Conference in London boycotted by Congress
1931		Gandhi–Irwin Pact

Memories of the Raj

Zareer Masani travelled extensively in India recording people's memories of the Raj for a series of BBC programmes. Here, Jatin Chakrabarti remembers playing football in India in the 1920s:

Source A

I do remember that in 1924 or '26, in the final of the Indian Football Association Shield, there was heavy rain. In that rain, the ground was practically flooded, and it was very muddy and slushy. The game ought to have been stopped; as the Indians were playing barefoot, they were greatly disadvantaged; but the referee gave the opinion that the ground was quite fit for a game. The Mohun Bagan team was defeated by three or four goals to nil. Whenever that notorious referee was used in any game, everybody took it for granted that whenever he gets any opportunity, he will find against the Indians.

From Zareer Masani, *Indian Tales of the Raj*, published in 1987

SKILLS BUILDER

1 What does Source A tell you about attitudes in 1920s India?

2 Football is only a game. Did it really matter that the referee was biased?

3 How reliable is this source as evidence of attitudes in India in the mid-1920s?

How did Congress consolidate its position in the 1920s?

Membership

During the period of non-cooperation, membership of Congress grew by leaps and bounds. From a base of 100,000, it rose to around 2 million by the end of 1921. True, some more conservative members left because they objected to seeing Congress turning from being a pressure group to one of open defiance to the British Raj and a large number of Muslims left when non-cooperation collapsed because of what they regarded as Gandhi's failure to support them in their concerns over Turkey and the break-up of the Islamic Ottoman Empire (see page 131), but overwhelmingly the membership trend was upwards.

Congress had achieved this support by extending its appeal into geographical areas and wooing interest groups that had hitherto been neglected. Many of it's new supporters came from the richer peasantry and the commercial castes, but it was also beginning to recruit support from railway workers, mill-hands and the poorer peasants, some of whom had organised themselves into peasant leagues.

Organisation

When Gandhi emerged as leader of Congress in 1920, the party organisation consisted of three administrative levels: local branches, provincial committees and an All-Indian Congress Committee (the AICC). This structure was revitalised in 1920 because of Gandhi's perception that a new sense of direction and purpose was needed. Co-operation with the Raj was to end and be replaced by non-violent non-cooperation. Membership of the All-Indian Congress Committee was increased from 161 to 350, and seats were re-allocated on a regional population basis. Great emphasis was

How would the new structure of Congress enable it to challenge the Raj more effectively than in the past? For example, were there more official ways of making the views of Indians known to the Raj? Did Indians have more or less power?

placed on recruiting from hitherto untapped groups like trade unions and from women. Around 100 additional provincial committees were set up and several hundred more local branches.

Gandhi set up a new unit within the All-Indian Congress Committee. This was the Congress Working Committee (CWC) and its job was to formulate policy. Gandhi used a clever analogy when he said, 'The Working Committee is to the Congress what a Cabinet is to Parliament'. This was no idle comparison. Gandhi intended Congress to develop an alternative administrative structure that could take over when, as he hoped, the Raj withered away.

After non-cooperation

Non-cooperation, as you have seen, collapsed in 1922 and, with Gandhi in prison, a seemingly leaderless Congress, with its strategy and tactics in tatters, might have been expected to fall apart. Far from it. Congress used the time as a breathing space within which to consolidate past successes and to expand into new areas.

While Gandhi was in gaol, leadership of Congress passed to the moderates C.R. Das (a barrister in the Calcutta High Court) and Motilal Nehru. Both Das and Nehru favoured taking advantage of the Government of India Act of 1919 (see page 69) and, in 1923, members of Congress were allowed to stand for election to the councils set up by the Raj. In this way, it was argued, the Montagu-Chelmsford reforms could be effectively undermined. In fact, there was a totally different outcome. Many congressmen were successful in local elections and their presence on the local councils lent those bodies an air of respectability. Their election also lent an air of respectability to the members of Congress and so increased the popularity of the Congress Party itself. Many middle-class Indians, alienated by Gandhi's campaigns, returned to the fold.

On being released from prison in 1924, Gandhi went back to basics. He set up the All-India Spinners' Association, with the intention of spreading the word about hand-spinning and weaving, as well as promoting the more general cause of village self-sufficiency. He persuaded Congress to embark on a programme of mass literacy and improvement of village sanitation – Congress did not take much persuading on this. And Gandhi himself began to campaign vigorously on behalf of the 'Untouchables', to enable them to enter fully into Indian society.

Many millions of Indians must have breathed a collective sigh of relief. Gandhi appeared to have abandoned his confrontational programme of non-violence and Congress was emerging as a responsible political party, determined to improve the lot of the Indian people. How wrong they were!

Enter the 'young hooligans'

Many members of Congress would have been happy to let the process of constructive development continue almost indefinitely. But two events changed all this.

- Three energetic, charismatic young men, whom Gandhi was later to call 'young hooligans', burst upon the political scene.
- The British government set up the Simon Commission (see pages 108–115).

The two events were not unconnected.

Who were these 'young hooligans'? They were **Subhas Chandra Bose**, **Jayaprakash Narayan** and Jawaharlal Nehru. Together and separately they lobbied on the All-Indian Congress Committee and the Congress Working Committee relentlessly for renewed action – for another great push towards the goal of independence. Why did Gandhi label them hooligans? Because they were attracted to Socialism, a doctrine they found fed their anti-imperialist sentiments and which Gandhi, deeply conservative at heart, regarded as dangerously radical.

Biography

Subhas Chandra Bose (1897–1945)

Anti-British and very militant in his ideas, Bose opposed Gandhi's tactics of non-violence. He also opposed the idea of liberal democracies, instead preferring totalitarian regimes and believing that India would benefit from a strong totalitarian leader.

Bose was born into an affluent Bengali family in Cuttack, Orissa and had a European education within India and at Cambridge University. He took the Indian Civil Service examination in 1920, coming second, but resigned from the Indian Civil Service a year later because he wanted to work for Indian independence.

Initially, he worked in Calcutta with Chittaranjan Das, the Bengali freedom-fighter, from where in 1921 he organised a boycott of the visit of the Prince of Wales and was imprisoned. In April 1924, he was elected to the post of Chief Executive Officer of the Calcutta Corporation. Over the next 20 years he held positions of authority in Calcutta and Congress, including being elected president of Congress, and was imprisoned 11 times by the British for 'terrorist' activities.

During the Second World War, Bose broadcast anti-British propaganda from Nazi Germany. He also formed an army of Indians who had been taken prisoner by the Germans, which penetrated eastern India and attacked British posts there.

Seen by many as a traitor and a puppet of the Germans and Japanese, Bose was killed in an air crash over Japan in 1945.

Biography

Jayaprakash Narayan (1902–79)

Usually known as J.P., Narayan was born in Sitabdiara, a village in Uttar Pradesh. He completed his higher education in the USA, where he became a Marxist. After returning to India he joined the Congress Party and was arrested and jailed several times by the British for his participation in the Independence Movement.

After his release from jail in 1932, he helped form the Congress Socialist Party (CSP), a left-wing group within Congress. Following independence and the death of Gandhi, J.P. led the Party out of Congress and it became the opposition Socialist Party.

Originally a supporter of physical force to eject the British from India, J.P. was won over by the non-violence arguments of Gandhi and became a strong supporter of *satyagrahas* as a tactic.

In 1920, J.P. married Prabhavati Devi, a freedom fighter in her own right and close friend and disciple of Kasturba Gandhi.

Definition

Dominion status

To be self-governing, but within the British Empire.

Bose, Narayan and Nehru eschewed the idea of settling for **dominion status**, which had been floated immediately after the First World War and discussed, on and off, by Congress ever since.

Source B

I submit to you honestly that if I have energy to serve the country, that energy oozes out of me at the very thought of dominion status. I cannot go about spending my energy and strength for dominion status. I do submit to you that there are many like me in this country who feel like that. You will find in all India groups of organisations that are springing up full of energy and militant spirit and they promise to attain an early freedom for India. The question is, are you going to help the development of the militant spirit in the country? Are you going to help the development of this revolutionary spirit in the country or are you going to damp it and kill it in trying to bring about a compromise? Certainly it damps my spirit if you talk of dominion status and I can only judge others by my standard. The real thing in the world is not so much the question of the struggle between India and England, the real conflict is between the two sets of ideals; and the question is, which set of ideals are you going to keep before the country? This is a conflict between imperialism and all that is not imperialism, and if you look at it from that point of view, you cannot for one moment think of dominion status so long as Great Britain has the Empire around her.

From Jawaharlal Nehru's speech to Congress in Calcutta on 27 December 1928

Question

Why was Jawaharlal Nehru so opposed to the acceptance of dominion status for India?

The Simon Commission and its impact

The Raj, too, drew breath after the collapse of the non-violent campaigns of 1920–22. British policy consisted in balancing the need to keep control at the centre while at the same time making concessions to Indian aspirations. The lines to be followed were those laid down by the Montagu-Chelmsford reforms (see pages 68–70). This meant that Britain retained responsibility for foreign policy and India's defence, and India's elected provincial and national assemblies took on responsibility for some financial and all social and welfare matters. A lot of good work was done by these assemblies, particularly in advancing a cholera and smallpox **inoculation programme**, despite Gandhi's opposition to them. Many Indians worked well with the Raj and had no problems in doing so, although a large section of Indian society regarded them as traitors.

Gandhi regarded vaccination against smallpox as a manifestation of the evil that the British Raj had unleashed on India. Vaccination, he said, was a 'filthy process that is little short of eating beef.' He advised smallpox sufferers that they would be cured if they used enemas, made sure they had plenty of fresh air, wrapped themselves in a wet sheet at night and changed their diet.

Definition

Inoculation programme

This was a systematic and well-organised programme aimed at protecting people from the killer diseases of cholera and smallpox. Those working on the programme inoculated thousands of men, women and children against cholera and vaccinated them against smallpox.

What was the political situation in Westminster?

The British government had to be mindful, too, of the political situation in Westminster. The Government of India Act of 1919, which embodied the Montagu-Chelmsford reforms, was due for review in 1929. But 1929 was the year scheduled for a general election. The Conservative government was worried that if the review was held after the general election and if the Labour Party won the general election, then policies on India would veer to the left. Labour Party politicians had strong links with Congress and Conservative Party politicians were afraid that any review undertaken under a Labour government would give Congress more or less what they wanted. What was to be done? The Secretary of State for India, Lord Birkenhead, had the solution. He simply brought the review forward so that it happened before the general election and under a Conservative government.

The Simon Commission

In 1927, the government sent a parliamentary delegation, headed by **Sir John Simon**, out to India to find out how the Government of India Act of 1919 was working and to make recommendations as to how, and indeed whether, it should be amended. The Labour MP Clement Attlee, who later led the Labour Party to victory in the 1945 British general election, was a member of the seven-man delegation. Significantly, there were no Indian members. The 'message' here was loud and clear. The future of India was to be decided by British politicians based in Westminster. Indians were to take no part in deciding their own future. This was not lost on the Indians themselves.

Biography

Sir John Simon (1873–1954)

Son of the Reverend Edwin Simon and his wife Fanny Allsebrook, and educated at Fettes College Edinburgh and Oxford University, Simon became a lawyer in 1899.

In 1906, he entered Parliament as a Liberal MP representing Walthamstow and, later, Spen Valley. He became Solicitor-General in 1910 and Attorney-General three years later. In 1915, he was made Home Secretary, but resigned in 1916 because he disagreed with conscription.

When the Liberal Party split, Simon supported Asquith against Lloyd George and, in 1922–24, was treated almost as deputy leader of the party.

After supporting Newfoundland in a boundary dispute with Canada, he retired from the bar and, in 1927–31, chaired the Simon Commission on India's constitution.

Simon served in Ramsay MacDonald's national government first as Foreign Secretary and then as Home Secretary, later working as Chancellor of the Exchequer under Chamberlain and Lord Chancellor in Churchill's government. However, he was seen as one of the 'guilty men' who had appeased Hitler and this, combined with his awkward and chilly manner, meant that he never held office after 1945.

Sir Tej Bahadur Sapru was the leader of the Indian Liberal Party, opposed to Congress, the non-violent campaigns and Gandhi. The Party favoured a dialogue with the British Empire and sought self-government reforms but not independence from the Empire.

Source C

I do not think a worse challenge has been thrown down ever before to Indian nationalism, notwithstanding the profuse assurances in Mr Baldwin's speech and the yet more profuse assurances in Mr Ramsay MacDonald's speech. Indian nationalists of the moderate school have been compelled to ask if the only way of recognising the spirit of co-operation is by telling Indians that their lot is to be none other than that of petitioners; that they cannot be trusted to participate in the responsibility of making recommendations to Parliament for the future of their country; and that all that they may aspire to is to put their proposals before the Commission, which may accept them or reject them, and again to repeat the same process of persuasion, argument and discussion before the Joint Committee of Parliament. Now, if this is what is meant by co-operation, if this is the new idea of equality of status on which we are to be fed, if our patriotism is a prejudice, and if the patriotism of the seven members of Parliament is to be treated as impartial justice, then we Liberals feel justified in telling the government here and in England, 'You may do anything you like in the assertion of your right as supreme power, but we are not going to acquiesce in this method of dealing with us. Neither our self-respect nor our sense of duty to our country can permit us to go near the Commission.'

From T.B. Sapru in his presidential address on 27 December 1927

SKILLS BUILDER

Read Source C.

1 On what grounds is Sapru opposed to giving evidence to the Simon Commission?

2 What arguments might members of the Simon Commission have used against him?

How was the Simon Commission received?

In a word: badly. When the Commission arrived in Bombay, they were greeted by booing, jeering crowds carrying banners, waving black flags and shouting slogans like 'Simon, go home!' It was the same in Calcutta, Delhi, Lahore, Lucknow, Madras and Patna. Everywhere the Commission went, they were met with mass demonstrations, which the police could barely control.

Source D

7.1
A demonstration in 1928 in Madras against the Simon Commission

In Masani's recordings for the BBC, Usha Mehta, a young schoolgirl at the time of the visit of the Simon Commission, remembers how she opposed its presence in India:

Source E

I remember the year 1928, when the Simon Commission was touring the country in connection with constitutional reforms. All the parties were in favour of boycotting the Commission, and the slogan that was very much in the air was 'Simon, Go Back!' We children also felt attracted to the movement, and we formed the '*Vanar Sena*' or monkey army. This was the volunteer corps in which mostly boys were involved. We girls felt that we must have an identity of our own, so we formed a separate Cat Army or '*Manjar Sena*'. We used to march in processions, shouting slogans like '*Vande Mataram*' (I bow to thee, my motherland), '*Inqilab Zindabad*' (Long live the Revolution) and 'Up, up the national flag; down, down the Union Jack'.

From Zareer Masani, *Indian Tales of the Raj*, published in 1987

Indian opinion divided

A wide range of Indian political opinion was clearly opposed to the Simon Commission. Members of Congress, Hindu leaders, liberal thinkers and a large section of the Muslim League led by Jinnah decided to boycott the Commission and refused to give evidence to its commissioners. On the other hand, Muslims from the provinces where they were in a majority decided to help the Commission's enquiries, as did a number of Anglo-Indians, Sikhs and 'Untouchables'. All of these minority groups

SKILLS BUILDER

1 How far are Sources C, D and E in agreement about their opposition to the Simon Commission?

2 Explain which source would be the most useful to an historian enquiring into opposition to the Simon Commission.

Question

Was the Simon Commission a great mistake? Debate this in your group.

Definition

The Commonwealth

A loose federation of countries and states that once formed the old British Empire. After the Second World War, it became usual to refer to what had been the 'Empire' as the 'Commonwealth', the thinking being that in this way countries like Canada, which were largely self-governing, would have their status recognised and valued. To refer to them as 'colonies' was outdated and wrong, particularly when they had dominion status.

SKILLS BUILDER

What is there in these recommendations to alarm (a) the Raj and (b) Muslims in India?

hoped for a better future than that which they were anticipating under a Hindu-dominated Congress. However, the Simon Report, when it finally emerged in draft form, did little more than re-assert the status quo and was abandoned before publication. Events, as will be seen, had overtaken it.

The Nehru Report

The boycotters met in 1928 at an All-Parties Conference, where a sub-committee produced a report that was really the first draft of a written constitution for India. It was the work of two eminent lawyers: Tej Bahadur Sapru, leader of the Liberal Party and a former member of the Indian government and, of course, Motilal Nehru. The Nehru Report recommended dominion status for India on the same terms as those laid down for white self-governing countries within the British Empire, in which Princely and British India were to be joined in a federation. There was to be no further devolution of power to the provinces. This meant, in effect, that Hindus would form a permanent majority within central government. Despite vague promises that religious freedoms would be safeguarded and new Muslim states would be formed, Muslims were deeply unhappy. Under the Nehru Report, they would lose the protection of their separate electoral status, perpetuated by the British as a result of the Lucknow Pact of 1916 (see page 67). The fragile Hindu-Muslim alliance, which C.R. Das, among others, had worked so hard to maintain, hung in the balance. Source F lists some of the main recommendations of the report:

Source F

1. India shall have the same constitutional status in the comity of nations known as the British Empire as the Dominion of Canada, the **Commonwealth** of Australia, the Dominion of New Zealand, the Union of South Africa and the Irish Free State, with a Parliament having powers to make laws for the peace, order and good government of India, and an executive responsible to that Parliament, and shall be styled and known as the Commonwealth of India.

...

4(i) All powers of government and all authority, legislative, executive and judicial, are derived from the people and shall be exercised in the Commonwealth of India through the organisations.

4(iii) Freedom of conscience and the free profession and practice of religion are, subject to public order and morality, hereby guaranteed to every person.

4(iv) The right of free expression of opinion, as well as the right to assemble peaceably and without arms, and to form associations or unions, is hereby guaranteed for purposes not opposed to public order or morality.

From the Nehru Report, 1928

How did Congress react?

Congress organised a boycott (see page 111) of everything to do with the Simon Commission as 'the only self-respecting course for India' and demanded immediate *swaraj*. Congress then took the initiative. At their annual conference, held in December 1928 under the leadership of Motilal Nehru, delegates backed two motions. They demanded instant dominion status (as recommended in the Nehru Report) even though Jawaharlal Nehru had grave doubts (see page 108). Jawaharlal and Subhas Chandra Bose proposed a second, far more radical motion, which delegates also backed, that the British were to withdraw completely from India by 31 December 1929.

What if this didn't happen? Then a renewed campaign of total disruption would begin. This was, of course, blackmail of the highest order and no one with any political sense would believe the British would fall for it. But it was also a clever political manoeuvre. The spotlight swung from the Simon Commission to Congress, and the British government would have to react.

The British response

In July 1929, a Labour government was elected in Britain and their response was probably very different from the response the previous Conservative government, which sent the Simon Commission, might have had. The new prime minister, Ramsay MacDonald, was sympathetic to Congress' demands and so was the new Secretary of State for India, William Wedgwood. Through the 1920s, British politicians had tried to accommodate nationalist feeling in Ireland and Egypt, and therefore it did not seem unreasonable to the new government to take account of nationalist feeling in India.

Irwin, a Viceroy bent on conciliation, travelled back to England on his mid-term leave with two suggestions to put to the new Labour government: a conference to discuss future reforms and a declaration that the Raj's goal was dominion status for India. He met with a supportive response from both MacDonald and Wedgwood as well as, somewhat surprisingly, from Stanley Baldwin, the leader of the Conservative Party.

Biography

Lord Edward Frederick Wood Irwin (1881–1959)

Son of the second Viscount Halifax, educated at Eton and Oxford University, Irwin served as an MP from 1910 to 1925. In 1926 he became Viceroy of India, a post he held until 1931. During his vice-royalty, India went through a period of great stress, initiated by the exclusion of Indians from the Simon Commission.

Irwin retired as Viceroy shortly after the Gandhi–Irwin Pact and left India to take up an appointment as British Ambassador to the USA. In 1924, he inherited his father's title and became Lord Halifax. He served as British Foreign Secretary from 1938 to 1940 and he was a member of the War Cabinet from 1939 to 1945.

Source G

There was support, too, from Stanley Baldwin, a bold step which distanced him from a substantial faction on the right of his party, which was determined to keep India, whatever the cost. Recent events indicated just what the cost might eventually be: a strong, unswerving line in Ireland had led to a three-year partisan war against the Irish Republican Army, which had ended in a compromise in 1922. Likewise, prolonged resistance to British control over Egypt had ended with a bargain that took heed of Egyptian feelings. Whatever the diehards said to the contrary, Ireland and Egypt could not be held by the sword alone, nor could India.

From Lawrence James, *Raj: the Making and Unmaking of British India*, published in 1997

Question

Do you agree with Source G that India could not be held by the sword alone? Set up a debate on the subject.

The Irwin Declaration, 31 October 1929

It was therefore with some degree of optimism that the Viceroy, Lord Irwin, issued what became known as the Irwin Declaration. This reiterated the Montagu Declaration of 1917 (see page 68) and asserted that its 'natural issue' was to be 'the attainment of dominion status'. Thus, insofar as the British propaganda machine was concerned, there was absolute continuity in British policy toward India: dominion status was now officially the natural outcome of all that had gone before. Furthermore, Indian representatives were invited to London to a round-table conference where details of a new Indian constitution would be hammered out.

The Congress Working Committee officially welcomed the announcement and called upon the British government to demonstrate its good faith by declaring an amnesty for all Indian political prisoners. This was a step too far for Irwin, who refused. Indian frustration at what they perceived as British stubbornness led to more terrorist attacks, including the bombing of the Viceroy's train and the destruction of the carriage next to the one in which he was travelling.

Gandhi's dilemma

Gandhi, like the rest of the Congress leadership, knew that to attend the London conference would be political suicide. Not only would they be on 'foreign' soil, but they would also be forced to follow a British agenda. What was worse, the British weren't just expecting representatives of Congress to attend the proposed conference. All representatives of Indian opinion were expected to be there: Sikhs and Untouchables, for example, as well as the princes, who Gandhi regarded as nothing better than pawns of the British. The chances of Congress getting what they wanted would, Gandhi believed, be severely compromised. On the other hand, not to go to London would probably result in a settlement being made with which Congress – and Gandhi – could not possibly agree.

There was a second problem. Gandhi knew that despite the resolutions passed the previous year (see pages 112–13), Congress really was deeply divided in what actually to do about the Raj. Threats were one thing, action was another. Gandhi knew that to embark on another campaign of mass civil disobedience would alienate the moderates in Congress and could end up, as previous ones had done, in bloodshed and bitterness. On the other hand, the 'young hooligans' had considerable support in the districts, particularly among the young and the trade unionists, and were building up a considerable following among younger congressmen. Was Gandhi to back the young militants against the moderate conservatives and risk wave after wave of bloodshed or was he to back the moderates, accept dominion status and risk dividing Congress forever?

Congress decides

Added to Gandhi's problems in deciding the strategy and tactics that would get him what he wanted was the general problem of Congress' need to re-assert its authority. It was essential, given the proliferation of small groups that were finding a voice, for Congress to re-emphasise its claim to speak for all India. Not to do so would run the risk of allowing the British to settle with individual factions and, in doing so, play them off against each other. Somehow, as many of the disaffected groups as possible had to be persuaded that to come under the umbrella of Congress was in their best interests. Somehow, a deeply divided Congress had to unite on the best way forward: co-operation with the Raj and Irwin's proposed round-table conference, or non-violent confrontation.

Congress met in Lahore in December 1929. A policy decision could no longer be shelved. Gandhi had made up his mind: he would support the young militants. He steered his policy through the various Congress committees and a militant open session and ended up with a working committee of his own choice to direct Congress' actions in the months ahead. Henceforward *purna swaraj* (complete independence) was to be India's new political demand. India stood poised for the next round of *satyagrahas*, due to begin on January 26, which was designated Independence Day.

Risk-takers both?

Neither Gandhi nor Irwin was secure in the claims they made. Congress certainly did not represent the opinion of all India any more than Irwin had wide support for the strategy he planned.

The salt *satyagraha*

Congress had left it to the Congress Working Committee to decide how and when the non-violent confrontation was to begin. The Committee, in turn, decided that because Gandhi and his followers were committed to non-violence, they should decide.

Why did Gandhi choose to oppose the salt tax?

In many ways, deciding to oppose the government's tax on salt was the most sensible decision Gandhi could have made. Making salt was a government monopoly and the salt tax was a hangover from the days of the East India Company, which brought in very little to the government – about 4 per cent of its total revenue. So the Raj was not likely to feel particularly challenged. The tax cost the average Indian 3 **annas** a year (about 1.5p), so there was no great issue there, either. But salt itself was an emotive issue – the one commodity everyone needed to make life itself sustainable – and the Raj controlled its production and exacted tax from its sale. What a symbol of power and oppression!

Definition

Purna swaraj
Total independence.

Question

How sensible was Gandhi in deciding to support the 'young hooligans' in their demands for complete independence?

SKILLS BUILDER

Use the sources and information in this section to explain why, in your judgement, both Gandhi and Irwin were prepared to be risk-takers.

Definition

Anna
Indian unit of currency.

The march

Gandhi set out from his house in Ahmedabad on 12 March 1930, accompanied by a posse of reporters and camera newsreelmen. His intention was to walk the 240 miles to Dandi on the Gujarat coast. As he walked, thousands joined him, including, at his request, Untouchables whose inclusion was supposed to demonstrate the universality of the mission. The march was a great publicity enterprise as the press dogged Gandhi's every footstep. Everywhere he stopped he preached the doctrine of non-violence and the world's press reported it faithfully.

On arriving at the coast in early April, Gandhi bathed and picked up a token piece of sea salt from the shore and Indian's poetess, Sarojini Naidu, shouted 'Hail, law breaker!' Gandhi issued a public statement, confessing that he had broken the law and urged Indians everywhere to help themselves to the natural salt found in creeks and along the seashore. They did. Across India thousands of peasants followed Gandhi's advice and broke the law to collect the salt they needed in their daily life. It was a declaration of war against the tax and the government that collected it.

Source H

7.2 Some of Gandhi's followers evaporating seawater to extract salt

In Masani's recordings for the BBC, Usha Mehta remembers the impact the Salt March had on Indian women:

Source I

Gandhi was a great emancipator. I remember, during the Salt March, many women of all ages came out to join the movement. Even our old aunts and great-aunts and grandmothers used to bring pitchers of salt water to their houses and manufacture illegal salt. And then they would shout at the top of their voices 'We have broken the Salt Law!'

From Zareer Masani, *Indian Tales of the Raj*, published in 1987

Across India, hundreds of peasants were arrested and imprisoned. There were mass arrests, too, of national and local Congress leaders. Jawaharal Nehru was sentenced to six months imprisonment on 14 April. In May, Gandhi himself was arrested and imprisoned. This sent shock waves throughout India, stimulating strikes and protests throughout the land. Particularly worrying for the government was the number of moderate men who seemed to be sympathising with Gandhi. In June, the entire Congress Working Committee was arrested.

Source J

7.3 A modern statue, in Delhi, of Gandhi leading the Salt March

SKILLS BUILDER

What conclusions can you draw from Sources H, I and J about the importance of the Salt March?

The civil disobedience campaign

The campaign entered its second phase after Gandhi's arrest in May 1930. Unlike the non-violent campaign of 1920–22, it was not master-minded and directed centrally. Provincial committees were authorised to organise their own *satyagrahas*. The nature and timing of the *satyagrahas* were to be determined by provincial imperatives, although Congress did recommend that the provincial committees should consider, in this order:

- salt
- a boycott of foreign cloth
- non-payment of taxes
- refusal to obey the authorities when they tried to prevent the *satyagrahas*.

In organising the civil disobedience campaign in this way, Congress cleverly papered over the cracks of potential divisions among its members as to just how disobedient civil disobedience should be. Furthermore, by allowing provincial committees such a large degree of autonomy, Congress hoped to demonstrate that it really was an umbrella organisation, sensitive to local needs. And, most importantly, the campaign was much more difficult for the Raj to stop because there was no central organisation to take out.

Was the campaign a success?

In 1930, the civil disobedience campaign became a formidable psychological weapon against the Raj and, in places, an actual physical threat. By the middle of the year, all provinces in India had been affected, with Bombay and Gujarat being the most turbulent. In Bombay, the Governor wrote of 'overt rebellion' and parts of the city became no-go areas for police. In the Bengal district of Midnapore, a salt *satyagraha* was followed by attacks on police and magistrates, intimidation of officials and a refusal to pay local taxes. In Bihar, an attack on the excise was catastrophic for government revenues. In the United Provinces, partly because of falling prices and oppressive landlords, a peasant anti-land tax campaign was particularly successful. Local politicians in the Central Provinces decided to back opposition to forest laws, which forbade peasants to fell trees and graze their animals at will, ensuring that the wishes and needs of the local landowners were paramount in this respect.

In the majority of areas, civil disobedience was often used by people as a way of expressing local grievances, but these were expressed on the national stage and, as such, were impressive. Different groups were mobilised at different times and in different places. Civil disobedience became the vehicle whereby a whole range of people from students to middle-class businessmen became politically aware and articulate. Women, in particular, became actively involved, often because their menfolk were imprisoned, but in their own right too and not as substitute males. By November 1930, nearly 360 women were in gaol for their participation in different *satyagrahas*.

Order restored?

By early 1931, the Raj had more or less restored law and order. Official estimates say that around 60,000 people passed through India's gaols in 1930. This had put an immense strain on the civil service, police and magistrates as well as causing intolerable overcrowding in the gaols themselves. Indeed, by the end of 1930, there were still some 29,000 people in prison, most of them adult Hindu men, although around 2000 were youths under the age of 17.

There had been a point in mid-1930 when Viceroy Irwin had seriously considered imposing martial law on the most disaffected regions as the only way of keeping some kind of order. However, the memory of the disaster at Amritsar 12 years earlier, together with the belief that to bring in the army would be an admission of failure on his part, made Irwin keep his nerve. This paid off, because by the end of the year Congress was also feeling the strain. Local *satyagrahas*, while initially successful, could not always be sustained. Once local grievances had been expressed and settled, even if temporarily, life frequently returned to normal. Furthermore, there had been an economic slump early in 1930 and many had relished the opportunity to withhold taxes and the payment of bills. The economic upturn later in the year changed that and the profit motive once again became paramount. People, too, simply ran out of energy and something like civil disobedience fatigue set in. By the end of 1930, the Raj and Congress were at stalemate.

The Gandhi–Irwin Pact 1931

The only way out of the stalemate was some form of truce that would save the faces of Congress in general, of Gandhi in particular and of the Raj, and enable them to move forward. The end of 1930 saw Gandhi in prison, developing his spiritual life, and Congress desperate to find some way of revitalising the civil disobedience campaign. Jawaharlal Nehru, released from prison in October, thought he had the answer when he announced that the 'conquest of power' was about to begin. The authorities viewed this as a call to arms and open rebellion. He went straight back to gaol.

Viceroy Irwin was afraid that Congress would find a way out of the stalemate by resorting to a campaign of violence. He wanted to create a situation in which Gandhi could leave prison and participate in the London conference as the representative of Congress, yet he couldn't be seen to negotiate openly with someone the authorities regarded as a terrorist. Furthermore, he had to be seen to support the Indian Civil Service and those who had stood aside from confrontation. And, possibly the biggest hurdle of all, he had to persuade Gandhi that his presence at the Round Table Conference was in Congress' best interests.

A meeting between Gandhi and Irwin was brokered by Indian businessmen, who were worried at the effect the civil disobedience campaigns were having on the Indian economy. They first approached Gandhi in July 1930, but it was only in February 1931 that Irwin and Gandhi met face to face.

Irwin had done his homework and recognised in Gandhi both a spiritual being and a shrewd politician, and was able to appeal to both sides of his nature. Indeed, Gandhi said of Irwin: 'He desires peace because he has been touched by the struggle.' Discussions were frank and open, and helped by the fact that both men genuinely wanted to find a way out of the impasse. In the end, this was the pact to which they both signed up:

- Congress' civil disobedience campaign was suspended
- Gandhi agreed to attend a second London conference
- 19,000 Congress supporters were released from gaol
- confiscated property was returned to its owners
- some emergency restrictions were relaxed.

Some time later, a series of conversations about Gandhi were broadcast on the radio. Here Irwin, by then Lord Halifax, is talking:

Source K

It is alarming and also nauseating to see Mr Gandhi, a seditious Middle Temple lawyer, now posing as a *fakir* of a type well known in the East, striding half-naked up the steps of the viceregal palace while he is still organising and conducting a defiant campaign of civil disobedience, to parley on equal terms with the representative of the King-Emperor. Such a spectacle can only increase the unrest in India and the danger to which white people there are exposed.

Comment by Winston Churchill to the House of Commons, on the meeting between Gandhi and Viceroy Irwin, in 1931

Definition

Fakir

Religious person who practises self-denial.

Question

What was Churchill's attitude to the meeting between Gandhi and Irwin?

SKILLS BUILDER

1 How would you describe the relationship between Gandhi and Viceroy Irwin?

2 How reliable is Source L as evidence of that relationship?

3 How far are the views expressed in Source M supported by Source L?

Source N

In the end, Irwin got what he was after: the suspension of Congress' civil disobedience and Gandhi's agreement to attend a second conference in London. The Raj had publicly acknowledged Gandhi's pre-eminence within Congress and India as a whole, and he had recognised that it would be better if it secured its independence relatively peacefully – with British co-operation rather than without it.

From Lawrence James, *Raj: the Making and Unmaking of British India*, published in 1997

Source L

Well, when I was finishing my talks with Mr Gandhi, we finished, I remember at two o'clock on a Thursday and at nine or ten o'clock he came back to me, and said that he had had a dreadful evening when he had returned to his *ashram* – that he had met others of his Indian friends and Jawaharlal Nehru had said that he had betrayed India and that he had – he, Jawaharlal, had wept on his shoulder, as Gandhi said he had never wept before, even when his mother died – over this tragedy of the betrayal of India, and the little man was quite upset at all that, and so I said: 'Well, don't be too discouraged because you happen to live on the spot, but in a few hours' time, I shall be getting furious cables from Mr Churchill and others in England, saying that I have betrayed England. Therefore if he thinks I have betrayed England, and your friends think you are betraying India, we are probably about right – in the middle.' So that cheered him up a bit.

From Francis Watson and Hallam Tennyson, *Talking of Gandhi*, published in 1969

Source M

The fact that Gandhi and Irwin both had to defend their Pact to those of their colleagues who felt they had given too much away showed that neither had gained outstanding advantage or lost face irretrievably. Government had won peace for its constitutional discussions to go forward, and the prospect of Congress co-operation in finding a new solution to the problem of Empire. Congress had gained enormously in prestige and respectability in the much publicised and prolonged parleys between its main spokesman and the head of the Raj.

From Judith M. Brown, *Modern India: the Origins of an Asian Democracy*, published in 1994

The Gandhi–Irwin Pact bought everyone a breathing space.

Unit summary

What have you learned in this unit?

You have learned that, during the 1920s, Congress reviewed its position and was able to retrench and gather its strength to the extent that it was able to launch a nationwide civil disobedience campaign at the end of the decade. Significantly, very few Muslims took part in this campaign. The Raj, despite making a serious mistake in the Simon Commission, was able to rethink its position, partly because of the election in Britain of a Labour government, which was sympathetic to the cause of Indian nationalism. By 1931, the Raj and Congress had reached an agreement whereby Gandhi was able to travel to London to take part in the Round Table Conferences that were to determine India's future.

What skills have you used in this unit?

You have worked with a range of secondary, primary and contemporary source material, evaluating and analysing them in order to understand the significance of the Nehru Report, the Salt March and the civil disobedience campaign in the consolidation of the position of Gandhi and Congress regarding Indian independence. You will have appreciated the significance of the lack of Muslim participation in the civil disobedience campaign. You have explored the reactions of the Raj to the situation in India and to the apparent conciliation between Viceroy Irwin and Gandhi that enabled Congress to be represented at the next Round Table Conference.

Exam tips

This is the sort of question you will find on the exam paper as a (b) question.

- Read Sources L, M and N, and use your own knowledge. Do you agree with the view that, in the Gandhi–Irwin Pact of 1931, Irwin had conceded too much?

This is a slightly different question from the previous (b) style questions you have worked on, in that the 'view' is not in the source but in the question.

You have worked on (b) question plans at the ends of Units 3, 4 and 6, so you should have a good idea of the sort of plan you prefer. As you draw it up, remember to:

- Be very clear about the view being put forward. Because it is asking you about Irwin's concessions, you need to be very clear about what he conceded and how this reflected, or ran counter to, British policy.
- Analyse the three sources for points that support and points that challenge the view that Irwin conceded 'too much'. You need to consider too, whether Indian or British opinion would think it was 'too much'.
- Cross-reference between the sources for points of agreement and points of disagreement.
- Combine these points with your own wider knowledge into an argument for or against the view given in the question.
- Reach a balanced, supported conclusion.

RESEARCH TOPIC

Winston Churchill resigned from his opposition front-bench position so that he could campaign around Britain against Congress. Research that campaign and the level of support it attracted.

8 Jinnah and the idea of separateness

What is this unit about?

Hindus and Muslims had coexisted in India for hundreds of years. There were always differences between the followers of each religion, but these worsened as the Indian people became more politicised at the end of the nineteenth and beginning of the twentieth centuries. This unit explores the reasons for the worsening of the relationship between Hindus and Muslims on both local and national levels. It considers the impact of the Muslim minority on political decision-making, the impact of both the Muslim League and the Khilafat Movement, and the importance of Muhammad Ali Jinnah in the development of the concept of a separate homeland for Muslims.

Key questions

- Why did the period of rapprochement between Hindus and Muslims not last?
- By the end of the 1920s, had the establishment of a separate Muslim state in the Indian sub-continent become inevitable?
- Did the involvement of Muhammad Ali Jinnah help or hinder the Muslim cause in India in the years to 1929?

Timeline

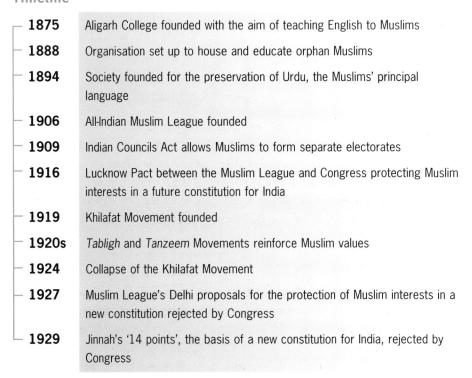

1875	Aligarh College founded with the aim of teaching English to Muslims
1888	Organisation set up to house and educate orphan Muslims
1894	Society founded for the preservation of Urdu, the Muslims' principal language
1906	All-Indian Muslim League founded
1909	Indian Councils Act allows Muslims to form separate electorates
1916	Lucknow Pact between the Muslim League and Congress protecting Muslim interests in a future constitution for India
1919	Khilafat Movement founded
1920s	*Tabligh* and *Tanzeem* Movements reinforce Muslim values
1924	Collapse of the Khilafat Movement
1927	Muslim League's Delhi proposals for the protection of Muslim interests in a new constitution rejected by Congress
1929	Jinnah's '14 points', the basis of a new constitution for India, rejected by Congress

Hindus and Muslims

Source A

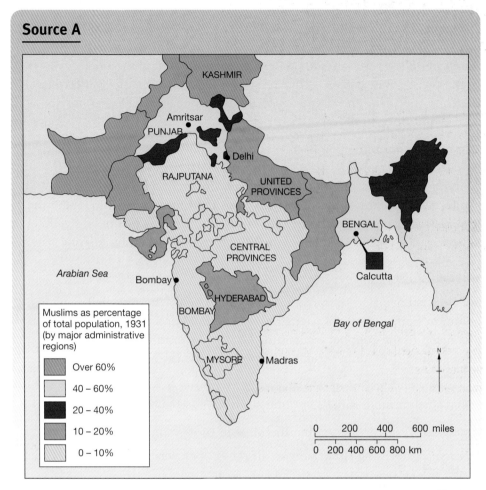

8.1 Map of India, showing Muslims as a percentage of the total population in 1931

Muslims as percentage of total population, 1931 (by major administrative regions)

- Over 60%
- 40 – 60%
- 20 – 40%
- 10 – 20%
- 0 – 10%

SKILLS BUILDER

Study the map carefully.

- Discuss the ways the distribution of the Muslim population in India might have affected relationships between Muslim and Hindu communities.

- If a homeland was to be created for Muslims, where would it be?

Why did Hindus and Muslims clash?

The Hindu and Muslim communities in India were divided by their beliefs and practices, and too frequently could find no areas of mutual toleration. The situation was exacerbated by the sheer size of the Hindu majority across India, which seemed such a threat to the Muslim minority that many Muslims believed they had to fight, not only for a political voice to be heard, but also on occasion for their very existence.

What do Hindus believe?

Many Hindus recognise one God, *Brahman*, who is the eternal origin and the cause and foundation of all existence. Most Hindus worship *Brahman* through deities that represent a particular aspect of this one God. There are thousands, some say millions, of individual deities used in this way. Three are particularly important because they represent three key aspects of God: as creating force (*Brahma*), as destroying force (*Shiva*) and as a

Definitions

Hindu holy books

Shrutis are the books of authority. 'Shruti' literally means 'that which is heard' because these scriptures were passed on by word of mouth. The main set of texts is called the *Vedas* and the parts of the *Vedas* that contain the philosophy of Hinduism are called the *Upanishads*. The *Bhagavad Gita* is a text that, although not part of the *Vedas*, is considered by most Hindus to be a text of authority. *Smritis* are scriptures of lesser authority. They consist of historic stories such as 'Ramayana' and 'Mahabharata', mythological stories called 'Puranas' and law books like the 'Manusmriti'.

Karma

Karma is the sum total of a person's actions, including their intended actions, which determine the state into which they will be reincarnated.

Islam

The word 'Islam' means 'submission to God'.

Qur'an

Islamic scripture as revealed to Muhammad.

preserving and protecting force (*Vishnu*). These divinities are frequently displayed in paintings and as statues.

Different Hindu communities worship their own divinities, but this isn't in any way divisive. These are simply different ways of approaching God. It therefore follows that Hindus do not have a problem with people worshipping other gods in other religions: they are all simply different routes to the same end. Similarly, Hindus do not have just one holy book, but several **holy books**.

The caste system in India is still intact but many of the rules are not as rigid as they were in the past (see pages 17–19). Hindus believe that everyone's soul is a tiny part of *Brahman*, the great world soul. The soul can be reborn many times. The body, and therefore caste, into which the soul is born depends on the quality of the life that has just been lived. Existence is a cycle of birth, death and rebirth, governed by **karma**.

What do Muslims believe?

Muslims believe that there is one God, Allah, and who revealed their faith, **Islam**, to humankind at various times. The final and complete revelation was made to the prophet Muhammad in the seventh century. It was through him that Allah set down his holy words in the **Qur'an**.

The central principles of the Muslim faith are the five pillars of Islam, which every Muslim must satisfy in order to live a good and responsible life:

- *Shahadah*: sincerely reciting the Muslim profession of faith
- *Salah*: performing ritual prayers in the proper way five times a day
- *Zakah*: giving alms to the poor and needy
- *Sawm*: fasting during the month of Ramadan
- *Hajj*: making a pilgrimage to Makkah.

Carrying out these obligations provides the framework of a Muslim's life and demonstrates that they are putting their faith first and not trying to fit it around their secular lives. Different communities might insist on certain different practices, but at the heart lies the relationship between the individual and Allah.

The key issue is that Muslims believe Allah wants no other gods, so images of living things are forbidden because people might be tempted to make them into idols and worship them rather than Allah: this extends to pictures of Allah or his prophets. This puts Islam into conflict with Hinduism with its many deities, represented by images and sculptures in every Hindu home and street. Islam also sees all Muslims in a community (*ummah*) of faith in which all people are equal: the caste system, which can be intimately intertwined with Hinduism, goes directly against this. There are other differences, too. Hindus hold the cow to be sacred; Muslims eat beef. Hindu men are usually clean-shaven; Muslims usually wear beards. There are also differences in dress (particularly for women).

The situation in early twentieth-century India was, of course, not that simple. 'Hindus' and 'Muslims' were not two solid, monolithic one-dimensional communities. Within each community were significant differences and antagonisms between respective factions and schools of thought, for example, between Shi'ah and Sunni Muslims.

Was coexistence possible?

From the late nineteenth century, the uneasy coexistence that had existed for hundreds of years seemed to be breaking down. This seems to have been partly due to the position of strict neutrality officially adopted by the Raj. This encouraged both Muslims and Hindus (and all other religious followers like Sikhs and Christians) to believe that they had equal rights to carry out whatever religious practices were appropriate to their religion, no matter what offence they gave. Neither Muslim nor Hindu communities seemed prepared to consider compromise.

Some of the princely states experienced less religious friction than the states that came directly under the Raj. This was probably because the governments of the princely states didn't feel it necessary to maintain a neutral position on matters of religion. They came down very firmly on one side or the other and everyone knew how much apparently extreme behaviour would be tolerated.

Could the two communities live together in the melting pot that was India? They had managed to do so more or less successfully for hundreds of years. Would pressure for Indian independence drive them apart or could some form of rapprochement be found?

Worship and festivals as flashpoints

It is clear that local communities were sharply divided by the very different belief systems held by Hindus and Muslims. These offered plenty of opportunity for irritation and mutual distrust, which spilled over into disruption and violence.

Hindus like to use gongs, bells and cymbals to create loud music when they are worshipping. Muslims prefer to pray in silence. Sometimes Hindus stopped playing music during the Muslim times of prayer and sometimes they did not. When they didn't, verbal abuse and violence resulted.

Festivals were another source of friction. At the Muslim festival of Bakr'Id, cows are ritually slaughtered. But the cow is sacred to Hindus. On the other hand, the Hindu festival of Holi is particularly noisome and troubling to Muslims. It is a very lively festival, lasting over two days. On the first day, bonfires are lit at night; on the second, people dance in the street, throwing coloured powder and water at each other and drink a liquid laced with cannabis.

Philip Mason, who joined the Indian Civil Service immediately after the First World War, recalls the efforts spent trying to prevent religious conflicts on a local level:

Source B

There was a record kept in the police station which it was part of one's duty to keep up-to-date. This recorded all the customs in connection with festivals; the route a procession would follow, whether it went near a particular temple or not, whether it went near some particular peepul tree which might become holy in the course of time. You had to see they followed the exact precedent. Then some stupid little thing would happen, a rumour that Pahans were abducting Hindu girls, or that somebody had killed a Mohammedan. Usually it was quite untrue, but then the trouble, which was always smouldering in certain cities, started. You'd get some stabbing incidents at night, and then everybody was out trying to keep the score up; if five Mohammedans were stabbed one night, six Hindus would be murdered the next.

From Charles Allen (editor), *Plain Tales from the Raj*, published in 1975

Organisations: contributors to tension?

The Hindu organisation Arya Samj was pro-active in the Muslim community in parts of northern India. Members openly criticised Islam and sought converts to Hinduism, converting more than a thousand between 1907 and 1910. They argued for the protection of cows, sacred to Hindus, and established the Cow Protection Society, which brought them into open conflict with Muslim butchers and tradesmen. They attempted to have Hindi replace Urdu as the language of administration, which frightened Urdu-speaking Muslims, who began to feel more and more threatened by the Hindu majority.

But it wasn't all one way. Hindus thought the Muslim *Tabligh* and *Tanzeem* Movements (see page 127) were just as provocative.

The situation worsened when it became known that the major donors to the Arya Samj cause came from the Hindu merchant and money-lending class, on whom lower-class Muslims depended for their economic security.

In 1915, a Hindu 'ginger group', **Mahasabha**, was established and aimed to make the Hindu community powerful and independent. The group was quite prepared to use force against people it thought were diluting the purity of the Hindu faith.

Propaganda: contributor to tension?

Russian agents working in Tashkent and Samarkand were aiming to help create a Pan-Islamic-Bolshevik axis. Although the success of this was extremely unlikely, Viceroy Chelmsford took the situation seriously. This was probably largely because the propaganda pouring into northern India was destabilising the region further.

Definition

Mahasabha

This Hindu nationalist organisation was founded in 1915 to bring together diverse local Hindu movements in order to counter the Muslim League and the secular Indian National Congress. In the 1920s, it had branches in most parts of India. In 1948, a member of *Mahasabha* murdered Gandhi.

Source C

Oh, working Muhammedans! The Soviet government has been formed to free you all. Are you aware that your fellow labourers in other parts of the world are being cruelly and shamefully strangled in cold blood by the British – the greatest enemy of Islam? The British government is the same which has enslaved 70 million Muslims in India, which rules Egypt with fire and sword, which has wiped out Tripoli and dismembered the Turkish Empire. You know that the Afghans have risen against them, and that the British are running like hares before the gallant Afghan troops. Send your friends to the Indian *sepoys*, who are deceived by British pay, and win them to your side, turning them against their infidel employers.

From a Turkish agitator working in Merv, Afghanistan in 1919

SKILLS BUILDER

Read Sources B and C, and the information about flashpoints and tensions. Which was the most dangerous for (a) the Muslim community and (b) the British Raj?

How did the Muslims try to counter Hindu dominance?

Educated and upper-class Muslims responded to what they saw as Hindu dominance by setting up various organisations. In 1875, a Muslim leader, Sir Sayyid Ahmad Khan set up Aligarh College where Muslims were educated and taught the English language so that they could deal with the Raj better and make their way professionally. In Lahore, in 1885, an organisation was established to house and educate orphans so that they retained Islam and became good Muslims. In 1894, a society was founded in Aligarh for the preservation of Urdu. In 1906, Muslim leaders meeting in Dacca founded the All-Indian Muslim League (see page 61). In the early 1920s, the *Tanzeem* and *Tabligh* Movements aimed to strengthen the Muslim community by weeding out all practices that encouraged greater understanding between Muslim and Hindu communities.

Less well-educated Muslims responded with violence, especially in areas where the Arya Samj and the Cow Protection Society were active.

The deadly round of riot, violence, retribution and revenge was played out time and time again throughout India. It would have taken a massive amount of political and religious will to turn this around, and the will was not there in sufficient strength among enough people to make this happen.

How did the Muslim minority impact on political decision-making?

The Muslims' main problem, politically, was that in nearly every state they were in the minority. The map on page 123 shows this clearly. In the heady days of the Raj, this had not been too much of a problem. As long as the governing elite ruled for the people and political decisions were not made by the people, the numbers didn't matter too much. However, the situation changed radically once the Raj began to move tentatively toward a more democratic situation. Unless protected, the Muslim minority would be out-voted by the Hindu majority at every level.

Education

There was a further dimension, unique to the Muslim, not the Hindu, community. Historically, Muslims had been slower than Hindus to take up the educational opportunities offered by the Raj. Consequently, by the beginning of the twentieth century, there was a considerable poorly educated and, indeed, uneducated Muslim underclass. The Muslim elite would never agree to this underclass having any sort of political control. As early as 1887, Sir Sayyid Ahmad Khan pointed out the problems:

Source D

Let us suppose that we have universal suffrage. And first suppose that all the Mahomedan electors vote for a Mahomedan member and all Hindu electors for a Hindu member. Now count how many votes the Mahomedan member has and how many the Hindu. It is certain the Hindu member will have four times as many because their population is four times as numerous. How can the Mahomedan guard his interests? It would be like a game of dice in which one man has four dice and the other only one.

In the second place, suppose that the electorate be limited. Some method of qualification must be made; for example, that people with a certain income shall be electors. Now, I ask you, oh Mahomedans! Weep at your condition! Have you such wealth that you can compete with Hindus? Most certainly not. Suppose, for example, that an income of Rs. 5000 a year be fixed on, how many Mahomedan electors will there be? Which party will have the larger number of votes?

From a speech made by Sir Sayyid Ahmad Khan in Lucknow in 1887

Gradually, the situation for Muslims improved insofar as education was concerned.

SKILLS BUILDER

Read Sources D and E. Why was education such a key issue for the Muslim community?

Source E

Under the 1919 reforms, education became a provincial subject transferred to the control of Indian ministers. Consequently it suffered from the absence of a co-ordinated continental policy. It was also the victim of the economies required in the provinces by the post-reforms distribution of government revenues. But there was marked improvement among certain previously backward groups. By the end of the 1930s there were more Muslims being educated than the average for all communities. In 1936–7, 26.1 per cent of all pupils were Muslims, while Muslims formed only 24.7 per cent of the population. Even Muslim girls were benefiting: 25.6 per cent of girl pupils were Muslim while Muslims were only 24.1 per cent of the female population. By then Muslims as an all-India community could no longer be considered educationally backward, though in provinces where they were a majority their standards still lagged behind the Hindus.

From Judith M. Brown, *Modern India: the Origins of an Asian Democracy*, published in 1994

What sort of democracy was proposed?

Most Muslims, right from the start, strongly opposed any extension of a democracy that was based on the principle of 'One man, one vote'. If this principle was to become the norm throughout India, there would be few, if any, Muslims elected to provincial or national assemblies. In this, the more conservative members of the British administration gave them tacit support. Congress, on the other hand, was increasingly pushing for the extension of the democratic principle of one man, one vote. How was this to be resolved?

Muslim leaders worked out a compromise position, which was accepted by Lord Minto (see pages 55–58) when he promised that the Muslim 'rights and interests as a community' would be safeguarded. This compromise was enshrined, to the dismay of many Hindus, in the Indian Councils Act of 1909 (see page 58) whereby the Muslims formed a separate electorate in order to protect their interests and for their voice to be heard.

How important was the Muslim League?

Initially formed in 1906 under the chairmanship of the *Nawab* of Dacca (see page 61), the Muslim League was to be the voice of the Muslim community, an organisation complementary to Congress, which was dominated by Hindus. It is easy, with hindsight, to see a direct line from the formation of the Muslim League to the creation of the separate state of Pakistan. But in 1906 a separate state was not a possibility considered by anyone in a position of power or influence.

Although conceived as an anti-Congress body, there were many instances when the Muslim League worked with members of Congress for the same outcome. In 1910, for example, the League, influenced by the Muslim 'Young Party' of Aligarh graduates and the vehemently anti-British seminary at Deoband in the United Provinces, moved to Lucknow and began discussing the possibility of a joint nationalist programme with Congress leaders. The outcome was the Lucknow Pact of 1916 (see page 67).

Source F

Province	Muslim population (%)	Planned seats (%)
Punjab	Over 50	50
Bengal	Over 50	40
United Provinces	14	30
Bihar	13	25
Central Provinces	4	15
Madras	7	
Bombay	20	33.3

8.2 Planned seats for Muslims in provincial councils as part of the Lucknow Pact of 1916. From Tim Leadbeater, *Britain and India 1845–1947*, published in 2008

SKILLS BUILDER

Match the proposals in Source F with the map, Source A (see page 123).

1 Do you think the proposed arrangement is a fair one?

2 Is there anything about these proposals that surprises you?

Of course, this working out of separate electorates was simply an agreement between Muslims and Hindus. They didn't have the power to impose it. Historian Judith Brown has views on the significance of the Pact:

Source G

The Congress-League Pact was emphatically not an agreement between Congress and the whole Muslim community, any more than the foundation of the League had signified the emergence of a unified Muslim community with a single political voice. At the time of the Pact, the League probably had between 500 and 800 members, and the Lucknow agreement did not even represent all of them because the negotiations were carried on by a clique led by UP [United Provinces] 'Young Party' Muslims. Under its terms, Congress and the League put forward a scheme of constitutional reform. Congress gained at least token Muslim backing, vital if it was to put real pressure on the raj; whilst the Muslim's quid pro quo was Congress' acceptance of their claim to separate political status which should be safeguarded by separate electorates for the provincial and all-India legislatures.

From Judith M. Brown, *Modern India: the Origins of an Asian Democracy*, published in 1994

Significantly, the Muslim League's chief spokesman at the discussions leading to the Lucknow Pact was an active Muslim member of Congress, the Bombay-based barrister Muhammad Ali Jinnah. It is ironic that the creation of a separate, Muslim electorate with reserved seats did not only allow Muslims a voice, but also gave them an enhanced sense of Islamic identity, which sat uneasily with the sincere secularism of men like Jinnah. Indeed, Jinnah himself did not like the idea of separate electorates.

SKILLS BUILDER

Read Sources G and H. What chances had separate electorates of succeeding as a solution to the Muslim minority problem?

Definition

Federal

A form of government in which states or regions have a measure of self-government while giving certain powers, for example for foreign affairs, to a central government.

Source H

A pragmatic politician, Jinnah realistically gauged how much the British were prepared to concede and reluctantly accepted separate electorates as a fact of political life for the time being but not necessarily for all time. He did not approve of the principle; he was against its extension, but he recognised that Muslim politicians were not yet ready to give it up.

From Ayesha Jalal, *The Sole Spokesman*, published in 1985

In December 1924, the Muslim League met separately from Congress for the first time since 1920, when Congress and the League had joined together in protest against the Amritsar Massacre and the Rowlatt Acts. It planned a future for India that was based upon a loose **federal** structure, in which provinces would be largely autonomous and Muslims would continue to have separate electorates.

What was the importance of the Khilafat Movement?

Events in the outside world impacted upon the Muslims' perception of themselves as a political as well as a religious community. Many Indian Muslims had long regarded the Sultan of Turkey as their Caliph, their most important spiritual leader. Turkey's decision to fight on the side of Germany, and therefore against Britain, during the First World War challenged Muslim loyalties to the extreme. The 1919 peace settlements did nothing to ease this tension as the Treaty of Sèvres greatly reduced the size of Turkey and removed the Sultan from power. The **Khilafat Movement**, set up to support the Caliph, spread rapidly throughout India. Using Islamic symbols to unite the diverse Muslim communities, it repudiated British rule in India and legitimised Muslim participation in the Indian Nationalist Movement.

Muslim leaders joined with Gandhi in mobilising the masses for the 1920 and 1921 civil disobedience and non-cooperation campaigns in response to the Amritsar Massacre and the Rowlatt Acts (see pages 98–101). At the same time, Gandhi endorsed the Khilafat Movement, thus bringing the weight of Hindu opinion behind what had originally been a solely Muslim movement.

> **Definition**
>
> **Khilafat Movement**
> This movement was set up by Indian Muslims to support the Sultan of Turkey, who was regarded by many Muslims as their Caliph, or spiritual leader.

Source I

The Khilafat question has now become a question of questions. It has become an imperial question of the first magnitude. I trust the Hindus will realise that the Khilafat question overshadows everything else.

Briefly put, the claim is that the Turks should retain European Turkey subject to full guarantees for the protection of non-Muslim races under the Turkish Empire and that the Sultan should control the holy places of Islam and should have suzerainty over Arabia as defined by the Muslim wise men subject to self-governing rights being given to the Arabs if they so desire. This is what was promised by Mr Lloyd George and this is what Lord Hardinge had contemplated. The Mohammedan soldiers would not have fought to deprive Turkey of her possessions.

To restore to Turkey, subject to necessary guarantees, what was hers before the war is a Christian solution. To wrest any of her possessions from her for the sake of punishing her is a gun-powder solution. The Allies of England in the hour of triumph must be scrupulously just. To reduce the Turks to impotence would be not only unjust. It would be a breach of solemn declarations and promises. It is to be wished that the Viceroy will take his courage in both his hands and place himself at the head of the Khilafat agitation as Lord Hardinge did at the time of the South African 'passive resistance' struggle and thus like his predecessor give a clear and emphatic direction to an agitation which under impulsive or faulty leadership may lead to disastrous consequences. But the situation rests more with us Hindus and Mohammedans than with the Viceroy and still more with the Muslim leaders than with the Hindus or the Viceroy.

From K.M. Gandhi (views dated 7 March 1920), *The Collected Works of Mahatma Gandhi Volume 17*

Jinnah, however, was opposed to Gandhi's support for the Khilafat Movement.

Source J

By declaring his support for the Khilafat, Gandhi secured the allegiance of an impressive array of Muslim spiritual leaders and political activists for his policy of non-violent non-cooperation. This fusion of religion and politics left Jinnah cold in the wings. He denounced Gandhi for causing schism and split. At the Congress' Nagpur session in December 1920, when Gandhi's non-cooperation programme was ratified, Jinnah alone had the courage of his convictions and spoke openly against non-cooperation.

Jinnah deplored the opportunistic alliance between the *Mahatma* [Gandhi] and the Khilafat Muslims. In Jinnah's eyes, that coalition, remarkable even in a country used to the oddest combinations, threatened the stability of the existing political structures and orderly progress along moderate and nationalistic lines. The alarming rise in communal tensions in the remaining three years of the Khilafat agitation is a commentary on the soundness of Jinnah's assessment.

From Ayesha Jalal, *The Sole Spokesman*, published in 1985

SKILLS BUILDER

Read Sources I and J. Discuss the following in your group.

1 Why do you think Gandhi, a Hindu, supported the Khilafat Movement?

2 Why do you think Jinnah, a Muslim, opposed of it?

3 Use Sources I and J, and your own knowledge. Why did the Khilafat Movement fail?

Despite apparently impressive achievements, the Khilafat Movement collapsed. Turkey rejected the caliphate and became a secular state. The religious, mass-based aspects of the Movement alienated western-orientated Indian politicians like Jinnah, who resigned from Congress. Finally, many Muslims had become uncomfortable with Gandhi's leadership.

The precarious alliance of the Muslim League, Khilafat committees and Congress collapsed once the non-violent campaigns ended. Congressmen began to regret the generous electoral arrangements agreed for Muslims under the Lucknow Pact and Muslims drifted away from Congress. By 1923, only 3.6 per cent of Congress delegates were Muslims; in 1921, the figure was 10.9 per cent.

The parting of the ways?

Despite unpromising circumstances, Jinnah continued to work to try to bring Congress and the Muslim League together to work out an agreed position for India's future.

Source K

8.3 Muhammad Ali Jinnah in 1947

Frank Moraes, knew Jinnah well:

Source L

He was tall, thin and elegant, with a monocle on a grey silk cord and a stiff white collar which he wore in the hottest weather. Jinnah was one of the very few intellectually honest politicians I have known. Humility was not one of his strong points, but there was no humbug in his make-up. Like every decent-minded, thoughtful Indian he wanted his country to be politically free. The British completely misread the character and aims of this dedicated man. They had been accustomed to deal with a type of Muslim leader whose dislike for the Congress could be encouraged by official favours. But Jinnah had no purchase price.

From F. Moraes, *Witness to an Era*, published in 1973

SKILLS BUILDER

Sources K and L are both descriptions, but of a different type. How useful are these sources to an historian? Discuss this in your group.

At the Muslim League's 1927 meeting in Delhi, Jinnah persuaded members to make a bold offer to Congress in the hope of bringing Congress and the League back together again. The League offered to end its support of separate electorates (which Jinnah had never liked) in exchange for a guaranteed one-third of the seats in the Central Legislative Assembly and the separation of Sind from Bombay in order to create a Muslim-dominated province. The offer was rejected out of hand by Congress, believing it to be the result of an awareness of the weakness of the Muslims' position. Viceroy Irwin had his doubts, too:

Source M

The whole position is one of obscurity. The meeting of Muslims held on 20th in Delhi was only an informal conference. The conclusions were communicated semi-officially to the press by Jinnah. It is therefore not clear in the first place how far they represented the real views of those present. In the second place, it remains to be seen what reception they will have from representative Mahomedan bodies.

From what I have heard, there are two very different forces at work. Firstly, Jinnah finds his position as nominal leader of what is practically a Mahomedan Party most precarious. Some form of compromise with the Hindus is not only demanded by his political beliefs, but is probably an essential condition of his retaining position as a political leader. Secondly, some Mahomedans may possibly have thought this move a useful means of sowing dissentions among the Hindus, reckoning the Congress Party must welcome it while the Nationalists would be unlikely to agree to the separation of Sind from Bombay.

It would show the Muslims in a reasonable light, and the subsequent failure to reach agreement would be attributed to the stubbornness of the Hindus.

At present my impression is that it is largely a question of manoeuvring for position, and that there is not much prospect of a real agreement emerging.

From Viceroy Irwin to the Secretary of State on 26 March 1927

In 1929, Jinnah tried again. This time he offered a 14-point compromise plan, eight of which are listed in Source N.

Read Source N. Which points do you think were the most important in protecting the interests of the Muslims living in India? Discuss this in your group.

> ## Source N
>
> - The future constitution of India should be federal.
> - A uniform measure of autonomy should be granted to every province.
> - In the central legislature, Muslim representation should be not less than one-third.
> - All legislatures in the country and all elected bodies should be constituted on the principle of adequate and effective representation of minorities in every province without reducing the majority in any province to a minority or even equality.
> - Any territorial redistribution that might be necessary should not affect the Muslim majorities in the Punjab, Bengal and the North West Frontier Province.
> - Full religious liberty should be granted to all communities.
> - Provision should be made in the constitution for Muslims to have an adequate share, along with other Indians in all the services of the state and in local self-governing bodies, whilst at the same time having due regard for the need for efficiency.
> - The Constitution should embody adequate safeguards for the protection of Muslim culture, education, language and religion.
>
> From M.A. Jinnah, *Indian Quarterly Register*, published in 1929

This offer was, again, rejected out of hand. Jinnah despaired. Referring to the situation as the 'parting of the ways', he left for England to work as a lawyer.

In fact, the Muslim League and the Indian National Congress continued to negotiate right down to independence in 1947. But never again would Congress receive a better offer for a peaceful settlement; never again would there be a Lucknow-style rapprochement.

Unit summary

What have you learned in this unit?

You have learned that the 1920s saw a hardening of attitudes of both the Muslim League and Congress. Extremist groups, such as the Hindu *Mahasabha* and the Muslim *Tabligh* and *Tanzeem* Movements sought to strengthen their two communities. Gandhi, while apparently embracing the Muslim cause through his support of the Khilafat Movement, may well have been using it for his own ends. Jinnah, while seemingly desperately trying to reach a rapprochement with Congress, in fact, probably did not have the support of the majority of Muslims. Basically, Congress was unwilling to grant the Muslims the concessions, such as separate electorates, that would guarantee their voice would be heard in whatever constitution emerged for an independent India. The majority of Muslims would not accept a constitution that provided for anything less.

What skills have you used in this unit?

You have worked with a range of primary and secondary source material to explore and analyse Hindu and Muslim antagonism, the importance of education to the Muslim community, the impact of the Khilafat Movement on both communities, the significance of Jinnah's Delhi proposals of 1927 and his 14 points, proposed two years later. Overall, you have explored the significance of the role of Muhammad Ali Jinnah in the 1920s.

Exam tips

This is the sort of question you will find on the exam paper as a (b) question.

- Read Sources J, M and N, and use your own knowledge. Do you agree with the view that Jinnah, in the 1920s, displayed sound political judgement?

This is, as with the (b) question at the end of Unit 7, a slightly different question from the previous (b) style questions you have worked on, in that the 'view' is not in the source but in the question.

You have worked on (b) question plans at the ends of Units 3, 4, 6 and 7, so you should have a good idea of the sort of plan you prefer. As you draw it up, remember the following points.

- Be very clear about the view being put forward. Because this question is asking you about the soundness of Jinnah's political judgement, you will need to use your knowledge of the ways in which he reacted to the situation in India in the 1920s.
- Analyse the three sources for points that support and points that challenge the soundness of his political judgement.
- Cross-reference between the sources for points of agreement and points of disagreement.
- Combine these points with your own wider knowledge into an argument for or against the view given in the question.
- Reach a balanced, supported conclusion.

RESEARCH TOPIC

Research the attitude of the Raj to the Muslim communities in India in the 1920s.

9 Consultation and conflict in the 1930s

What is this unit about?

India did not gain its independence through one swift revolution, but rather through a process of evolution. The British government, the Raj, Congress and the Muslim League were the main players. This unit explores the evolution of the idea of independence in the 1930s. Proposals were made, countered and adapted; sometimes they were adopted, sometimes they were thrown out and sometimes they were ignored. Individuals followed their own agendas; compromise did not always seem possible but sometimes broke a deadlock. All this was being played out against a background of riot and repression, death and revolt in the Indian sub-continent. However, by the end of the 1930s, Indian independence was no longer a far away dream: it was seen by Indians and British as an achievable reality.

Key questions

- Who was to blame for the failure of the Round Table Conferences?
- The Government of India Act 1935 generated opposition in Britain and in India. How far was that opposition justified?
- In December 1938, Jinnah claimed that Congress had killed every hope of a Hindu–Muslim settlement. To what extent was he correct?

Timeline

	1930	First Round Table Conference in London; Gandhi doesn't attend
	1931	Lord Irwin replaced as Viceroy by Lord Willingdon
		Second Round Table Conference in London; Gandhi attends, representing Congress
	1932	Third Round Table Conference in London; no representatives from the UK's Labour Party or India's Congress Party attend
	January	Gandhi arrested and Congress outlawed; terrorist activity in India increases
	August	Ramsay MacDonald announces Communal Award, whereby separate electorates are to be incorporated into the Indian Constitution
		Gandhi begins a 'fast-unto-death'
		Yeravda Pact between Gandhi and the Untouchables accepted by the British government and ends Gandhi's fast after one week
	1935	Government of India Act

1937	Provincial elections in India; Congress sweeps the board
	Muslim League experiences unprecedented support
1938	The militant Bose elected as president of Congress
	Bose–Gandhi–Jinnah talks about conciliation collapse because of Congress' refusal to accept the Muslim League as the sole voice of Muslims in India
	Bose argues with Gandhi and Nehru, leaves Congress and forms the Forward Bloc Party, dedicated to the revolutionary overthrow of the Raj

The Britain–India relationship

Source A

A QUESTION OF CONTROL.

INDIA. "WHAT ABOUT CHANGING PLACES?"

JOHN BULL. "WELL, YOU'RE WELCOME TO SEE WHAT YOU CAN DO AT THE WHEEL; BUT I THINK I'D BETTER SIT BESIDE YOU—WITHIN REACH OF THE BRAKE."

9.1 Cartoon 'A question of control', *Punch*, January 1931

SKILLS BUILDER

Study Source A carefully.

1 How does the cartoonist portray Britain and India?

2 What point is the cartoonist making about the relationship between Britain and India?

How successful were the Round Table Conferences?

The First Round Table Conference (see page 114) was held in London in 1930. All shades of Indian political opinion were represented with the exception, of course, of Congress. Despite this or perhaps because of it, considerable progress was made. It was decided that:

• India would be run as a type of dominion

• the dominion would take the form of a federation that would include the princely states as well as the 11 British provinces

• there would be Indian participation in all levels of government.

Question

How far do you think the changed political situation would affect any subsequent Round Table Conferences? Discuss this in your group.

Source B

All the parties at this Conference represent sectional interests. Congress alone claims to represent the whole of India, all interests. Congress knows no distinction of race, colour or creed; its platform is universal. And yet here I see that Congress is treated as one of the Parties. I do not mind it; I do not regard it as a calamity for the Congress; but I do regard it as a calamity for the purpose of doing the work for which we have gathered together here. I wish I could convince all the British public men, the British Ministers, that the Congress is capable of delivering the goods.

From a speech made by K.M. Gandhi at the Second Round Table Conference on 30 November 1931

Between the First and Second Round Table Conferences, the political situation changed. The Viceroy, Lord Irwin, who was respected, conciliatory and well-liked, left India in April 1931 when his tour of duty came to an end. He was replaced by Lord Willingdon, a rigid Conservative who had been Governor of Bombay, when he had had differences with Gandhi. Back in Britain, the first Labour government had been voted out and replaced by a Tory-dominated coalition (the National government) with a Cabinet facing a depression, unemployment and the collapse of the economy. The new Secretary of State for India, Sir Samuel Hoare, had more reservations about self-government for India than his predecessor, Wedgwood Benn.

The Second Round Table Conference had a similar mix of delegates, but this time Gandhi was there, as the sole representative of Congress. In that way, Gandhi hoped to symbolise the unity of the Indian Nationalist Movement, insisting his attendance was 'with God as my Guide'. All it did symbolise was his arrogance in assuming he could represent such a vast and diverse organisation alone and his lack of judgement in maintaining that he could speak for India (see Source B).

Iqbal, the Aga Khan (the spiritual leader of the Ismailis, a small Muslim sect) and Muhammad Ali Jinnah attended the Conference representing the Muslim League; Master Tara Singh represented the Sikhs and Dr Ambedkar, the Untouchables. All of them demanded separate electorates for their communities, and it was at this point that the Conference began to unravel. The well-known and well-rehearsed arguments began again, focusing on the desirability, or otherwise, of reserving seats for racial and religious minorities and how this would affect the resulting balance of power. Again, Hindus and Muslims could not agree. Congress had the additional worry of the possibility of an alliance between the princes and the Muslims, which could outweigh any recommendations that Congress might make. Unsurprisingly, this Second Round Table Conference couldn't agree on a workable constitution.

Source C

9.2 Gandhi leaving a session of the Second Round Table Conference, September 1931

Source D

Gandhi made the fatal error of claiming to speak for the Muslims and depressed classes. The spokesmen of both communities repudiated him, and since the Muslims then numbered nearly thirty per cent of the population and the depressed classes about twenty per cent, it was difficult for him to sustain his claim that he represented ninety-five per cent of India. Gandhi had, in fact, come to a tentative agreement with the Muslims on the basis of joint electorates for Hindus and Muslims, but when it came to an apportionment of seats between Hindus, Muslims and Sikhs, he yielded to the pressures of the extremist Hindu leader, Pandit Madan Mohan Malaviya, who insisted that the only seat in dispute should go to the Sikhs and not to the Muslims. That Gandhi's efforts at a Hindu-Muslim settlement should have failed was bad enough. That they failed over the allocation of one seat made the attempt ridiculous. The minorities, comprising the Muslims, depressed classes, a section of Indian Christians, the Anglo-Indians and the British community, then confronted the British government with a document embodying an agreement arrived at between themselves. Whitehall had no alternative but to announce that the government would make its own award.

From Frank Moraes, *Witness to an Era*, published in 1973

The Third Round Table Conference was held in 1932. By this time, Prime Minister Ramsay MacDonald had lost the support of his own Labour Party and was able to continue in office only through a National government, supported by his political opponents. The British Labour Party didn't send any representatives to the Conference and neither did India's Congress Party. Because the British Labour Party had been the main driver behind the Round Table Conferences, this third Conference was doomed before it started. It discussed the franchise, finance and the role of the princely states, but again couldn't reach any definite conclusions. The Conference collapsed.

How did India react to the collapse of the Round Table Conferences?

In India, the situation was deteriorating and Viceroy Willingdon decided to take a tough line. Lacking the temperament to engage in discussions with Gandhi, he followed the British government's instructions that he should conciliate only those elements of Indian opinion that were prepared to work with the current administration. So on 4 January 1932, just one week after Gandhi returned to India, he was arrested and imprisoned. Congress was outlawed and all members of Congress' Working Committee and the provincial committees were rounded up and imprisoned. Youth organisations were also banned.

Within four months, over 80,000 Indians, mostly members of Congress, were in prison. The reaction of the Indian population was swift but, in the absence of local and national Congress leaders, and especially of Gandhi, uneven and disorganised. Boycotts of British goods were common and so was non-payment of taxes; youth organisations, although banned, became very popular; and terrorist activity increased, with more and more women becoming involved. Indeed, the United Provinces and the North-West Frontier Province became little more than armed camps, and troops in

SKILLS BUILDER

1 Look at Source C. It was clearly wet and cold in London in September 1931. Why, then, did Gandhi dress as he did?

2 How far do Sources A, B and D explain why the Second Round Table Conference failed?

Definition

Fast-unto-death

This was a common Middle Eastern way of registering a deep personal protest. An individual would refuse all food until they died. Sometimes a person would refuse water as well and this hastened death. However, most people adopting this dramatic form of protest would accept water because it made the process of dying longer and so have more impact on their cause. Other examples of hunger strikers are the suffragettes and the IRA internees.

Question

How should the British government have reacted to Gandhi's letter to Ramsay MacDonald? Discuss this in your group.

Peshawar and Meerut were kept on armed alert. But the police never lost control of the streets or rural areas for very long and the authorities kept overall control of the situation.

Intervention from Westminster: the Communal Award

On 16 August 1932, British Prime Minister Ramsay MacDonald announced the Communal Award, which was to be incorporated into any new Indian constitution. This designated Sikhs, Indian Christians, Anglo-Indians and Untouchables as separate classes, along with Muslims, and entitled to separate electorates, as were the Muslims.

Gandhi was furious. He wasn't in favour of separate electorates anyway, but he regarded the inclusion of Untouchables as the final straw. The removal of the stigma of untouchability had long been one of his missions and, in his mind, all Untouchables were Hindus. Thus, Gandhi reasoned, the British government was trying to weaken Congress further by separating off the Untouchables as a group worthy of a separate electorate. He reacted in a dramatic fashion, launching a **fast-unto-death**. 'As a man of religion,' he said, 'I have no other course left open'. Of course he had, but he chose to blackmail the government into withdrawing the Communal Award in this way.

The authorities hate this form of protest because they believe it creates martyrs. Usually at a loss as to what to do, they have swung from one extreme to the other, from force feeding though to early release and then to simply ignoring the situation and removing the individual to hospital at the point of organ failure. The main objective has always been to prevent an individual dying in prison.

Source E

I have read the British government's decision on the representation of the minorities and have slept over it. In pursuance of my letter to Sir Samuel Hoare and my declaration at the meeting of the Minorities Committee of the Round Table Conference on 13 November 1931, at St James' Palace, I have to resist your decision with my life. The only way I can do so is by declaring a perpetual fast unto death from food of any kind, save water, with or without salt and soda. This fast will cease if, during its progress, the British government, of its own motion or under pressure of public opinion, revise their decision and withdraw their scheme of communal electorates for the Depressed Classes whose representatives should be elected by the general electorate under a common franchise, no matter how wide it is. The proposed fast will come into operation in the ordinary course from the noon of 20th September next, unless the said decision is meanwhile revised in the manner suggested above.

From a letter written by K.M. Gandhi to Ramsay MacDonald on 18 August 1932

Neither Viceroy Willingdon nor Congress wanted Gandhi to die. Willingdon didn't want to make Gandhi a martyr and so, in his view, inflate the importance of his cause. He had plans in place to release Gandhi once he got to the point of no return so that at least he would not die in prison. Congress, of course, did not want to lose their iconic leader. In the event, Gandhi and Ambedkar, the Untouchables' leader, came to an agreement in Yeravda Jail. They agreed that the number of seats available to Untouchables on provincial councils would be 147, as opposed to the 71 allocated by the British government, and that Untouchables would be allocated 18 per cent of Central Assembly seats as long as they ran for election by the general electorate.

The British government accepted the Yeravda Pact, Gandhi ended his fast a week after it began and the following week was celebrated as Untouchability Abolition Week. Although Hindu leaders declared that henceforth, among Hindus, no one should be regarded as an Untouchable by reason of their birth and would have the same rights as other Hindus to use wells, schools, roads and other public institutions, it took another 20 years before untouchability was abolished by law.

Leadership problems

Gandhi and Jinnah, as well as other leaders of various different Indian groups, faced enormous difficulties in trying to lead and develop Indian opinion, as well as represent it on a world stage (see Source F).

Jinnah was also open to criticism. In 1942, M.R. Jayakar, a liberal Hindu politician, recalled Jinnah's style of negotiation at the Round Table Conferences to C. Rajagopalachari, a lawyer and chief minister of Madras from 1937 to 1939:

Source F

It seemed as if Gandhi's speeches in London were directed to India rather than to Britain. He could not be persuaded to speak to a prepared text, and his habit of speaking *extempore* made his speeches unnecessarily long-winded and sometimes irrelevant. He ignored the opportunity to carry on private negotiations with the British leaders and left England with his political image badly dented. Possibly the *Mahatma* might have felt that in Britain, as in India, it was more important to open a dialogue with the people than with the politicians: the only British politician he was anxious to meet was his stormy critic, Churchill, but Churchill refused.

From Frank Moraes, *Witness to an Era*, published in 1973

Source G

Jinnah's attitude at the Round Table Conference surprised every one of us including the British Delegation. His one effort was, and a deceitful one too, to accept all the concessions that were made to him on behalf of the Hindus and subsequently to take them privately to the Prime Minister of England, Ramsay MacDonald, and to say to him in a bargaining spirit: 'This is what the Hindus are prepared to give; how much more will the British Government give the Muslims?' This method of bargaining became in course of time so notorious that ultimately MacDonald telephoned to me asking me to stop this process of bargaining, for it was most deceitful and led nowhere. I am citing this incident as proving the unscrupulous way in which Jinnah will bargain for the Muslim cause. As you are dealing with him, I have to warn you to be very careful.

From a letter written by M.R. Jayakar to C. Rajagopalachari on 21 January 1942

Questions

Read Sources F and G.

1 For what are Gandhi and Jinnah being criticised?
2 How far do these criticisms explain why the Round Table Conferences failed?

Biography

Biography

Harold Harmsworth, 1st Lord Rothermere (1868–1940)

The younger brother of Alfred Harmsworth (who became 1st Baron Northcliffe), Harold became the business manager in the newspaper empire they founded together.

As newspaper proprietor, he started by launching the *Daily Record* in Scotland, and then bought out his brother's interest in the *Daily Mail* and finally the *Sunday Pictorial*. He controlled the Associated Newspapers group from Alfred's death in 1922 until 1932. He used this opportunity to write a series of articles supporting Hitler and Mussolini, defending the retention of the British Empire as a collection of dependent territories and attacking Stanley Baldwin on the issue of Empire free trade.

Definition

Babu

A clerk; used by the British to describe western-educated Indians.

Why was the government of India Act passed in 1935?

Back in the corridors of Whitehall, and faced with the apparent inability of the Indians to agree on their own constitution, British politicians set to and created one of their own. It wasn't that easy.

Opposition in Westminster

A determined group of Conservatives fought the Government of India Bill every inch of the way. They joined forces with ex-generals and former civil servants, some of whom had served in India, and together they formed the India Defence League. Rudyard Kipling (see page 28) was a vice-president and Winston Churchill its most vociferous supporter. Churchill's views on India were formed when he had been stationed there as an army subaltern in 1897, and they hadn't changed since. He refused to accept that Indians were capable of running their own affairs.

Media support for the India Defence League came from the *Daily Mail*. Its proprietor **Lord Rothermere** wrote a series of scurrilous articles under the general heading of 'If We Lose India'. These were laced with entirely erroneous 'facts', for example, that Gandhi and Congress were a 'numerically insignificant group of 400,000 semi-educated **babus** who hankered after the spoils of minor office', and photographs of British troops quelling riots with lorries piled high with corpses. The message was clear: Indians were unfit to govern themselves and only the paternalistic British could effectively manage the sub-continent. If Britain was to leave India, carnage would follow. Furthermore, the *Daily Mail* warned, India was essential to the British economy and to lose India's trade at a time when every economy in the western world was struggling would be the height of folly. In fact, Churchill, taking up the tale of doom and gloom, was of the opinion that 'England, without her Empire in India, ceases to be a Great Power'.

Source H

We have as good a right to be in India as anyone there except, perhaps, the Depressed Classes, who are the original stock. It is a government responsible to the Crown and to Parliament. It is incomparably the best government that India has ever seen or ever will see. . .

We are confronted with the old choice of self-government versus good government. We are invited to believe that the worst self-government is better than the best good government. . .

The protection and security [Britain has given] cannot be removed from India. They have grown with our growth and strengthened with our strength. They will diminish with our diminution and decay with our decay. If this external aid is withheld, India will descend into the squalor and anarchy of India in the sixteenth and seventeenth centuries. It seems to me that the present infatuation of the liberal mind, and I must say of the more intellectual part of the Socialist mind, is at this moment very serious. Their error is an undue exaltation of the principle of self-government. They set this principle above all other principles; they press it to the destruction of all other principle.

From a speech by Winston Churchill on the second reading of the Government of India Bill on 11 February 1935

Source I

The question that we should be putting is this: does this Constitutional scheme provide a medium through which the living forces of India can operate, for what we have to deal with are the forces of modern India, a living India, and not the dead India of the past. If we are to do anything with India, we have to bring modern influences into play. For good or ill, the Congress Party is one of the dominating factors in the situation. We may disagree with it, but within it are very many of the forces that are going to make for modern India.

. . .

Is this bill going to be accepted and worked by the people of India? I do not think so. The indications are that if it is to be worked at all it will be in a grudging spirit and that it is only too likely that its provisions will be used, not for seeing how far it can be made useful for self-government, but as a means of getting something more.

From a speech by Clement Attlee to Parliament on the Government of India Bill on 4 June 1935

Prime Minister Stanley Baldwin steered the Bill through the Commons with quiet determination. He stuck to the position he had taken up when he supported the Irwin Declaration (see page 114) and never wavered from it. A pragmatic prime minister, he managed to convince the majority of his party that the British Empire was an organic organisation that had to change and develop, or die. In the Commons, the bill was attacked by Winston Churchill and by Clement Attlee (see Sources H and I) but for different reasons. In the event, fewer than 50 MPs followed Churchill into the 'No' lobby and the Bill became law in August 1935. The Secretary of State for India, Sir Samuel Hoare, acknowledging the furore created by the Bill, countered by arguing: 'No one in India has produced a workable alternative.'

> **SKILLS BUILDER**
>
> Read Sources H and I. How different were the grounds on which Churchill and Attlee attacked the Government of India Bill?

What was the impact on India of the Government of India Act 1935?

The Government of India Act was the final British-written constitution to be imposed on India.

What did the Act say?

A Federation of India was proposed but never put into effect because the requisite number of states, mainly the princely bloc, would not join. Therefore, only the clauses dealing with provincial governments actually happened. The main features of these were:

- India was divided into 11 provinces, which would control almost everything, except defence and foreign affairs
- each province would have a legislative assembly, a provincial government and a governor, who retained the power to act in an emergency
- dyarchy (see page 69) was abolished
- separate electorates were to continue as before

- Burma was separated from India and given its own government
- two new states of Sindh and Orissa were created
- the Viceroy would still be appointed by the British government and would be in control of defence and foreign affairs; he would have to follow the advice of an Executive Committee, which was made up mostly of Indians.

SKILLS BUILDER

Read Sources J and K. How far is Judith Brown's assessment of the 1935 Government of India Act supported by Viceroy Linlithgow's report to London in mid-1936?

Why did both Congress and the Muslim League reject the Act?

Congress objected to the Act because the members wanted *swaraj* – full independence – and were not interested in what they saw as a half-way house. It wanted a strong central government, which would inevitably be predominantly Hindu, and not strong provincial governments, some of which the Muslims would probably be able to control. It also objected to the Act because it continued the practice of reserved seats for minority groups.

The Muslim League objected to the Act because it did not offer enough power to Muslims and because most provinces were controlled by Congress with no guarantee that the rights of Muslims would be protected.

Source J

It is vital that the impetus of the new law and the completion of provincial autonomy should carry us straight on into federation. For indeed there would be grave danger in allowing any prolonged interval of time to elapse between achieving provincial autonomy and the final phase, which is federation. However, federation has few enthusiastic friends. The Princes, I believe, for the most part regard it as inevitable but do not welcome it. Congress hates it, and the provinces will soon develop a degree of local patriotism. This means they will easily agree with the progressive weakening of central authority, such as would most certainly happen if the reconstruction of the centre is unduly delayed.

An adaptation of Viceroy Linlithgow's report to London on 15 June 1936

Source K

For all its limitations, the 1935 Act was a major experiment in the devolution of power in a non-white part of Britain's empire. Its imperial framers hoped it would channel the interests and forces in Indian public life through institutions that would protect Britain's diminishing interests on the sub-continent and require from Britain a much lighter exercise of imperial control and decreased expenditure of resources. However, by the time of its enactment it seemed a battered and much cobbled measure, disliked by most Indian politicians and a significant group of British MPs.

Despite the long-term failure to provide a federal solution to the imperial problem of ruling the sub-continent, the 1935 Act succeeded as a temporary solution to the problem of governing British India. For two years the British tactic of retreat to the centre, leaving the provinces to run themselves under Indian ministers, paid off spectacularly.

From Judith M. Brown, *Modern India: the Origins of an Asian Democracy*, published in 1994

The 1937 elections

Both Congress and the Muslim League were faced with an immediate dilemma: should they participate in the provincial elections set for 1937? Not to participate would be consistent with their rejection of the Act, but the elections were going ahead anyway and a total boycott would cut them off from government. Furthermore, to participate might give them the opportunity to work within the system to create change. Both Congress and the League decided to take part.

How did Congress fare?

Congress virtually swept the board. The Congress Party gained overall control of the United and Central Provinces, Orissa, Bombay and Madras, and it became the largest single party in Assam and the North-West Frontier Province. Although fewer than half of the 1585 provincial legislative seats contested throughout India were open to the general electorate, Congress won them all, together with 59 more from the separate electorate contests, ending up with 716 legislative members. To all intents and purposes, Congress was a partner in government with the Raj.

How did the Muslim League fare?

In a word, badly. Jinnah only returned to India in 1935 from his self-imposed exile in London. He worked hard before the elections to build up a powerbase but, in the limited time available to him, he wasn't even able to find enough candidates to contest all the reserved Muslim seats. An analysis of polling figures shows that Muslims gave little support to Congress candidates, even though they had to be Muslim to stand for the restricted seats. Indeed, the only overwhelmingly Muslim province that voted strongly for Congress was the North-West Frontier Province.

How did the Muslim League revitalise itself?

Jinnah realised that the Muslim League had two alternatives. It would have to attract mass support to enable it to win control in some provinces, especially the Punjab and Sind, where Muslims were in a majority or it would have to enter into some kind of power-sharing agreement with Congress. This, Congress refused to contemplate. And then Congress Party members played straight into the Muslim League's hands.

Many of the new Congress provincial council ministers, starved of power and recognition for so long, threw caution to the winds. They took advantage of their new offices and appointed relatives and caste brethren to jobs they had at their disposal; they ignored minorities and often behaved spitefully to their enemies. In some provinces, fiscal policies were drawn up to hurt Muslim landowners; in Bihar, cow-slaughter was banned; and Congress flags were hoisted on public buildings where there was a substantial Muslim minority. Many Muslims felt that they were living in a Hindu Raj. Now, as never before, many Muslims believed they needed the electoral safeguards that Jinnah and the League had long been demanding.

Jinnah rose to the occasion. He began a series of carefully orchestrated personal appearances, mass rallies and press interviews. The rallies and processions deliberately harked back to the glory days of the Mughal Empire and included, among other memorabilia, the inauguration of a **Tipu Sultan** Day. But Jinnah and his 'spin doctors' looked to the future too, deliberately targeting university students. Jinnah himself became the embodiment of Muslim identity, hopes and dreams. In spite of all the endeavours of Gandhi, Nehru and even Jinnah, Muslims could never be persuaded that the Hindu-dominated Congress party was their natural home. In the 1930s, they turned to the Muslim League in their thousands. Jinnah (inadvertently helped by Congress members) had at last given the Muslims a sense of identity and purpose.

Source L

The Congress has now killed every hope of Hindu-Muslim settlement. The Congress does not want any settlement with the Muslim of India. There are four forces at play in this country. Firstly, here is the British government. Secondly there are the rulers and people of the Indian States. Thirdly, there are the Hindus and, fourthly, there are Muslims. The Congress leaders may cry as much as they like that Congress is a national body. But I say it is not true. The Congress is nothing but a Hindu body. That is the truth and the Congress leaders know it. The presence of the few Muslims – the few misled and misguided ones and the few who are there with ulterior motives – does not and cannot make it a national body.

From Jinnah's presidential address to the Patna session of the Muslim League in December 1938

Biography

Fateh Ali Tipu (Tipu Sultan) 1750–99

Tipu Sultan became a symbol of what Muslims, given the chance and the right conditions, could achieve. This Muslim ruler and Sultan of Mysore challenged British power by developing a new state and an army that could, and initially did, defeat the British. Taught European military and administrative skills by French officers, he defeated the British at the Battle of Coleroon River in 1782 and then negotiated with them for recognition as Sultan of Mysore. He turned Mysore into a strong and wealthy state by introducing new crops and industries (for example, growing pineapples and manufacturing silk).

In 1789, Tipu attacked the adjacent British protectorate of Travancore. The resulting war ended in humiliation for Tipu in 1791 when he lost half his lands to the British East India Company. He sought revenge by allying himself with the French, but even so the Mysore wars ended in defeat and his own death.

There was one last-ditch stand to achieve unity between Congress and the League. Subhas Bose was elected Congress president in 1938. Jinnah met briefly with Gandhi, Nehru and Bose in that year, but talks broke down because of Jinnah's insistence that the Muslim League be recognised by Congress as the sole party of India's Muslims. Congress liked to think they were an inclusive party, capable of representing the entire nation (see Source L).

British officials watched with a kind of bemused bewilderment, mixed with satisfaction. Older men remained convinced that the British alone were best suited to running India. Younger men, like Maurice Zinkin of the Indian Civil Service, believed that 'most accepted the inevitability of self-government at some time'.

Source M

I think the basic mistake of the Congress leadership was its continued insistence that the Congress represented all Indians. By translating democracy in terms of mere majority, the Congress sidestepped the fact that in a plural society such as India's only a government which enjoyed the support of both Hindus and Muslims could be considered democratic or representative. It aggravated this lapse by claiming that only Congress Muslims represented Muslims as Indians, and therefore no separate Muslim representation was necessary. From this line of reasoning proceeded its disastrous conclusion that a coalition with the Muslim League could not be entertained.

From Frank Moraes, *Witness to an Era*, published in 1973

Congress divided against itself

At the end of 1938, Congress itself was torn apart by in-fighting over its presidency. There was considerable pressure on Bose to quit: Gandhi didn't trust him and neither did the old guard. However, Jawaharlal Nehru refused to stand in his place and Bose refused to step aside for the Gandhi faction's nominee, Pattabhi Sitaramayya. Bose knew he had the support of student, peasant and worker delegates and, in the first ever contested election for the presidency of Congress, he had won by 1580 votes to 1375. Twelve members of the Gandhi faction immediately resigned from the Working Committee in protest against the democratic election of their own president. Bose was left as president of a party that could not function because of a huge rift in its senior echelons. Gandhi ignored his pleas for help and Nehru's attempts at mediation failed. Finally, Bose was forced to resign and was replaced by Rajendra Prasad, 'elected' by the Working Committee of which he was a member. Bose and his brother Sarat Chandra walked away from Congress altogether. Back in their homeland of Bengal, they formed the Forward Bloc Party, dedicated to the revolutionary overthrow of the Raj.

Throughout this period, between the passing of the 1935 Government of India Act and its partial implementation in India up to 1939, the Raj experienced a brief period of popularity. More and more people, and in particular Congress chief ministers, looked to the administrative structures of the Raj for practical guidance and professional help on a daily basis. For all the potential leaders of an independent India, the realisation that freedom alone would not solve the sub-continent's complex problems was sobering.

Unit summary

What have you learned in this unit?

You have learned that, although all shades of Indian political opinion were represented, the Round Table Conferences failed. They failed largely because the various parties attended with different aims and objectives. The biggest stumbling block seemed to be how the minority groups (particularly the Muslims) were to be treated in any new constitution.

Because the Indians couldn't agree among themselves, the British government imposed a constitution (the Government of India Act 1935) that aimed at creating a federal India. However, both Congress and the Muslim League were opposed to the Act. By 1939, a discernable shift had taken place. Indian independence no longer seemed to be an impossible dream but an achievable reality. The problem was that the structure and composition of an independent India was far from clear.

What skills have you used in this unit?

You have worked with a range of primary, contemporary and secondary sources in order to explore and analyse the different tensions that were present at the Round Table Conferences. You have explored the reasons for the imposition of the 1935 Government of India Act and the reasons it was opposed in Britain and in India. You have considered and evaluated the complexity of the relationships between the different racial and religious groups in India, in particular the relationships between Hindus and Muslims, Congress and the Muslim League.

Exam tips

This is the sort of question you will find appearing on the exam paper as a (b) question.

- Study Sources B, L and M, and use your own knowledge. Do you agree with the view that, by the beginning of 1939, the only obstacle to Indian independence was the Indians themselves?

Draw up the sort of plan that works for you when answering a (b) style question. As you draw it up, remember to:

- Be very clear about the view being put forward. It is not contained in one of the sources, so you will have to work out how the sources relate to that view.
- You will need to use your knowledge of the obstacles in the way of Indian independence, including the attitudes of the British.
- Analyse the three sources for points that support and points that challenge the view that the only obstacle to Indian independence was the Indians themselves.
- Cross-reference between the sources for points of agreement and points of disagreement.
- Combine these points with your own wider knowledge into an argument for or against the view given in the question.
- Reach a balanced, supported conclusion.

RESEARCH TOPIC

Research the reaction of the British press and public to the Round Table Conferences and to Gandhi's presence in Britain.

10 The impact of the early years of the Second World War

What is this unit about?

The First World War (1914–18) had the effect of bringing Hindus and Muslims together and so unifying India's Nationalist Movement. Events in the 1920s and 1930s drove Congress and the Muslim League further and further apart, while at the same time making it more and more clear that India's independence from the Raj was achievable. The Second World War (1939–45) confirmed both of these developments: the ending of the Raj and the separation of Muslim and Hindu. It shattered all hopes of Congress and the Muslim League coexisting in an independent India. In this unit, you will find out just how this happened.

Key questions

- Why did Congress and the Muslim League react to the outbreak of war in Europe in 1939 in different ways?
- To what extent was Gandhi's 'Quit India' campaign a mistake?
- What was the significance of the Second World War to the fortunes of the Muslim League?

Timeline

1939	**3 September**	Viceroy Linlithgow announces that India is at war with Germany
	14 September	Congress Working Committee declares it will not support the British in war unless self-determination is granted to India
	23 October	Congress asks all Congress provincial ministries to resign; all resign by the end of the month
	22 December	Observed by the Muslim League as Deliverance Day from Congress rule
1940	**20 March**	Congress demands complete independence and a constituent assembly
	23 March	Lahore Resolution of the Muslim League demands separate Muslim homeland
	7 August	August Offer from the Viceroy on India's constitutional development
	15 September	Congress rejects the August Offer
	28 September	Muslim League rejects the August Offer

1942	23 March	The Cripps Mission arrives in India
	2 April	Congress and Muslim League reject Cripps' proposals
	11 April	Cripps leaves India
	8 August	Congress endorses Gandhi's 'Quit India' campaign
	9 August	Gandhi, Nehru and Congress leaders arrested

War!

On 3 September 1939, British Prime Minister Neville Chamberlain declared war on Nazi Germany. Lord Linlithgow, India's Viceroy, followed suit. On the same day, and acting (just) within his legal powers, he committed over 300 million Indians to war without consulting a single one of them.

SKILLS BUILDER

1 Is there anything in Viceroy Linlithgow's comments that surprises you?

2 Which do you think Indians resented most – that war was declared without consulting them or that they were being committed to fighting for liberty and democracy by a power that was denying these principles to them?

Source A

Confronted with the demand that she should accept the dictation of a foreign power in relation to her own subjects, India has decided to stand firm.

. . .

Nowhere do these great principles [of morality and international justice] mean more than in India.

Comments made by Viceroy Linlithgow after declaring war on India's behalf

How did Congress and the Muslim League react to the outbreak of war in 1939?

What did Congress do?

Congress' first reaction was one of shock and horror. What was the Government of India Act 1935 about if not some form of power-sharing? How could the Raj behave as if India was still in the nineteenth century? Wasn't Viceroy Linlithgow demonstrating clearly that Britain still considered itself to be master in India? Had the previous 20 years been in vain? This initial reaction was complicated by a feeling of deep sympathy with Britain in its struggle with European Fascism.

Gandhi urged the British government to negotiate with Hitler, using peaceful means, of course. Those members of Congress, like Nehru, who were at all familiar with events in Europe knew just how futile this suggestion was. As hostilities commenced, Gandhi gave his wholehearted support to the British people: 'We do not seek our independence out of Britain's ruin. That is not the way of non-violence.' Nehru and other Indian Socialists sympathised completely with the British approach to Fascism. They were not, however, prepared to commit themselves openly to support a government that had not consulted them prior to the declaration of war nor, or so they said, were they prepared to fight unless they were granted immediate *swaraj*.

Source B

The Congress considers the declaration, by the British Government, of India as a belligerent country, without any reference to the people of India, and the exploitation of India's resources in this war as an affront to them, which no self-respecting and freedom-loving people can accept or tolerate.

The recent pronouncements made on behalf of the British Government in regard to India demonstrate that Great Britain is carrying on the war fundamentally for Imperialist ends and for the preservation and strengthening of her Empire, which is based on the exploitation of the people of India as well as of other Asiatic and African countries. Under these circumstances, it is clear that the Congress cannot, in any way, directly or indirectly, be party to the war, which means continuance and perpetuation of this exploitation.

This Congress, therefore, strongly disapproves of Indian troops being made to fight for Great Britain and of the drain from India of men and material for the purpose of the war. Congressmen and those under the Congress influence cannot help in the prosecution of the war with men, money or material.

The Congress hereby declares that nothing short of complete independence can be accepted by the people of India. The people of India alone can properly shape their own constitution and determine their relations to other countries of the world, through a constituent assembly elected on the basis of adult suffrage.

From the Resolution passed by the Indian National Congress at Ramgarh on 20 March 1940

Congress withdrew the Ministries from the provinces where Congress had a majority in order to dissociate India from the war and to enforce Congress determination to free India from foreign domination.

Source C

10.1 Indian soldiers in the Second World War

SKILLS BUILDER

Read Source B.

1 Why was Congress opposed to involvement in the Second World War?

2 What did Congress hope to achieve by withdrawing its members from provincial assemblies?

3 How far does Source C challenge Source B about Indian participation in the Second World War?

In the early months of the Second World War, however, British politicians had other preoccupations, and demands for *purna swaraj* (independence now) fell upon deaf ears. As a consequence, as you can see from Source B, Congress' leaders ordered all Congress members to resign from provincial ministries throughout India. This was not necessarily the most sensible thing they could have done since it removed hundreds of Indians from official positions where they could ameliorate the effects of war for their people and, to some extent, influence events internal to India. India's provinces reverted to a form of direct British government, something that they hadn't known since 1919.

What did the Muslim League do?

Jinnah could hardly believe his luck. Congress had, of its own volition, virtually retired from the political scene. The way lay open for the Muslim League to strengthen its position.

The last Congress provincial ministry abandoned its posts on 22 December 1939, as required to do by Congress leaders. Jinnah had earlier designated this day as Muslim India's Day of Deliverance and called on all Muslims to celebrate their release from Hindu bondage. This they did with gusto.

SKILLS BUILDER

Read Source D. What, in your view, was the purpose of the Muslim Day of Deliverance?

Source D

I wish the Musalmans all over India to observe Friday 22 December as the 'Day of Deliverance' and thanksgiving as a mark of relief that the Congress regime has at last ceased to function. I hope that the provincial, district and primary Muslim Leagues all over India will hold public meetings and offer prayers by way of thanksgiving for being delivered from the unjust Congress regime. I trust that public meetings will be conducted in an orderly manner and with all due sense of humility, and nothing should be done which will cause offence to any other community, because it is the High Command of the Congress that is primarily responsible for the wrongs that have been done to the Musalmans and other minorities.

From M.A. Jinnah, in his appeal for the observation of Deliverance Day, given on 2 December 1939

Source E

Two days ago I sent you a letter informing you that I intended going to Bombay soon and hoped to meet you there. Yesterday morning I read in the newspapers your statement fixing December 22nd as a day of deliverance and thanksgiving as a mark of relief that the Congress government have at last ceased to function. I have read this statement very carefully more than once and have given 24 hours thought to the matter. What has oppressed me terribly since yesterday is the realisation that our sense of values and objectives in life as well as in politics differs so very greatly. I had hoped, after our conversations, that this was not so great, but now the gulf appears wider than ever. Under these circumstances, I wonder what purpose will be served by our discussing with each other the problems that confront us. There must be some common ground for discussion, some common objective aimed at, for that discussion to bear fruit.

From a letter written by J. Nehru to M.A. Jinnah on 9 December 1939

Source F

I am in receipt of your letter of 9th December. I quite agree with you 'that there must be some common ground for discussion to yield fruit'; that is the very reason why I made it clear in our conversation at Delhi in October last to Mr Gandhi and yourself. First, that as long as the Congress is not prepared to treat the Muslim League as the authoritative and representative organisation of the Muslims in India it was not possible to carry on talks regarding the Hindu–Muslim settlement. If happily we could settle the Hindu–Muslim question then we would be in a position to evolve an agreed formula for a demand of a declaration by H.M. Government [on H.M. Government's war aims in respect of democracy and imperialism] that would satisfy us. I can only say that if you desire to discuss the matter further I am at your disposal.

From a letter written by M.A. Jinnah to J. Nehru on 13 December 1939

SKILLS BUILDER

Read Sources E and F. How likely was it that Nehru and Jinnah would find common ground for talks?

There seemed to be no way back, now. With Congress out of the political picture, the Muslim League worked with the Raj and the British government to support the war effort and to strengthen their own position within India.

The Lahore Resolution, March 1940

Freed from the necessity of coping with Congress, Jinnah focused on the Muslim League and the challenging problems of formulating its constitutional goals – goals with which all Muslims could agree. He called a meeting of the League in Lahore in March 1940, which was attended by approximately 100,000 Muslims.

Source G

If the British Government is really in earnest, and sincere to secure peace and happiness for the people of the sub-continent, the only course open to us all is to allow the major nations separate homelands by dividing India into autonomous national states. There is no reason why these states should be antagonistic to each other.

The Hindus and Muslims belong to two different religious philosophies, social customs and literature. They neither inter-marry, nor dine together and indeed they belong to two different civilisations, which are based on conflicting ideas. To join together two such nations under a single state, one as a minority and one as a majority, must lead to growing discontent and the final destruction of such a state.

Muslim India cannot accept any constitution which must necessarily result in a Hindu majority government. Hindus and Muslims brought together under a democratic system forced upon the minorities can only mean Hindu Raj.

From the presidential address by M.A. Jinnah at the Lahore session of the
All-Indian Muslim League in March 1940

The word 'separate' had not only been said, it had been driven home relentlessly. The genie was out of the bottle. It seemed that Jinnah could no longer see any possibility of a Hindu–Muslim rapprochement.

Source H

Resolved that it is the considered view of the session of the All-Indian Muslim League that no constitutional plan would be workable in this country, or acceptable to the Muslims unless it is designed on the following basic principles, viz., that geographically contiguous units are demarcated into regions which should be so constituted with such territorial readjustments as may be necessary that the areas in which Muslims are numerically in a majority, as in the north-western and eastern zones of India, should be grouped to constitute independent states in which the constituent units shall be autonomous and sovereign.

That adequate, effective and mandatory safeguards should be specifically provided in the constitution for minorities in these units and regions for the protection of their religious, cultural, economic, political, administrative and other rights and interests, in consultation with them, and in other parts of India where the Muslims are in a minority.

This session further authorises the Working Committee to frame a scheme of constitution in accordance with these basic principles, providing for the assumption, finally, by the respective regions of all powers such as defence, external affairs, communications, customs and such other matters as may be necessary.

From the Resolution of the Muslim League at Lahore, 24 March 1940

SKILLS BUILDER

Read Sources G and H, and use your own knowledge. What, in your view, did Jinnah and the Muslim League really want in March 1940?

It is, however, by no means certain that at this point the Muslim League envisaged that two separate states of East and West Pakistan would eventually emerge. It is by no means certain that Jinnah himself wanted this: he may have been using the idea of separate states as a bargaining tactic to gain separate representation within a united sub-continent. If so, he was playing a dangerous game, risking his bluff being called. However, the involvement of Fazul Huq, the eminent Bengali politician and strong proponent of a separate Pakistan, in the drafting of the Lahore Resolution makes it more than likely that this was a possibility in the minds of the drafters when they wrote of 'independent states in which the constituent units shall be autonomous and sovereign'.

What was the reaction of Congress?

A battle of words between Jinnah and Gandhi ensued, with Gandhi maintaining that the Lahore Declaration was tantamount to the vivisection of India and appealing, over the head of Jinnah, to the commonsense of Muslims to draw back from the obvious suicide that Partition would mean for India. Mini-*satyagraha* campaigns broke out and the perpetrators were jailed.

Nehru denounced the idea of Pakistan as a mad scheme and toured India trying to strengthen the will of Congress supporters. The young were already drilling and wearing pseudo-uniforms, ready for the supposed conflict with the Muslims. Nehru inspected one such body, carrying an imitation Field Marshal's baton, and was promptly thrown into gaol for his trouble.

In reality, Congress was suffering from a self-inflicted wound: the withdrawal of congressmen from positions of authority and influence in the provinces had completely weakened their hand politically.

What were the threats to India?

Source I

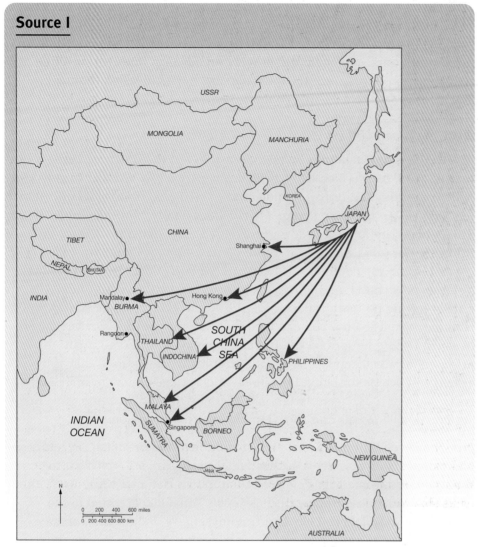

10.2 Map showing the advancement of the Axis forces in the Pacific theatre

External threats

By the beginning of 1942, the Allies' position in all war zones was desperate. Hitler's armies controlled the Balkans and had invaded Russia, Rommel was within striking distance of the Suez Canal and France had fallen to the Nazi onslaught as had most of Western Europe. In the Pacific theatre, Japan launched a lightening strike on the US naval base of Pearl Harbor in December 1941. The Japanese then swept through South-East Asia and, in a series of lightening strikes took Shanghai, Hong Kong, the Philippines, Malaya, Indochina and Thailand. On 15 February 1942, the 'unconquerable' island of Singapore fell. The whole of Asia now lay open to the Japanese. They pushed on into Burma, capturing Rangoon in March and Mandalay six weeks later. With Japan's declared aim of freeing Asians from European rule, Malays and Burmese welcomed the invading troops as liberators. The Japanese ships cruised at will around the Indian Ocean, once the unchallenged province of the British navy. Japanese forces were, quite literally, lapping at India's eastern boundaries.

Early in March, Viceroy Linlithgow confessed that he did not have sufficient armed forces in India to hold out against a Japanese landing on the Cuttack coast and could not prevent an advance into Orissa. All he could suggest, in response to a possible land-borne invasion through Bengal, was a scorched earth policy.

Bose: the enemy within?

In 1939, Subhas Chandra Bose (see page 107) left the Congress Party and formed the Forward Bloc Party, which was basically a terrorist organisation aimed at getting the British to quit India. The organisation was banned by the Raj in 1941 and Bose fled to Afghanistan, finally ending up in Berlin. There, his reception was lukewarm. Hitler feared that any collapse of the British Raj in India would lead to Russia moving into the power vacuum created in the sub-continent. However, Bose was encouraged to broadcast propaganda to India, urging Indians to rise up against British tyranny. Finally having no more use for him, the Nazis agreed that he could work with the Japanese on a possible land invasion into India. Bose was moved to Japan, where he formed the Indian National Army from Indian prisoners of war taken by the Japanese. Initially, Japan used this army as a source of agents for behind-the-lines sabotage and spying in mainland India. Most of these agents were picked up by the Indian authorities; many became double agents and some simply took the train home.

Bose, however, still planned for a full-scale invasion of India. The Japanese had more limited objectives, centred on a push against Imphal. In the spring of 1944, some 6000 soldiers of the Indian National Army went into action with Japanese troops. Of these 6000, some 600 deserted to the British, 400 were killed, 1500 died from dysentery and malaria, and a further 1400 were invalided out of the war zone. The rest surrendered. Bose, escaping in the last Japanese plane to leave Rangoon, died from burns shortly after the plane crashed.

Source J

The arrival from Europe of a politician of Bose's calibre was enough to generate considerable support amongst the two million Indians in the region. Huge rallies were held in Singapore pledging support and money, with crowds waving 'Liberty or Death' banners. Bose told them he wanted recruits for 'the liberation of India. . . I am confident that with the help of my countrymen in east Asia, I shall be able to organise such a gigantic force as will be able to sweep away the British power from India, in conjunction with those who have already been fighting at home. *Inquilab Zindabad! Azad Hind Zindabad*! [Long Live Revolution! Long Live Free India!]' They would march to the Red Fort in Delhi, he told them, and their war cry would be '*Dilli Chalo*!' [On to Delhi], like the Meerut mutineers of 1857. He gave radio broadcasts in English and Bengali, telling his listeners in Churchillian tones that all he had to offer them was 'hunger, thirst, forced marches and death'.

From Patrick French, *Liberty or Death*, published in 1997

Source K

10.3 Propaganda leaflet aimed at the Indian National Army, employed during the campaign in Burma, 1943–45

SKILLS BUILDER

1 How far does Source K support what Source J says about the activities of Bose?

2 Use your own knowledge and Sources J and K to explain whether, in your view, Bose was a patriot or a traitor.

Enter the Americans

The seaborne threat to India was only removed when the US navy defeated the Japanese at the battle of the Coral Sea at the beginning of May 1942. The lesson was there for the world to see: a shift in power had happened. In future, India's seaborne security could only be guaranteed by the US, not the British, navy.

Early in 1941, before the USA entered the war, President Roosevelt and Prime Minister Churchill met on board the US cruiser *Augusta* in Newfoundland Bay and agreed the Atlantic Charter. This was basically an affirmation that all peoples should enjoy the right of self-determination when the war was over. Indian hopes were raised by what seemed like another commitment to their independence, only to have those hopes dashed when Churchill reassured the House of Commons that this did not, of course apply to 'India, Burma and other parts of the British Empire'. When this was discussed in the Viceroy's Legislative Council, an Indian member, Jammadas Mehta, pointedly reminded the Viceroy that Indians were dying to bring freedom to others when that very same freedom was denied to them. Vinayak Savarkar, President of the All-Hindu *Mahasabha*, appealed directly to Roosevelt, asking him to guarantee India's post-war freedom.

The US government, soon to become the senior partner in the war against Nazi Germany and the Axis powers, viewed the situation in India with some alarm. Roosevelt saw it as essential that India was fully behind the Allied war effort. True, thousands of Indian troops were fighting in the various theatres of war, but it was the situation within India that worried him. India simply could not fall to the Japanese, who had overrun the rest of South-East Asia. Furthermore, Roosevelt was very wary of committing American troops to fighting a war in Asia that could be seen as a last ditch attempt to prop up the British Empire. Americans had not forgotten that they had formed part of the first British Empire, against which they had run a successful revolution in 1776.

Roosevelt began putting what pressure he could on the reluctant Churchill to agree to some form of self-government for India in order to unite the country. This was supported from within the British War Cabinet by Clement Attlee and Leo Amery, who were convinced that India's future safety depended on the creation of a popularly supported national government – not after the war, but immediately. This was not the same as self-government, but they were travelling in the same direction as Roosevelt. Churchill, cornered by colleagues on whom he depended, reluctantly gave in. He appointed the Lord Privy Seal, Sir Stafford Cripps, to lead a delegation to India.

Why did the Cripps Mission fail?

Sir Stafford Cripps and his delegation initially seemed to have everything going for them. He was a Labour Party minister, a friend of Nehru and Gandhi, and personally sympathetic to Indian aspirations. Well-known and well-liked in Congress circles, there was much optimism on the Indian side when he arrived in New Delhi on 23 March 1942. Viceroy Linlithgow, however, was less than impressed, fearing that some sort of settlement would be imposed by the British government over his head.

But the Cripps Mission was doomed. It was doomed because what he had to offer was not what Congress wanted to hear. He came to offer what the British government believed was a bargain:

- after the war, India would be offered full dominion status
- the Indian people would elect an assembly, which would frame a new constitution
- if any province or princely state wanted to disassociate itself from the new India, they were free to go their own way.

And in return, because there are two parts to every bargain, all Indian parties were invited to join in an interim government of national unity under the Viceroy and his Council, which would operate until the end of the war.

Gandhi was furious. 'Why did you come, if this is all you have to offer?' he demanded of Cripps, 'I advise you to take the first plane home.' Congress rejected the first part of the bargain – they were not willing to accept a situation where states were allowed to opt out of a united India. They were, however, willing to join the proposed interim government provided it behaved like the Westminster one, with the Viceroy acting as prime minister and with the defence ministry under the control of an Indian. Churchill and Linlithgow were having none of it. The Raj had to remain in control while the war against Germany continued. Indian opinion was affronted, believing that this was yet another sign that Britain would cling onto India at all costs and would not accept Indians as equal partners. Jinnah, on the other hand, while being ready to accept the Cripps' bargain because of its implication that a separate **Pakistan** would not be a problem, did have to reject it if the Muslim League was to remain part of the constitution-making process.

President Roosevelt was desperate to keep the Cripps Mission in India:

Source L

I hope most earnestly that you may be able to postpone the departure from India of Cripps until one more effort has finally been made to prevent break-down of the negotiations.

The feeling, held here almost universally, is that the deadlock has been due to the British government's unwillingness to concede the right of self-government to the Indians, despite the willingness of the Indians to entrust to the British authorities technical, military and naval defence control. It is impossible for American public opinion to understand why, if there is willingness on the part of the British government to permit the component parts of India to secede after the war from the British Empire, it is unwilling to permit them to enjoy during the war what is tantamount to self-government.

I feel that I am compelled to place before you this issue very frankly. Should the current negotiations be allowed to collapse because of the issues as presented to the people of America and should India subsequently be invaded by Japan, with attendant serious defeats of a military or naval character for our side, it would be hard to over-estimate the prejudicial reaction of American public opinion.

From President Roosevelt's message to the British Prime Minister Winston Churchill on 12 April 1942

Cripps flew home on 11 April. Churchill had won a victory at too great a cost and Roosevelt had been wrong-footed. The Indians would not accept what had seemed to them both to be a perfectly reasonable proposition.

What was the impact of Gandhi's 'Quit India' campaign?

In 1942, Gandhi launched his last great *satyagraha* campaign. On 3 May, he declared: 'I am convinced that the time has come for the British and the Indians to be reconciled to complete separation from each other. There is no common interest left to unite such distant and different nations.' When asked by reporters to whom the British should relinquish their authority, he replied: 'Leave India to God. If that is too much, then leave her to anarchy.' Of the intervention of a deity we have no evidence; of a descent into anarchy, he was so very nearly correct.

Definition

Pakistan

The name Pakistan is an acronym of the names of the states that were to make up the new country: Punjab, Afghan Frontier, Kashmir, Sind and Baluchistan. Put together, the whole word meant 'Land of the Pure'.

Source M

You know the weight which I attach to everything you say to me, but I did not feel I could take responsibility for the defence of India if everything has again to be thrown into the melting pot at this critical juncture.

That I am sure would be the view of Cabinet and of Parliament.

From Winston Churchill's reply to President Roosevelt on 12 April 1942

Questions

1 Why did Roosevelt become involved in the situation in India?
2 Why was Churchill so determined to oppose all moves towards Indian independence?

What did Congress do?

Congress prevaricated. To commit to a *satyagraha* at such a critical time in Britain's struggle against Nazi Germany and the Axis powers seemed, on the one hand, like an act of great folly, even treachery. It would set the Raj against Congress and make any reconciliation after the war (assuming an allied victory, which in the dark days of 1942 seemed fairly unlikely) very difficult indeed. On the other hand, to remain dormant now might give the upper hand to Jinnah or to Bose. Congress had to make its position clear and had to rally its supporters to the cause of *swaraj*.

Finally, on 8 August 1942, Congress officially sanctioned Gandhi's *satyagraha*, his great 'Quit India' campaign.

Source N

The All-Indian Congress Committee would yet again, at this last moment, in the interest of world freedom, renew this appeal to Britain and the United Nations. But the Committee feels that it is no longer justified in holding the nation back from endeavouring to assert its will against an imperialist and authoritarian Government, which dominates over it and prevents it from functioning in its own interest and in the interest of humanity. The Committee resolves, therefore, to sanction for the vindication of India's inalienable right to freedom and independence, the starting of a mass struggle on non-violent lines on the widest possible scale, so that the country might utilise all the non-violent strength it has gathered during the last twenty-two years of peaceful struggle. Such a struggle must inevitably be under the leadership of Gandhi and the Committee requests him to take the lead and guide the nation in the steps to be taken.

From the 'Quit India' demand, in a resolution of the All-Indian Congress Committee on 8 August 1942

Question

What, in the context of the Second World War, were the risks involved in starting the 'Quit India' campaign?

'Quit India' was the shout that greeted every English man, woman and child as they went about their daily lives in India. 'Quit India' was shouted at the troops who were desperately trying to defend India's frontiers against the Japanese. Correctly guessing that the response of the Raj would be repression, Congress leaders, before they could be imprisoned and silenced, called on their supporters to make India ungovernable.

Congress versus Raj

Congress had spent three months arguing as to whether the Congress Party should, or should not, support Gandhi's 'Quit India' *satyagraha* and the Raj had plenty of time to prepare contingency plans. On 9 August, the day after Congress officially sanctioned the campaign, Gandhi, Nehru and most of the Congress Party's leaders were arrested and interned. Within the next fortnight, thousands of local activists were rounded up and imprisoned. Offices were raided, files taken and funds frozen.

Gandhi, anticipating that this would happen and realising that it would thus be impossible to organise the *satyagraha* from above, told his followers to 'Go out to die, not to live', urging every demonstrator to become their own leader. So began a horrific round of riots, killings, attacks on Europeans, and damage to, and destruction of, government property. There were the usual targets: revenue offices and police stations, but, alarmingly in time of war and with India daily expecting an invasion from the Japanese troops massing on its borders, stations and signal boxes were wrecked, railway tracks were torn up, and telegraph and telephone lines were pulled down. Over 1000 deaths and over 3000 serious injuries were directly attributed to the 'Quit India' campaign.

The Raj did not stand idly by. The threat to the transport of troops and war supplies was so great that on 14 August the RAF began flying sorties against the crowds threatening railway lines in the United Provinces and Bihar. They were ordered first to drop flares and, if that didn't disperse the crowds, machine-gun them. During one of the sorties, a plane crash-landed and two of its crew were murdered. Thirty-five thousand British troops were made available to support the police. Some were rushed between trouble spots; others guarded lines of communication, munitions stores and public buildings.

The authorities reckoned that they had about six weeks to get India under control before the monsoons stopped and a Japanese invasion could be expected from the east and a German one from the west and north-west.

Viceroy Linlithgow wrote to Prime Minister Churchill on 31 August: 'I am engaged here in meeting by far the most serious rebellion since that of 1857, the gravity and extent of which we have so far concealed from the world for reasons of military security. Mob violence remains rampant over large tracts of the countryside. I am by no means confident that we may not see in September a formidable effort to renew this widespread sabotage of our war effort.'

Churchill, always an opponent of Congress, made his position clear to MPs in the House of Commons: 'We mean to hold our own. I have not become the King's first minister in order to preside over the liquidation of the British Empire.'

Linlithgow may have been a little over-dramatic in comparing the situation to the Indian Mutiny. In 1942, British Intelligence knew what was likely to happen and had forces waiting to be deployed. Raids on Congress branch offices yielded more information about the positioning of local disturbances. Undercover CID agents and informers had penetrated most of Congress' networks and, as a result, Congress' room for manoeuvre was severely limited. In 1857, the Mutiny came as a terrible shock. The 'Quit India' campaign may have come as a shock, but the Raj was more than ready. Even so, there were brief losses of control everywhere.

At Chinur, in Bengal, on 14 August, a crowd assembled to attack a police station even though the ring leaders had been arrested a couple of days

Questions

Was the 'Quit India' campaign Gandhi's great mistake? Think about the expectations and outcomes of the campaign. What did Gandhi anticipate would happen? How realistic was this expectation? What were the intended outcomes of the campaign? What were the unexpected outcomes?

earlier. The local police inspector was murdered and two magistrates burned alive. Order was restored by 20 August by soldiers from the Green Howards. Afterwards, they were accused of murder and rape. At Sasaram, in Bihar, the railway line from Lucknow to Calcutta was attacked by a body of school children, university students and criminals. Local Hindu policemen refused to intervene because they were heavily outnumbered and order was only restored when a battalion of the Bedfordshire Regiment arrived on the scene. At Ballia, in Uttar Pradesh, the outnumbered magistrate burned banknotes worth 400,000 rupees to stop them falling into the hands of the mob. Later, charred and burned notes were found to be in circulation. At Madhuban, in the United Provinces, local policemen barricaded themselves inside the police station. Ranged against them were 4000 angry villagers armed with spears, saws, spades and two elephants. The standoff lasted two hours and ended with the rebels running away. The defenders had fired 119 rounds and killed 40–50 villagers; there were no police casualties.

By November 1942, the worst of the attacks were over. What, if anything, had been achieved? Congress analysts showed that the 'Quit India' *satyagraha* had failed to paralyse the government, even in militant Hindu areas like Bihar. The reason they gave was that the military had remained loyal to the Raj. Even among Indian regiments, only 216 soldiers had gone absent without leave. The campaign had not attracted support throughout India in terms of geography, religion or caste and non-cooperation had brought detention, despair and death.

How did the Muslim League handle the war?

Back in 1940 (see page 153), Jinnah and the Muslim League had come out conclusively in favour of a separation of Hindu and Muslim after the war, as expressed in the Lahore Declaration. Whether this was to be as a state within India or as a separate country altogether remained unclear then. But since then the Muslim League's commitment to separateness had been openly stated and the proposed Muslim state had been given a name – Pakistan.

Throughout the war years, Jinnah proved to be a much cleverer operator than either Gandhi or Nehru. He showed himself and the Muslim League to be prepared to co-operate with, and even support, the Raj, but without making any firm commitments. In doing so, he pointed up the contrast between the League and Congress, providing the Raj with ample reasons to prefer to negotiate with the League.

The August Offer

In May 1940, Linlithgow invited Jinnah to Simla, with the aim of discussing with him a whole range of issues relating to India and the war. Two months later, Jinnah submitted a list of tentative proposals to Linlithgow, which were welcomed. Linlithgow made these proposals the basis of his 1940 August Offer:

- 'representative' Indians would join his Executive Council
- a War Advisory Council would be established, which would include the princes and 'other interests in the national life of India as a whole'
- an assurance that the government would not adopt any new constitution without the prior approval of Muslim India.

The Viceroy accompanied this offer with a statement that seemed to place the Muslim League at the centre of any decision-making about the future of India: 'It goes without saying that His Majesty's Government could not contemplate transfer of their present responsibilities for the peace and welfare of India to any system of government whose authority is directly denied by large and powerful elements in India's national life.' The message was clear. The wishes and needs of the Muslim community would have to be taken into account in any post-war settlement. It was obvious that the vital role played by Muslims in the Indian army at home and abroad greatly strengthened Jinnah's hand, particularly when compared to what was perceived by the British government as the obstructive attitude of Congress. The Secretary of State for India, L.S. Amery, complained to the House of Commons, 'If only Congress could, in fact, speak for all main elements in India's national life then, however advanced their demands, our problem would have been in many respects far easier.' Here, indeed, was recognition of the fact that Congress did not speak for the whole of India and an understanding that the millions of Muslims had to have their interests safeguarded. The huge problem that remained for the British was not so much whether power should be transferred, but to whom?

Unit summary

What have you learned in this unit?

You have learned that the Second World War was in many ways a watershed. Before the war there was the possibility, however faint, that Hindus and Muslims could work out some sort of rapprochement. Afterwards, that possibility had gone.

During the war, Congress had shown that it still had control and influence over millions of Indians and that these Indians had irrefutably demonstrated that the Raj no longer had the consent of its Congress-supporting Indian subjects and should go. The Muslim League had greatly strengthened its position, gaining tacit agreement from Britain that some sort of separateness for the Muslim community was possible, inevitable and even desirable. The Raj, in turn, had demonstrated that it could hold India by force if necessary and that it was more resilient than any had thought possible.

What skills have you used in this unit?

You have worked with a range of source material to explore the impact of the war on India and in particular on Congress and the Muslim League.

This evaluation has led you to an understanding of the motives underpinning the actions of Gandhi, Nehru and Congress, as well as Jinnah and the Muslim League. You have considered whether the actions of Subhas Bose were traitorous or not, and you have assessed whether Gandhi's 'Quit India' campaign helped or hindered Congress' cause. Perhaps most importantly, you have begun to consider the ways in which the possibility of a separate Muslim state was emerging in the thinking of Congress, the Muslim League and the Raj.

Exam tips

This is the sort of question you will find appearing on the exam paper as an (a) question.

- Study Sources D, E and F. How far do the sources support the view that Congress and the Muslim League were working toward a separate state for Muslims?

You have tackled (a) questions at the end of Units 2 and 5. Now let's develop what you learned there about approaches to the (a) question.

- What is the question asking you to do? It is asking how far the sources support a view.
- What is the view?
- Consider the sources carefully and make inferences and deductions from them rather than using them as sources of information. You might put these in three columns, one for each source.
- Cross-reference points of evidence from the three sources by drawing actual links between evidence in the three columns. This will enable you to make comparisons point by point and so use the sources as a set.
- Evaluate the evidence, assessing its quality and reliability in terms of how much weight it will bear and how secure the conclusions are that can be drawn from it.
- Reach a judgement about how far the sources can be said to support the given view.

RESEARCH TOPIC

You read something about the interest the USA took in the Cripps Mission (see pages 157–59). Explore further the attitudes the USA had towards the British Empire in general and India in particular.

1   What attitudes did the US President, Congress and public opinion express towards the Empire and India in the years from 1939 to 1945?

2   Why did the USA find the continued existence of the British Empire troublesome?

UNIT 11 The end of the Raj: dreams and nightmares

What is this unit about?

In October 1943, Field Marshal Wavell was appointed Viceroy of India and remained in the post until he was replaced in March 1947. During this time, Wavell tried to pave the way for independence and the British government, by sending out the Cabinet Mission (see pages 174–76), made one final attempt to resolve India's constitutional problems. They failed. In the end, Wavell was recalled and replaced as Viceroy by Lord Louis Mountbatten of Burma, great-grandson of Queen Victoria and close friend of the British Royal family, whose charm offensive was supposed to smooth the way to a peaceful handover of power. It didn't work. The Raj's withdrawal from India after imposing Partition resulted in terrifying rioting, mass destruction of property and the uncontrollable bloodletting and murder of thousands upon thousands of Hindus, Muslims and Sikhs.

Key questions

- Why, after the Second World War, did Britain need to lose its Indian Empire?
- Why did independence for the Indian sub-continent involve Partition?
- Who was to blame for the terrible violence that accompanied Partition: Jinnah, Gandhi, Nehru or Mountbatten?

Timeline

1943	June	Field Marshal Wavell appointed Viceroy of India
	August	Bengal famine begins
1945	May	VE day marks the end of war in Europe
	June	Simla Conference to consider Wavell's proposals to advance India towards self-government
	July	Simla Conference fails
		Labour government comes to power in the UK
	August	Japan surrenders
	November	Trial of Indian National Army officers begins in Delhi
1946	Winter	Indian general elections
	March	Cabinet Mission arrives in India
	May	Second Simla Conference results in conditional agreement between Congress, Muslim League and the British government
	July	Muslim League denounces Congress and declares Direct Action Day

	August	Muslim League's Direct Action Day resulting in the Calcutta killings
	September	Congress forms an interim government with Nehru as prime minister
		Muslim League joins interim government
1947	**January**	Wavell removed as Viceroy and Admiral Viscount Lord Louis Mountbatten agrees to take over
	February	British Prime Minister Attlee announces Indian independence no later than June 1948
	March	Mountbatten arrives in Delhi
	June	Final plan for Partition of India accepted by Congress, Muslim League and Sikhs
		Boundary Commission arrives in India
		Bengal Legislative Assembly opts for Partition of Bengal
		Punjab Legislative Assembly opts for Partition of Punjab
	July	Indian Independent Act, setting up two independent dominions of India and Pakistan receives royal assent
		Mass carnage begins
	August	Jinnah sworn in as Governor-General of Pakistan
		Mountbatten sworn in as Governor-General of India
		Liaquat Ali Khan becomes Prime Minister of Pakistan
		Nehru becomes Prime Minister of India

Enter Viceroy Archibald Wavell

In October 1943, General **Archibald Wavell** was appointed Viceroy of India. He was a soldier. Defeated by the German Field Marshal Rommel in North Africa and replaced there by Field Marshal Sir Claude Auchinleck, he was in command in the South-West Pacific and Commander-in-Chief of India when Malaya, Singapore and Burma fell to the Japanese. So why was he chosen by Churchill to be Viceroy of India? The appointment could be seen as an appropriate sideways move for an able man who was in command against impossible odds and who was, quite simply, the wrong person in the wrong place at the wrong time. Or it could be seen it as an indication of Churchill's lack of understanding that a person with political and negotiating skills was needed – not a military man who could, presumably, be controlled from Whitehall. But in Wavell, Churchill was to get more than he had bargained for.

Biography

Archibald Wavell (1883–1950)

Wavell served in the Boer War and both world wars as a soldier and administrator. After his 1941 counter-offensive in North Africa failed, he exchanged posts with Auchinleck to become Commander-in-Chief of India. Following the fall of Malaya and Burma to the Japanese, Wavell's main objective was to maintain India's boundaries to prevent a Japanese invasion from the east and an Axis one from the west. He succeeded.

It was made clear to him, on being made Viceroy of India in 1943, that his role was to hold the line: to keep India within the Empire as a bulwark against the Japanese until the war ended and some kind of settlement could be reached with the Indians regarding their independence.

As Viceroy, he is best remembered for the measures he took to relieve the terrible famine in Bengal in 1943 and for the Simla Conference of June 1945, where he tried to bring about a rapprochement between Congress and the Muslim League, but failed. He hated the idea of Partition, but came to regard it as inevitable.

Wavell worked hard to prepare the ground for independence and, ultimately, for Partition. He was relieved of his post in March 1947 and replaced by Lord Mountbatten, who oversaw the final months of the Raj and Indian independence.

Source A

11.1 Cartoon, commenting on Wavell as Viceroy in India, published in the *Daily Mail* 2 September 1946

SKILLS BUILDER

What point is the cartoonist making about Wavell's arrival in India as Viceroy?

Wavell as Viceroy: first moves

Wavell started his time in office by touring the sub-continent on a fact-finding mission, travelling as many as 1500kms a week by plane and train, jeep and car. He focused particularly on the troubled areas: the Punjab, Bengal and the United Provinces, trying to allay fears, settle disputes and boost morale.

Meetings of governors

One of Wavell's first moves was to reinstate regular meetings of the 11 governors of the provinces of British India. During his seven years as Viceroy, Linlithgow had not called a single such meeting. Wavell's action enabled the Indian government to present the British government with coherent advice and a unified point of view. It also made it much more difficult for the British government to dismiss the views of provincial governors out of hand. But this was easy compared to the disaster that overcame Bengal, which was to become one of the greatest tests of Wavell's leadership of the Raj.

The Bengal famine, 1943–44

The Bengal famine was caused by a multiplicity of factors: a run of poor harvests and distribution failures, loss of imports, wartime price inflation and severe weather conditions. The crop yield in 1943 was the worst that century and the recorded annual death rate rose from an average of 1.2 million to 1.9 million. Men, women and children were dying from smallpox, malaria, cholera, pneumonia and the diseases associated with malnutrition. The starving were crowding into Calcutta in their thousands in desperate hope of finding relief, begging and dying in the streets. Fear of a Japanese invasion encouraged hoarding by those who could afford to buy and there was fear, too, that the famine would work as a recruiting agent for the Indian National Army. By May 1943, the price of rice had risen tenfold and Wavell took immediate action to co-ordinate rationing and to try to stop profiteering, diverting troops from the war effort to do so. Churchill originally refused to divert British merchant shipping in order to take grain to starving Bengal and Roosevelt, when asked to loan American ships to bring in wheat from Australia, refused. Both leaders were afraid of damaging their own war effort.

Source B

Wavell began a running battle with London, trying to buy more grain for India. Churchill was not inclined to be helpful, since he followed the advice of his crony, Lord Cherwell, who claimed that the Bengal famine was a statistical invention. Cherwell, an established bigot, who apparently felt 'physical repulsion' when non-whites were in his presence, took the line that the famine was a figment of the Bengali imagination, and could be solved by better food distribution. Wavell thought of him as an 'old fraud and menace'. The Viceroy's request for the guarantee of a million tons of grain during the course of 1944 was answered with an offer of a quarter of that amount, and a reciprocal demand from London for Indian rice. Before long, Wavell was writing, 'I expect the PM is regretting that he ever appointed me', but by late June 1944 he had extracted 450,000 tons from the War Cabinet.

From Patrick French, *Liberty or Death*, published in 1997

It has been estimated that between one and three million people died in the three years of the Bengal famine and in some areas whole villages were wiped out. Jinnah accused the British government of incompetence and irresponsibility, pointing out that Churchill's government wouldn't have lasted five minutes if people had been dying of starvation in the streets of London as they were on the streets of Calcutta. Congress blamed the crisis on the diversion of foodstuffs to British troops. Both Congress and the Muslim League made political capital out of the crisis. Wavell spoke his mind to Leo Amery, the Secretary of State for India:

Source C

Bengal famine was one of the greatest disasters that has fallen any people under British rule and damage to our reputation here is incalculable. Attempt by His Majesty's government to prove on the basis of defective statistics that we can do without help demanded would be regarded here by all opinion British and Indian as utterly indefensible. They must either trust the opinion of the man they appointed to advise them on Indian affairs or replace him.

From a telegram written by A. Wavell to L. Amery in February 1944

Source D

At a time when Indian opinion was already incensed at being plunged into a British war without any consultation, the Bengal famine seemed to offer gruesome evidence that the Raj regarded the Indians as mere fodder for its military machine; and Indian loyalty to the Empire reached its lowest ebb at the very moment when Britain most desperately required it. Many relatively non-political Indians remember tuning in enthusiastically to Japanese and German wartime broadcasts and rejoicing over British defeats.

From Zareer Masani, *Indian Tales of the Raj*, published in 1987

Why was the British government ready to grant Indian independence after the war ended in 1945?

The ending of hostilities in 1945 saw Britain in an apparently contradictory situation. Outwardly, there was the image of a victorious nation. Unlike continental Europe, Britain had not been invaded; Britain was one of the 'Big-Three' who had won the war and who would dominate peacetime reconstruction. Reality, however, was somewhat different.

Changing economics

Britain was facing a desperate economic situation. Britain's industries, geared up to war-time production, had to wind down and change direction to meet the demands of peace-time. Furthermore, six years of war had drained Britain's financial reserves. War-time debts had run at £70 million per day towards the end, and by 1945 Britain owed £2730 million. On top of this, an enormous programme of reconstruction had to be undertaken, ranging from reforming the health and education services to rebuilding bombed and damaged ports, offices, factories and homes. Could maintaining an empire in India be afforded? Was maintaining an empire in India desirable?

> ## SKILLS BUILDER
>
> Read Sources B, C and D.
>
> 1 What impact did the Bengal Famine have on Indian politics?
>
> 2 Which source would you trust to give you the most reliable information about the Bengal Famine?

There were many reasons why India was ceasing to be important to Britain and many of the economic arguments for maintaining the Raj no longer held good:

- British investment in India had fallen during the 1930s. Indian capitalists were taking the lead in investing in their country, often in partnership with British investors.
- India was importing less and less from Britain. In the years 1928–29, Indians spent £83 million on imported British goods. In the years 1935–36, this had fallen to £39 million. In order to help Indian manufacturers develop their own markets, Indian governments had put increasingly high tariffs on imported goods. Indians found that, for example, home produced cotton goods were cheaper than imported Lancashire cotton ones. Lancashire cotton exports to India collapsed.
- Japanese competition further squeezed British goods out of the Indian market. This was because the cost of production in Japan was less than in Britain and so, even given the high import duties, Japanese goods were selling in India more cheaply than British ones.
- The USA was also exporting goods to India, further squeezing out the British exporters. In 1929, India imported 2887 buses, lorries and cars from Britain. This rose to 7726 by 1936. However, at the same time, India imported more from the USA: 6352 in 1929 and more than 12,000 in 1936.
- In 1931 the Reserve Bank of India had been established. This meant that India could set the value of its own currency without reference to sterling. The rupee was no longer tied to the value of sterling in the world's money markets.
- From 1933, Britain paid £1.5 million a year towards the running costs of the Indian army and in 1939 the British government agreed to pay for an army modernisation programme.
- Indian troops had been mobilised in the war against Japan, in North Africa and in Italy, and Britain had shouldered most of the costs. This meant that the Indian government had built up enormous savings and, by 1945, had a sterling balance in the Reserve Bank of India of £1300 million. And this was all because the Indian government had not had to meet the cost of their troops abroad.

Shifting loyalties

The old argument that Britain needed India as a bulwark of British power in Asia no longer carried much weight at a time when Indian politicians were protesting against the deployment of Indian forces in Indonesia and Indo-China. The politicians regarded it as unacceptable that 'their' forces were being used to, in their estimation, prop up decaying French and Dutch empires at a time when they were trying to free themselves from the grip of the Raj.

Two and a half million Indian men and women had joined the armed forces and by 1945, there were 15,740 Indian officers. But not all of them were loyal to the Raj. Rather, they were loyal to their concept of 'India' as Commander-in-Chief Auchinleck recognised: 'It is no use shutting one's eyes to the fact that any Indian soldier worth his salt is a Nationalist, though that does not make him anti-British.'

The Indian Civil Service, too, had undergone a sea change. Originally (see pages 39–42) the province of the British, by 1945, it was severely undermanned because of the need for able-bodied men to work in the armed forces and ancillary services. But even so, there were 429 British and 510 Indian Indian Civil Service officers remaining in India.

So it would seem that, by 1945, neither India nor the British had much need for each other in an imperial context. How, then, were they to extricate themselves from a situation in which they had once been mutually dependent?

Political manoeuvrings

The ending of the Second World War and the prospects of elections in both Britain and India created a political situation that was temporarily unstable and one in which political manoeuvrings by the main players became evident as they prioritised their various agendas and prepared for the transfer of power from the Raj to India.

The Simla Conference, 1945

In the spring of 1945, Viceroy Wavell travelled to London for a series of lengthy meetings with the British coalition government. The British Cabinet was ready, for two main reasons, to make a fresh attempt at an Indian settlement. Britain was millions of pounds in debt to India for goods and services borrowed to help win the war and this, combined with terrorist activity and unrest in India, convinced Wavell and Secretary of State Amery that another attempt at a constitutional settlement had to be made. Wavell returned to Delhi with a new scheme, loosely modelled on that of Sir Stafford Cripps (see pages 158–59). The major change Wavell was to propose concerned the composition of his Executive Council. This was to be chosen in a way that would give 'a balanced representation' of the main communities.

Source E

During the recent visit of Field-Marshal Viscount Wavell to this country, His Majesty's government reviewed with him a number of problems and discussed particularly the present political situation in India.

His Majesty's government are most anxious to make any contribution that is practicable to the breaking of the political deadlock in India. While that deadlock lasts, not only political but social and economic progress is being hampered.

It is proposed that the Executive Council should be reconstituted and that the Viceroy should in future make his selection for nomination to the Crown for appointment to his Executive from amongst leaders of Indian political life at the Centre and in the Provinces, in proportions which would give a balanced representation of the main communities, including equal proportions of Muslims and Caste Hindus.

The members of the Executive would be Indians with the exception of the Viceroy and the Commander-in-Chief, who would retain his position as War Member. This is essential so long as the defence of India remains a British responsibility.

From *India, Statement of Policy of HMG*, cmd publication 6652, published in 1945

From the outset, it seemed unlikely that Congress would be happy with this arrangement. Parity with Muslims would, in their view, inflate the importance of the Muslim constituency in India and the phrase 'Caste Hindu' implied that Untouchables were not Hindus.

Notwithstanding, a conference of Indian political leaders was held at Simla on 25 June 1945 to discuss the proposals. Congress leaders were released from prison so that they could attend and all in all some 21 Indian political leaders travelled to Simla, including Gandhi, Jinnah, Nehru – and Azad, the Muslim President of Congress, sneered at by Jinnah as a 'show case Muslim'. As could have been anticipated, the conference reached deadlock on the issue of how Muslim members of the newly reconstituted Executive Council were to be chosen. Jinnah insisted that they must all be nominated by the Muslim League; Congress could not accept such a restriction, maintaining that as it was an inclusive party, Muslims should be able to represent Congress as well as the Muslim League.

On 14 July, Wavell adjourned the conference, deadlock between Congress and the Muslim League not having been broken.

Source F

Jinnah flatly refused to co-operate unless he received a categorical assurance that all the Muslim Members would be drawn from the League and that, once the Council was formed, decisions to which the Muslims objected would be made only on a vote of a specified majority – say, two-thirds. I could not accept either of these conditions. The right of communal veto, if granted to the Muslims would also have to be granted to the Hindus, and the Sikhs and the Scheduled Caste members. The working of Council would become impossible.

Now that Jinnah had rejected a move within the present Constitution based on parity, it is not clear what he would be prepared to accept short of Pakistan. Gandhi's final comment to me was that His Majesty's Government would have to decide sooner or later whether to come down on the side of Hindu or Muslim, of Congress or League, since they could never reconcile them. A discouraging comment, but true under present leadership.

From a letter written by Viceroy Wavell to Secretary of State, Leo Amery on 15 July 1945

Source G

Wavell's quest for an interim government of national unity ended in tears at Simla at the beginning of July. From start to finish, Jinnah had been unbending in his insistence that all the fifteen Muslims on the new Council should be nominees of the League. His intransigence was part of a calculated political manoeuvre designed to exclude from power the League's rival, the Muslim Unionist Party, which controlled the provincial government of the Punjab. The League desperately needed the Punjab for without it Pakistan would be a house of straw. This explains why, when Wavell made his last appeal to Jinnah, he found him in 'a high state of nervous tension'. 'I am at the end of my tether,' he told the Viceroy, and appealed to him 'not to wreck the League'. Wavell did not budge and again rejected Jinnah's demands; the League had wrecked the chances of a ministry which offered some hope of national cohesion in what would turn out to be a period of unprecedented trauma in India's history.

From Lawrence James, *Raj: the Making and Unmaking of British India*, published in 1997

SKILLS BUILDER

Work in threes. Each person selects either (a) the Raj, (b) Congress or (c) the Muslim League.

1 Using Sources E, F and G, and the information in this section, tease out the arguments that would have been presented by each group at Simla.

2 Whose arguments are the most convincing?

The British general election

On 26 July 1945, the results of the British general election were announced: the Labour Party had swept into power with a 12 per cent swing and 393 seats in the Commons as against the Conservative Party's 213. Nehru was jubilant at Labour's victory. He had always felt ideologically closer to Clement Attlee, the Labour Party leader, than he had to the Conservatives. Just as there were new beginnings for Britain, there might, too, be radical changes for India.

Source H

At the end of July 1945, Labour won a landslide victory in Britain. Wavell was cautiously optimistic: 'I think Labour is likely to take more interest in and be more sympathetic towards India, but they will have some weird ideas about it.' In fact, the ideas of Clement Attlee were close to Wavell's. Britain would disengage from India after having agreed a political settlement, which would transform the country into a friendly partner within the Commonwealth. The undertaking was known by an official euphemism as the 'transfer of power', which suggested a smooth passage of authority from donor to recipient. Nothing was further from the truth: the 1942 Quit India movement and Jinnah's haggling at Simla were the opening rounds in a scramble for power. Indians now sensed as never before that the days of the Raj were numbered; as a Congress politician remarked to Wavell, 'No one worships the setting sun.'

From Lawrence James, *Raj: the Making and Unmaking of British India*, published in 1997

The Labour–Congress axis

Congress had, throughout the twentieth century, forged links with the British Labour Party and with individual Labour MPs. It relied on the Labour Party to give voice to the opinions of Congress in the British press and the House of Commons, and it relied on personal friendships to enable this to happen.

Perhaps the most important friendship was that between Stafford Cripps and Jawaharlal Nehru. Both men were highly educated, highly intellectual and dedicated to the radical reform of their respective countries. They gathered around themselves like-minded politicians who worked well together because of their shared ideals. One such man was Khrishna Menon, a London-based Socialist who did much to create and maintain

Labour–Congress links and who, at the same time, was a strong advocate of Nehru as India's future leader.

This rapport between Congress and the Labour Party obviously made some things easier, but it created difficulties, too. The Muslim League had no such relationship with any British political party and, within the ranks of their leadership, there grew the strong suspicion that Labour was anti-Muslim. As events progressed, mutual suspicion took hold.

Indian elections

The new British Cabinet's India Committee, dominated by Stafford Cripps, decided to recommend that elections should be held throughout India to allow people to choose their own representatives to a constituent assembly. This would give a clear indication as to Indian opinion and pave the way for negotiations about a final political settlement.

The elections of 1945–46 gave Jinnah the mandate he had been looking for: the Muslim League won all 30 of the seats reserved in the Central Assembly for Muslims. Congress won 90 per cent of the general electorate seats. The 15 remaining seats were divided among Sikhs, Europeans and independents. This pattern was reproduced in the provinces. Congress retained control of Bombay, Madras, the North-West Frontier Province, Orissa and the United and Central Provinces. The League held Bengal and the Sind and, although it gained 79 out of the 175 seats in the Punjab, was kept out of power there by a combination of Sikhs, Hindus and the Muslim Unionist Alliance.

All this was carried out against a background of street violence, murder and mayhem. Indian National Army members (see page 156) were being court-martialled in Delhi's Red Fort; seven million Indians were being demobbed from the armed services and were looking for work in industries that were laying off workers as they returned to peacetime production levels; drought threatened to produce famine in southern India; and some sailors and their officers in the Indian Navy mutinied.

The Cabinet Mission

It was into this maelstrom that Attlee sent his three-man Cabinet Mission to try to resolve India's constitutional problems.

What were the Cabinet Mission's proposals?

The 'three wise men' – Lord Pethick-Lawrence, a peer with Liberal views; Stafford Cripps, now president of the Board of Trade; and A.V. Alexander, First Lord of the Admiralty and a Co-operative Movement sponsored MP – arrived in India on 24 March 1946. Attlee had insisted that the Mission did everything possible to maintain a united India – a united India that could play a key role in Britain's plans for security in Asia. This would seem to rule out a separate Pakistan, but did not preclude the existence, within Hindu-dominated India, of separate Muslim-dominated states.

The three men stayed in India for more than three months, determined to break the deadlock between Congress and the Muslim League. And they so nearly succeeded.

A second Simla Conference was held in early May, to which Congress and the League were each invited to send four representatives. The purpose of the Conference was to work through the Cabinet Mission's proposals. These, basically, provided for a three-tier federal structure within a united India. Partition was not acceptable. This is what was proposed:

- an All-India Union, responsible for defence, foreign policy and internal communication, together with powers to raise finances to fund these three elements
- the All-India Union would be governed by an executive and legislature
- there would be three clusters of provincial governments:
  o Congress' Hindu heartland of Madras, Bombay, Orissa and the United and Central Provinces
  o the Muslim and predominantly Muslim areas of Baluchistan, the North-West Frontier Province, Sind and Punjab
  o Bengal and Assam, where the balance of religions was slightly in favour of the Muslims
- each provincial group would elect its own government to be responsible for the day-to-day running of provincial affairs
- the All-India Union would comprise elected representatives from each provincial group.

This did seem to be the last best hope of a peaceful transfer of power.

Were the Cabinet Mission's proposals acceptable?

After a great deal of debate and prevarication, both the Muslim League and Congress accepted the Cabinet Mission's proposals. The League stated that they were acceptable because the basis of Pakistan was inherent in the Mission's proposals. Congress, convinced by its Muslim president, Azad, that the proposals were in Congress' best interests, voted on 6 July to accept them, but promptly removed Azad from his position, voting in the Hindu, Jawaharlal Nehru, in his place. Then Nehru scored an own goal. Or did he?

Snatching defeat from the jaws of victory

A few days after Congress' acceptance of the Cabinet Mission's proposals, Jawaharlal Nehru held a press conference. Flushed with victory and trying to woo the left wing of his party, he promised that once Congress controlled the All-India Union, it would act as it pleased. He predicted that the provincial groupings would fall apart because they were not liked by large numbers of Hindus and basically were only supported by the Muslim League. The impact of this collapse of the Cabinet Mission's proposed groupings would be that India would become, in effect, a Hindu Raj.

The whole concept of Pakistan, Nehru insisted, would wither and die in the face of political reality. Alarmingly, this was an interpretation that Cripps declined to rule out.

Jinnah was horrified. His worst nightmare was coming true. He said that Nehru's comments were 'a complete repudiation of the basic form upon which the long-term scheme rests and all of its fundamentals'. Jinnah felt betrayed by Nehru and Congress – and betrayed by the Cabinet Mission, too, which had flown home, leaving him to deal with the collapse of what they had so carefully built up. Jinnah convened his council of the Muslim League in Bombay on 27 July 1946 and, denouncing the bad faith of both Congress and the Raj, repudiated the agreement with the Cabinet Mission. Two days later, he called upon Muslim India to prepare for 'direct action'. 'Direct Action Day' was to be 16 August 1946.

Source I

Whereas Muslim India has exhausted without success all efforts to find a peaceful solution of the Indian problem by compromise and constitutional means; and whereas the Congress is bent upon setting up Caste-Hindu Raj in India with the connivance of the British; and whereas it has become abundantly clear that the Muslims of India would not rest contented with anything less than the immediate establishment of an independent and fully sovereign state of Pakistan; the Council of the All-Indian Muslim League is convinced that now the time has come for the Muslim nation to resort to direct action to achieve Pakistan, to assert their just rights, to vindicate their honour and to get rid of the present British slavery and the contemplated future Caste-Hindu domination.

From the Muslim League's call for direct action, 29 July 1946

Source J

So the Muslim League has run out, thanks to the Mission living in the pocket of Congress while out here, the dishonesty of Cripps, my stupidity and weakness in not spotting his dishonesty earlier and standing up to it, and the irresponsibility of Nehru in making the statements he has since the Mission left.

From Viceroy Wavell's journal entry on 29 July 1946
)

SKILLS BUILDER

Read Sources H, I and J, and use your own knowledge. How far, in your view, was Lawrence James correct when he said that, after 1945, a 'scramble for power' would begin in India?

What were the effects of direct action?

It wasn't just Muslim India that was preparing for 'direct action', it was the Raj, too. Commander-in-Chief Auchinleck, having made discreet enquiries among his Indian officers, found them to be loyal to their own concept of 'India', but he privately warned Viceroy Wavell that he could not envisage Hindu firing at Hindu and Muslim shooting Muslim in any ensuing conflict.

Wavell had his provincial governors to worry about, too. Congress effectively controlled three-quarters of India. With the days of the Raj numbered, police loyalty would be swayed towards those who would inherit power and control. Wavell could not be sure he could contain the gathering storm.

16 August 1946

Source K

Never have we in the whole history of the League done anything except by constitutional methods and by constitutionalism. But now we bid goodbye to constitutional methods. Throughout the negotiations, the parties with whom we bargained held a pistol at us, one with power and machine guns behind it, and the other with non-cooperation and the threat to launch mass civil disobedience. We also have a pistol. We have exhausted all reason. There is no tribunal to which we can go. The only tribunal is the Muslim nation.

From a statement made by Jinnah on 29 July 1946, after the Muslim League's call for direct action

With these chilling words, Jinnah took India's Muslims into the horror and bloodletting of civil war. In Calcutta, the police were ordered by the Muslim League to take a special holiday and the streets were given over to the mob. Within 72 hours, more than 5000 lay dead, at least 20,000 were seriously injured and 100,000 residents were homeless. Muslim and Hindu murdered each other in an orgy of killings and bloodletting, looting and arson that spread across India.

Wavell's appeals to Congress and the Muslim League to call a halt to the killings fell on deaf ears. Growing increasingly irritated by Gandhi, whom he had come to regard as a malevolent manipulator, Wavell was genuinely appalled when Gandhi remarked that if India wanted a blood bath, she could have it. In similar tone, Jinnah had assured him that Pakistan was worth the sacrifice of ten million Muslims.

Question

Do you agree with Jinnah, in Source K, that he had no alternative but to 'bid goodbye to constitutional methods'?

Forming a government and losing a Viceroy

It was against this background of uncontrollable violence that Nehru was sworn in as prime minister of an interim government. Wavell finally managed to persuade a reluctant Jinnah to join the government. He did so only because he believed that the presence of five League members would be as good a means as any to pursue the goal of an independent Pakistan.

Wavell was worn out. He was himself having severe doubts about his ability to cope with the increasing strains that 1947 would bring as India moved closer to independence. It gradually became clear to Cripps and Attlee, partly because of Congress' wire-pulling behind the scenes and partly through their own dealings with Wavell, that a man with fresh ideas was needed to complete India's independence. Attlee wrote to Wavell on 31 January 1947, removing him from his post and offering him an earldom in recognition of his services to the Raj. Earlier, in the first week of January, Admiral Viscount **Louis Mountbatten of Burma**, had agreed to become India's last and, as it turned out, most controversial, Viceroy.

In the middle of February 1947, Attlee announced to the House of Commons that His Majesty's government had resolved to transfer power 'to 'responsible Indian hands' no later than 30 June 1948. By 'responsible hands', Attlee meant an Indian government that was capable of maintaining the peace. How was that to be managed? The race was on.

Lord Louis Mountbatten of Burma (1900–79)

A great-grandson of Queen Victoria and a close friend to the British royal family, Mountbatten was renowned for his charm, self-confidence, ambition and conceit.

Mountbatten had a spectacular career in the navy and in London society. In August 1943, he was made Supreme Allied Commander for South-East Asia and led the campaign to rid Burma and Malaya of the Japanese.

Known for his sympathies towards nationalist movements and for his slightly left-of-centre approach to politics, Mountbatten became Viceroy of India in 1947, charged with overseeing the transfer of power from the Raj to a responsible Indian government. The resultant Partition of the Indian sub-continent into India and Pakistan was accompanied by a horrendous bloodbath.

In 1949, Mountbatten resumed his naval career and was First Sea Lord at the Admiralty at the time of the Suez crisis (1956), over which he clashed dramatically with the Eden government. He was Chief of the Defence Staff from 1959 until his retirement in 1965. In 1979, he was murdered by the IRA.

Why, and with what success, was India partitioned in 1947?

The brief given to Mountbatten by Attlee and the British government was clear. Partition was to be avoided; if Congress and the League couldn't agree terms by the given deadline, then Britain would devolve power to the existing central and provincial governments – and go.

Politicians, such as Ernest Bevin, the Foreign Secretary, together with the chiefs of staff anticipated an attempt by Russia to expand into South-East Asia in the years after 1945 and viewed with foreboding the possibility of a prolonged armed conflict should this happen. If it happened, then Indian co-operation was essential if Britain was to maintain effective contact, not only with the Commonwealth in the Pacific, but with the oil fields of the Middle East. This made the argument for a united India even stronger: Auchinleck gloomily predicted that an independent Pakistan would need a British garrison to defend it against Russian encroachments through Afghanistan.

The 'charm offensive' begins

One of the reasons for sending Mountbatten to negotiate the final stages of India's independence was that he was totally different from any of the previous Viceroys. His flamboyance, left-wing tendencies and determination not only to be, but also to be seen as, a man of action brought a refreshing change to Indian politics and a hope that the Congress–League deadlock could be broken.

Mountbatten spent his first four weeks in India consulting with Indian ministers, politicians and his own staff. With some, his charm and flattery worked, as did his clear determination to cultivate the friendship of men with whom he had to bargain. Cordial relations were quickly achieved between the Mountbattens and Gandhi, Nehru and other Congress leaders. By marked contrast, Mountbatten's first meeting with Jinnah was decidedly frosty. Jinnah was not in the least seduced by the charms of the Viceroy or Vicereine. Mountbatten was later to refer to him as an 'evil genius', a 'psychopathic case', a 'lunatic' and, that old defamatory label, 'a bastard'. These epithets were duly relayed to Jinnah by staff who were trying to double guess how events would turn out and where their loyalties should lie, and did nothing to improve Jinnah's view that Mountbatten had strong pro-Congress sympathies. This view was strengthened by the very clear and much reported infatuation **Lady Mountbatten** held for the widower Nehru.

Lord Mountbatten was the first Viceroy to appoint a press attaché (the 1940s version of a spin doctor). Alan Campbell-Johnson's job was to make sure the Raj ended in a blaze of favourable publicity. The carefully posed photograph of Gandhi with the Viceroy and Lady Mountbatten in Source L delighted Campbell-Johnson almost as much as it enraged Jinnah.

Biography

Edwina, Countess Mountbatten of Burma (1901–60)

Born Edwina Cynthia Annette Ashley, she was the favourite granddaughter of the great Edwardian magnate, Sir Ernest Cassell. He was one of the richest men in Europe and left the bulk of his fortune to her when he died in 1921. She inherited £2 million, the country seat of Broadlands in Hampshire and a London town house.

She met Louis Mountbatten in 1920, when his salary was £610 a year, and they married at St Margaret's Westminster in July 1922 with all the Royal family present. The future Edward VIII was best man.

Her fashionable and privileged life ended with the onset of war in 1939 and particularly when her husband was made Viceroy of India. During the period of dreadful carnage following Partition, she tried desperately to ameliorate the suffering and misery of Hindus and Muslims.

Her affair with Jawaharlal Nehru is well documented and continued until her death. At her request, she was buried at sea. Nehru sent two Indian destroyers to accompany her body to its final resting place.

Source L

11.2 Gandhi with the Viceroy and Lady Mountbatten in March 1947

Source M

Mountbatten and his staff flew into Delhi on March 22, 1947, with all the promise of a monsoon's first downpour after months of blistering drought. He met at once with Nehru and Liaquat Ali [General Secretary of the Muslim League] seeking to break the deadlock between them that had paralysed the interim government. Nehru found himself thoroughly captivated by Mountbatten's personal diplomacy, soon falling under the spell, not only of the Viceroy but of his charming wife Edwina as well. Liaquat Ali was less easily charmed, for he and Jinnah feared that Mountbatten had been sent to India to placate Congress and knew that Wavell had been 'sacked' because of strong protests voiced against him to Attlee and Pethick-Lawrence by Nehru and Gandhi, both of whom considered him pro-Muslim.

From Stanley Wolpert, *A New History of India*, published in 1977

Pamela Mountbatten, the younger daughter of Lord and Lady Mountbatten and then 17 years old, remembers the months leading to independence:

Source N

Mr Jinnah – my father rarely called him anything else – was a fastidious man. He was extremely sophisticated and, unlike the other Indian leaders, always dressed in immaculate English style rather than national dress. He was a Muslim, but only spoke in English, whenever he condescended to speak. He had been intent on creating Pakistan ever since he had been introduced to the concept in London in 1933.

He did not fall for my father's charm offensive in those first days – which must have been working at full power. I was obviously ousted when the going got rough as my diary entry for 6 April reads 'Had dinner with the ADCs as Jinnah and his sister came to talk business.' At first my parents were very optimistic about the chance to mediate between Nehru and Congress, and Jinnah and the Muslim League. As my mother wrote in her diary of that same evening: 'Fascinating evening. Two very clever and odd people. I rather liked them but found them fanatical on their Pakistan and quite impractical.' Within a few meetings this optimism lapsed.

My father could talk of nothing else because he could not crack Jinnah and this had never happened to him before. He later admitted that he didn't realise how impossible his task was going to be until he met Jinnah. He has since often been accused of being anti-Muslim League, but that was not the right way of looking at the problem. Congress made themselves open to my father and courted his help. Jinnah was the opposite and rejected my father's involvement whenever he could.

From Pamela Mountbatten, *India Remembered*, published in 2007

SKILLS BUILDER

1 Look at Source L and read the caption and the information preceding it carefully. Why do you think that Alan Campbell-Johnson was particularly pleased with this photograph and Jinnah was enraged by it?

2 How far do Sources L, N and M, taken together, help explain the problems facing Viceroy Mountbatten?

3 How useful to an historian investigating the last months of the British Raj is Pamela Mountbatten's diary? How useful, in general, are diaries to historians?

Towards Partition

What Mountbatten heard during his four weeks of consultation made him believe that Partition was the only solution. This was most certainly not what Attlee wanted to hear. For the whole of its time in India, the Raj had tried to govern impartially between Muslim and Hindu, and, indeed, one of its major successes had been that its rule was secular. To fall back, now, on a primitive division of a huge landmass along religious lines was, so Attlee and his government believed, a seriously retrograde step.

So what had happened to make Mountbatten decide that Partition was the only answer? Alan Campbell-Johnson gave an explanation:

Source O

In his first talks with Lord Mountbatten, the Muslim League leader, Mr Jinnah, gave a frank warning that unless an acceptable political solution was reached very quickly, he could not guarantee to control the situation from his side. A similar warning was given by Congress leaders.

Unity had been Britain's greatest achievement in India, but by March 1947 the only alternatives were Pakistan or chaos. Lord Mountbatten discovered from personal discussions with the leaders of the Muslim League that they would insist on Partition at all costs and fight a civil war rather than accept transfer of power to a Hindu majority union, while Congress showed themselves as champions of unity, but not at the price of coercion.

From A. Campbell-Johnson, *Mission with Mountbatten*, published in 1951

SKILLS BUILDER

How far are the views of Alan Campbell-Johnson in Source O supported by those of Pamela Mountbatten in Source N and Stanley Wolpert in Source M?

Death and destruction

While Mountbatten was talking in Delhi, riots broke out in the Punjab. Although about 56 per cent of Punjab's inhabitants were Muslim, it had been administered by a shaky alliance of Hindus, Sikhs and non-League Muslims under Khizr Hayat Khan. His resignation in March 1947 and the attempt by the League to form its own administration led to militant Sikhs calling for direct action against the Muslim League – and the subsequent explosion of violence. Amritsar and Lahore were centres of carnage, while murder, arson and looting were common throughout the province. In the North-West Frontier Province, the League launched a civil disobedience campaign of its own against Congress.

What was Gandhi doing?

Gandhi was in despair. His dream of a single, united India in which all religions could coexist seemed to be evaporating before his eyes. He fell back on his belief in the power of truth and love, and began one of his long-distance walks. This time he walked through the Noakhali and Tiperah districts of East Bengal, trying through this 'act of love' to stop the mass killings that had left thousands dead. As always, he aimed to communicate directly with the illiterate masses, trying to explain what the politicians were doing. He then turned his attention to Bihar, where Hindus were killing Muslims on a large scale. As a practical gesture, it was a futile one. He had become an anachronistic figure and from this time on was sidelined in the search for an acceptable formula for independence.

Meanwhile, back in Delhi

Mountbatten and his staff were racing against the clock. Everyone involved, Indian and British, were exhausted, tense and sometimes, inevitably, bad-tempered. The momentum had to be maintained and the deadline had to be met. Ismay, Mountbatten's right-hand man, reported on 2 April that India was like a ship full of combustible material. The following months would show whether or not the ship would explode.

Plans for Partition

The plan for Partition and the reallocation of power was drawn up in April and May 1947.

Plan Balkan

The first draft, known as 'Plan Balkan', basically allowed the Indian states and provinces to decide their own future. This was a recipe for total anarchy, as past history had demonstrated and as Nehru forcefully pointed out when the plan was unofficially and improperly revealed to him in a private meeting with Mountbatten. This was yet another example of Mountbatten's perceived partiality because Jinnah had been given no such preview. However, Nehru was essentially correct when he pointed out: 'The inevitable consequence of the proposals would be to invite the Balkanisation of India; to provoke certain civil conflict and to add to violence and disorder; to cause a further breakdown of the central authority, which alone could prevent the growing chaos, and to demoralise the army, the police and the central services.'

Nehru went on to say that Congress would be sure to reject such a plan as it would both weaken India and also weaken the Congress Party itself. Furthermore, if Pakistan was to be a viable state, it needed to contain, in Jinnah's oft-stated opinion, an undivided Punjab and Bengal. To allow these states to decide their own futures would undoubtedly lead to their partition. In the face of this, and mindful of Jinnah's constant and consistent refusal to accept any arrangement that would produce an impoverished Pakistan, Mountbatten and his advisers tore up 'Plan Balkan' and started again.

The final plan

In great speed and with no little embarrassment, Mountbatten and his staff cobbled together a new partition plan. They were desperate to placate Congress and, at the same time, to get Jinnah 'on-side'. They were desperate, too, to get out of India before the sub-continent went down in flames. The remnants of the Raj were fast losing control of the domestic situation and Mountbatten was afraid the British would be swamped by events they could no longer control. Vast areas of north-west India were in a state of riot and rebellion; the 'steel frame' of the Indian Civil Service, which had held India together in the heyday of the Raj, was now reduced to a mere skeleton of mainly Indians to whom their friends and relations looked for patronage; Attlee's declaration that the British would be out of India by July 1948 had led to bloody contests for supremacy in mixed Hindu–Muslim areas like the Punjab.

The authorities' capacity for controlling the situation was severely compromised and collapsed altogether in Bihar. Almost the only form of authority that could go any way toward holding the situation together was the army. And Partition would mean that the army would no longer be a national body, but Hindu would be split from Muslim, officers from men. When Viceroy Mountbatten, whom Auchinleck called 'Pretty Dickie', asked him how long it would take to split the army between Pakistan and India, he said two, possibly five, years. In the event, Auchinleck was given four weeks to complete the separation.

Jinnah, too, was in a hurry. His persistent cough and debilitating physical weakness had been diagnosed as symptoms of a terminal disease – tuberculosis. If he wanted to see the birth of a separate Muslim state, events had to move fast.

On 18 May, Mountbatten carried his plan for Partition, involving the complete separation of India and Pakistan, to London for government and then parliamentary approval. On 15 July, it was announced in the House of Commons that in precisely one month's time, two separate dominions of India and Pakistan would be created on the Indian sub-continent.

The Boundary Commission

The work of the Boundary Commission was to draw a boundary between India and Pakistan that would, as far as possible, accommodate Hindus and Muslims in separate states. The Commission comprised equal numbers of Hindu and Muslim judges, chosen by Congress and the Muslim League, and a chairman, Sir Cyril Radcliffe, who was a legal expert. His impartiality was guaranteed because he had no previous experience whatsoever of India; neither, his work being done, did he ever return. Using out-of-date maps, anecdotal stories of land ownership and dusty boundary charts, the Commission was given just five weeks to complete its work.

Rumours, leaks and pressure

With so much at stake, it was inevitable that some decisions were leaked to interested parties, who then applied what pressure they could to make the Boundary Commission change its collective mind. One of the worst offenders here was Mountbatten himself. A leak would reach Nehru, who applied pressure on Mountbatten, who in turn attempted with some success to nobble the Boundary Commission. This was certainly true in the case of Firozpur. The town controlled the only bridge over the River Sutlej as well as playing a strategic part in the irrigation system of the area. Radcliffe's first draft of the boundary in the area, flown to Lahore on 10 August, placed Firozpur firmly inside Pakistan, which resulted in intensive lobbying by Nehru and Congress to have the boundary moved. On the evening of 11 August, Radcliffe had dinner with Mountbatten and Ismay. The following day, Firozpur appeared on the Indian side of the boundary.

Mountbatten was certainly not acting in an even-handed way. This may have been due in part to his personal dislike of Jinnah and to the warm relationship he, and particularly his wife, had with Nehru, but it was also

Question

It is often said that Mountbatten, too, was in a hurry. He wanted to get back to Britain to attend the wedding of his nephew, Philip, to the Princess Elizabeth (the future Queen Elizabeth II) in November 1947. Do you think it likely that this affected his decision to partition India? Discuss this in your group.

due to the fact that he simply didn't believe Pakistan would last. He likened it to a 'nissen hut' that would soon collapse and be reabsorbed into India. It may be this belief that led him to strengthen India at the expense of Pakistan.

What about the princes?

The princes had been unstinting in their support of the Raj during the Second World War. The *Maharajah* of Travancore had bought the Royal Indian navy an armed patrol boat; the *Nawab* of Bhopal bought fighter aircraft, as did the *Nizam* of Hyderabad, who also bought a whole squadron of planes; and the *Maharajah* of Kashmir gave 18 field ambulances. Altogether, the princes invested in the war effort by buying 180 million rupees-worth of war bonds. Of their subjects, 300,000 Indian volunteers had joined India's armed forces. Now, faced with the sub-continent being split between Muslim and Hindu, India and Pakistan, they felt ignored. Worse than ignored, they felt threatened by Congress, a party dedicated to removing their sovereign powers. As the *Nawab* of Bhopal remarked in 1946: 'The British seem to have abdicated power and what is worse, have handed it over to the enemies of their friends.'

Mountbatten took no notice of the *Nawab* of Bhopal and he took no notice of Conrad Corfield, the Head of India's Political Department, either. Corfield had little time for India's professional politicians and sympathised with the princes' desire to remain autonomous in their own lands and to keep meddling Congress politicians out. Corfield got the new Secretary of State for India, Lord Listowel, to agree that neither India nor Pakistan would inherit the princely states when the Raj ended, but the princes would become, in effect, independent rulers. Having won this concession, Corfield authorised the burning of four tons of documents listing the princes' misdemeanours over the years. He wanted to prevent the papers from falling into the hands of Congress, the members of which, he suspected, would use them for political blackmail.

Nehru was furious when he heard what Corfield had done. If carried through, it would mean the disintegration of India and a complete reverse for Congress, which intended quietly to take over the princely states. Mountbatten, who deeply resented being outwitted by an official, called Corfield a 'son-of-a-bitch' and had no problems in giving in to Nehru's demands that Corfield be dismissed as 'an enemy of India'.

Mountbatten then called a conference of Indian princes on 25 July at which he explained that when British rule ended on 15 August, they should have acceded to either India or Pakistan, depending on to which state they were nearer. By shamelessly exploiting his royal connections and playing on the princes' loyalty, fear and superstition, and by cajoling and flattering, browbeating and threatening, Mountbatten had them all signed up to either India or Pakistan by the time of the transfer of power from the Raj.

Source P

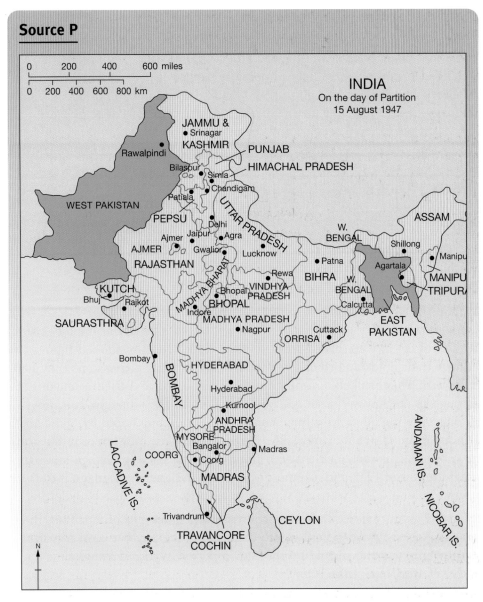

11.3 Map showing the Partition of the Indian sub-continent on 15 August 1947

Question

Why was the Indian sub-continent partitioned, and partitioned in this way?

You will need to think about:

- the role of Congress in trying to become an inclusive party for all Indians, Hindu and Muslim
- the ways in which the Muslim League tried to protect the interests of the Muslim minority
- the actions of Jinnah, Gandhi and Nehru, and the motives behind those actions
- the role of Mountbatten.

Dividing the spoils

A vast amount of administrative work had to be done before Partition could come into effect. The desk of every official in Calcutta, Delhi and Lahore was piled high with seemingly impossible paperwork. The assets and liabilities of British India had to be divided between India and Pakistan on the basis of 82.5 per cent for India and 17.5 per cent for Pakistan. The army and police, civil service and revenue service, all had to be reallocated, as did everything from railways and schools through to trucks, paper, pens and paperclips. In just one month, the accumulation of centuries of British hoarding, storing, building and creating was turned up, turned out and meticulously divided between the two soon-to-be dominions. But these were, in essence, things. Yet the division of these 'things' impacted on the lives of millions of people, too often with devastating effect.

Carnage

Millions of Hindus, Muslims and Sikhs were terrified that, after independence, they would wake up on the wrong side of the India-Pakistan border, living in a country hostile to their faith. They abandoned their homes, their fields and their livelihoods, packed what possessions they had and went. They walked, crammed into bullock carts and tried to make it through to the railway system. They travelled, so they thought, to safety. And as they travelled, Muslims heading west were butchered by Sikhs and Hindus in India. Hindus and Sikhs moving east were murdered by Muslims in Pakistan. It is reckoned that ten million people tried to change lands in that summer of 1947 and around one million Indians never made it to their promised land. They were massacred in an orgy of senseless bloodletting.

Source Q gives two eye-witness accounts of the outcomes of Partition, the first by Robert Payne, a British jute merchant travelling between Amritsar and Lahore, and the second by the BBC reporter, Wynford Vaughan Thomas, who was in the Punjab:

Source Q

I saw mile upon mile of people going east and going west, carrying their belongings. The Hindus and Sikhs from Pakistan moving on one side of the road, the Mohammedans on the other. We stopped and were watching the people go by when a figure came out from the huge line of refugees, stood to attention and asked me to help him. He then said that he'd been with the 4th Indian Division through the desert and in Italy. What could I do to help him? All I could do was look at him and say, 'Your politicians asked for *swaraj*, and this is *swaraj*.'

. . .

I used to see these massacres taking place. People tried to cut people down. It was most extraordinary, in the middle of all these scenes, that nobody for a moment touched me or any European. The trains ran a serious risk. Drivers would shunt into a siding and go off to water the engine. That would give the Sikh bands a chance to come in and they would go right through the train and kill everybody. And the train would shunt on to Lahore where in a siding they would have to take the dead out. They were a terrible sight. You could see them coming with the fly swarms around them. And when the bodies were taken out and laid down, there would be about two thousand at a time. One station official turned to me, he'd obviously been used to order – the pride of British India was the railways – and in a voice I will never forget, he said 'Sir, it is hardly worth issuing tickets any more.' A good man horrified by the collapse of order.

From Charles Allen (editor), *Plain Tales of the Raj*, published in 1975

Source R

11.4 A town in the Punjab ruined as a result of post-Partition rioting

Source S

It is doubtful whether more could have been done had more time been available. British troops were not used. The instructions of the Government were that they were only to be used to protect European lives. No Indian leader would have agreed to use British troops. Military action alone cannot stop large-scale disturbances in the Indian sub-continent. The form of the disturbance and the areas involved make the soldiers' task an impossible one.

From a report written by L. Mountbatten in September 1948

The British military withdrawal began in August 1947 and continued until mid-1948; at the very time when violence in the Punjab was at its height, the majority of British troops were kept in their barracks and then evacuated from the country. A totally inadequate force of 50,000 troops was dispatched to bring order along the new frontiers. They mostly kept their heads down in their barracks, totally unable to do anything to control the situation. Indeed, Mountbatten himself believed that the British were powerless to prevent the violence of 1946–48 (see Source S).

Source T

Jinnah in fact did not want the sort of Partition that occurred in 1947. It was not a popular Muslim demand at the time, made little sense to Muslims secure in provincial majorities, and offered nothing to the millions of Muslims scattered as minorities throughout the sub-continent. Furthermore, it made little sense in terms of economics and defence. It probably, therefore, was designed as a bargaining counter, vague enough to unite Indian Muslims behind it, in order to achieve recognition for Muslims as a 'nation' and therefore as equal with Congress in negotiations about the future.

From Judith M. Brown, *Modern India: the Origins of an Asian Democracy*, published in 1994

SKILLS BUILDER

How far do Sources Q and R support the view expressed in Source S that the British were powerless to stop the inter-communal violence?

Independence at last

As midnight on 14 August 1947 approached, Jawaharlal Nehru spoke:

Source U

Long years ago we made a tryst with destiny, and now the time comes when we shall redeem our pledge, not wholly or in full measure, but very substantially. At the stroke of the midnight hour, when the world sleeps, India will awake to life and freedom. A moment comes, which comes but rarely in history, when we step out from the old to the new, when an age ends, and when the soul of a nation, long suppressed, finds utterance. It is fitting that at this solemn moment we take the pledge of dedication to the service of India and her people and to the still larger cause of humanity.

From a speech by J. Nehru to Delhi's Constituent Assembly on 14 August 1947

What of the other main players? Mountbatten, hoping to be the first Governor-General of both India and Pakistan, had to be content with being Governor-General of India alone. Jinnah flew from Delhi to Karachi on 7 August to become Pakistan's first Governor-General himself. And Gandhi? He did not want to stay in Delhi for independence celebrations but left for Bengal. On Independence Day, he wrote: 'The rot began with the alien government. We, the inheritors, have not taken the trouble to rectify the errors of the past.'

Unit summary

What have you learned in this unit?

The granting of independence to the Indian sub-continent came at a point when Britain could no longer, for a variety of reasons, sustain an Indian empire. The election of a Labour government in Britain and the rapport members of that government had with members of Congress in many ways facilitated the moves to Indian independence, but at the same time tended to alienate the Muslim League. The League, suspicious of Congress and fearing a Congress Raj after independence, put forward various proposals for safeguarding the Muslim minority in the Indian sub-continent.

You have learned how the Cabinet Mission's proposals, tentatively accepted by both Congress and the Muslim League, were in the end rejected by the Muslim League, and about the consequences of that rejection. The orgy of killings and bloodletting that accompanied the League's Direct Action Day was repeated over and over again in the months that led to independence and subsequent Partition. Exhausted, Viceroy Wavell was replaced by Lord Louis Mountbatten, whose 'charm offensive' brought about independence by August 1947. But this was independence at a price: the Partition of India and Pakistan, the displacement of ten million people and the deaths of a million.

What skills have you used in this unit?

You have used your skills of comprehension, inference-making, evaluation and analysis to explore the complexity of the demands of Congress, the Muslim League and the British, and to begin to understand the motives of the main players. You have used these skills to reach judgements about events on the Indian sub-continent and you have supported and justified those judgements.

Exam tips

This is the sort of question you will find appearing on the exam paper as a (b) question:

- Study sources K, O and T, and use your own knowledge. Do you agree with the view, expressed in Source T, that Jinnah never really wanted a separate state of Pakistan, but used the demand for one as a 'bargaining counter'?

You worked on (b) style questions at the end of Units 3, 4, 6, 7, 8 and 9, and you have experimented with different sorts of plans and different styles of question. You should now have a good idea of the way in which you prefer to plan your answer. So go ahead and plan an answer to this question.

Now test yourself! Look at your plan and check what you have drawn up. Have you:

- *Analysed* Sources K and O for points that support and points that challenge the view expressed in Source T that Jinnah never really wanted a separate state of Pakistan, but used the demand for one as a bargaining counter, and noted these points in your plan?
- Remembered to look behind the surface features and consider *inferences*?
- Shown how you will *cross-reference* between the sources for points of agreement and disagreement?
- Shown where you will use your *wider knowledge* both to reinforce and challenge the points you have derived from the sources?
- Thought about how you will combine the points you have made into an *argument* for or against the view that Jinnah never really wanted a separate state of Pakistan, but used the demand for one as a bargaining counter, and noted this on your plan?
- Shown how your *evaluation* of the points you have used in your argument has considered the *quality of the evidence* used?
- Noted what your conclusion will be and how you will ensure it is *balanced* and *supported*?

RESEARCH TOPIC

What role did Gandhi play in the eventual Partition of India?

Epilogue

Indian independence gave 400 million people freedom from the largest empire the world has ever known. But, as you have seen, it was freedom at a price. That price was Partition and riot, dislocation and destruction, rape, abduction and death.

The speed with which independence was granted and the way in which it was managed left a number of unresolved issues, but in many ways 1947 was a year of transition rather than one of abrupt closure.

Continuity

- Many British people stayed on in India after 1947 as ordinary civilians and as officials. The governors of the Punjab, Madras, Bombay and the North-West Frontier Province, as well as some service chiefs and 83 civilian officers stayed in their jobs at least until the early 1950s. Indeed Mountbatten himself, at Nehru's request, stayed on for a year as India's constitutional Governor-General.

- For at least 30 years after 1947, the Indian tea industry remained in British hands.

- The Indian Administrative Service took over from the old Indian Civil Service. In the mid-1960s, when there were 23 central secretariat departments, Indian Civil Service-trained men headed 19 of them.

- The constitutions of both India and Pakistan were framed in accordance with the old 1935 Government of India Act: there are 250 identical clauses.

- The vast number of manuals and handbooks, forms and certificates, maps and gazetteers that were part of the Raj's bureaucracy remained in place for the use of the new administrators.

Unresolved issues

- Partition resulted in an enormous refugee problem; displaced people, once they had relocated themselves in Hindu India or Muslim Pakistan, had to find somewhere to live and somewhere to work. The refugee problem didn't only result in these practical issues. Enormous psychological damage was done to families who were decimated by death or who lost each other in the mass exodus and were never reunited.

- A member of the Hindu *Mahasabha*, angered at Gandhi's insistence that the Congress government should continue transferring assets to Pakistan, killed him. On 30 January 1948, Naturam Godse shot Gandhi as he addressed a prayer meeting in Delhi.

- The creation of the separate state of Pakistan did not bring unalloyed joy to all Muslims living in the sub-continent. Many of them, particularly those living in the south, simply couldn't make it to Pakistan. More than 30 million remained behind in India, either through force of circumstance or through choice. Bengali Hindi-speaking Muslims had problems too; most would have preferred to live in an independent Bengal defined by culture rather than religion and were alarmed when the Pakistan government announced that Urdu would be the official language of Pakistan.

- Muslims who did make it through to Pakistan tended to be better educated and richer than the local Sindhis and Punjabis, and they filled most of the responsible posts in the new government. This caused considerable friction and many *muhajirs*, as they were called, were attacked and had their property looted and burned. One of the first victims was Pakistan's first prime minister, Liaquat Ali Khan, who was assassinated in 1951.

- The separation of the state of Pakistan into East and West Pakistan did not make for ease of government or appropriate distribution of resources. In 1971, Pakistan suffered Partition again when East Pakistan became the independent state of Bangladesh.

- Conflict between Pakistan and India over Kashmir, caused largely by the inability of the Hindu *Maharajah* Hari Singh to make up his mind as to whether to plump for India or Pakistan, resulted in mass killings in 1947–48 and remained unresolved for decades.

In 1947, all the people involved in Partition agreed that power should be transferred on the basis of dominion status; hence both India and Pakistan had a constitutional Governor-General. In the case of India, this was Lord Louis Mountbatten and, in the case of Pakistan, Jinnah. But Britain made it clear that there would be no objection if either state decided, at a later date, to sever all allegiance to the Crown. In 1950, India became a republic, followed, six years' later, by Pakistan.

Thematic review: source-based debate and evaluation

It is important, especially when dealing with a topic that addresses change over time, to stand back and review the period you have been studying. You need to ask yourself not only what happened, but why it happened and why it happened then and not, say, 100 years earlier or 20 years later. What had driven change? Which factors were significant and which were not? Were there any events that were critical turning points? Thematic review questions, spanning the whole time period, will help to focus your thinking.

Here are the thematic review questions that relate to Britain and the Nationalist Challenge in India 1900–47. You can probably think of more, but for the moment these are the ones with which you will be working.

- To what extent would you agree with the view that the Second World War was a key turning point in the moves toward Indian independence?
- How far would you agree with the view that Indian independence would not have happened without the input of Gandhi?
- To what extent was the emergence of a separate state of Pakistan the work of Jinnah alone?
- How far would you agree with the view that the violence and bloodletting that accompanied Partition meant that Gandhi's non-violent methods, as advocated by him in his *satyagraha* campaigns, were useless?
- How far would you agree with the view expressed by Gandhi in 1947 that 'The rot began with the alien government. We, the inheritors, have not taken the trouble to rectify the errors of the past'?

Choose one of these thematic review questions that you plan to answer. Working through this section will make much more sense if you have an actual question in mind.

Answering a thematic review question

There are two keys to answering a thematic review question: *select* and *deploy*.

Select   You need to select appropriate source material. You need to select appropriate knowledge.

Deploy   You need to deploy what you have selected so that you answer the question in as direct a way as possible.

Unpacking 'select'

You will see that all the thematic review questions are asking for an evaluation. They ask 'How far. . .', 'To what extent. . .', 'How significant. . .', which means that you will have to weigh up the evidence given by the sources you have selected. You will, therefore, have to select sources that will give you a range of evidence. Six diary entries, for example, will not give you the range you want. You will also need to select sources that seem to provide evidence that pulls in different directions. Eight sources saying more or less the same thing but in different ways will not help you weigh up the significance of different sorts of evidence and reach a reasoned, supported conclusion.

So now go ahead.

1 Look back through this book and select the sources, primary and secondary, that you think will give you the appropriate range, balance and evidence.

2 Make notes of the knowledge you will need to use to contextualise the sources and create an argument.

You can't, of course, simply put some sources into an answer and hope that whoever is reading what you have written can sort things out for themselves. You need to evaluate the sources you have selected and use that evaluation to create the argument you will be making when you answer the question. You have already had practice of doing this, but here is a reminder of some of the questions you will need to ask of a source before you can turn it into evidence:

- Is the *content* appropriate for the question I am answering?
- Can I supply the appropriate *context* for the source?
- How *reliable* is the source as evidence? Was the author or artist *in a position to know* what he or she was talking about or drawing?
- What was the intended *audience* of the source? What was the *purpose* of the source?
- If the source is a photograph or cartoon, did the photographer or cartoonist *pose* the people in the picture/cartoon? Was the photographer or cartoonist *selective* in what he or she chose to photograph or draw?
- How *useful* is this source in developing an answer to the question? Remember that a source that is unreliable can still be useful.

Now you have your selection of source material, you need to think about it as a package. Does it do the job you want it to do? Does it supply you with enough evidence to argue your case, while at the same time providing you with enough evidence of different points of view so that you can show you have considered what weight the evidence will bear in reaching a reasoned, supported conclusion? In other words, can you effectively *cross-reference* between the sources, showing where they support and where they challenge each other?

Unpacking 'deploy'

The key to successful deployment of evidence and knowledge in answering a question like the one you have selected is always to keep the question in the forefront of your mind. Keep focused! Don't be tempted to go off into interesting by-ways.

Make every paragraph count as you build your argument.

You have already had a lot of practice in essay planning and writing, so this is just a reminder of the main things you need to bear in mind:

Plan

Plan carefully how you are going to construct your answer and make out your case.

Structure

Structure your answer. You could use the following framework as a guide.

Introduction

'Set out your stall', briefly outlining your argument and approach.

Paragraphs

The main body of your answer should develop your argument, using the evidence you have gathered by questioning the sources. As you outline your case, remember to cross-reference between the sources you are using so as to weigh the evidence, showing on which you place the greater weight.

Conclusion

Here you should pull your case together, giving a supported summary of the arguments you have made and coming to a reasoned, supported judgement.

In other words, say what you are going to do, do it, and show that you have done it.

You do not, of course, have to respond to these thematic review questions by writing an essay all by yourself. You could work collaboratively in a small group or you could use one or more of the questions to prepare for a class debate. In whatever way you are going to use these thematic review questions, the approach will be the same: select, deploy and keep to the point.

Good luck!

Exam zone

Relax and prepare

Hot tips: What other students have said

From GCSE to AS level

- I really enjoyed studying modern world History at GCSE, but I am glad that I had the chance to look at some nineteenth- and twentieth-century British history at AS level. It has been challenging but enjoyable to study a different period.

- Many of the skills that I learned at GCSE were built upon at AS level, especially in Unit 2 where the skills of source evaluation and analysis are very important.

- AS level History seems like a big step up at first with more demands made on independent reading and more complex source passages to cope with. However, by the end of the first term I felt as if my written work had improved considerably.

- The more practice source-based questions I attempted, the more confident I became and quite quickly I picked up the necessary style and technique required for success.

- I found it really helpful to look at mark schemes in the textbook. It was reassuring to see what the examiners were looking for and how I could gain top marks.

What I wish I had known at the start of the year

- I used the textbook a lot during the revision period to learn the key facts and to practise key skills. I really wished that I had used it from the beginning of the course in order to consolidate my class notes.

- I wished that I had done more reading and taken more notes from other material such as the photocopied handouts issued by my teacher. Reading around the subject and undertaking independent research would have made my understanding more complete and made the whole topic more interesting.

- AS History is not just about learning the relevant material but also developing the skills to use it effectively. I wish that I had spent more time throughout the year practising source questions to improve my style and technique.

- I wish I had paid more attention to the advice and comments made by my teacher on the written work I had done. This would have helped me to improve my scores throughout the year.

How to revise

- I started my revision by buying a new folder and some dividers. I put all my revision work into the folder and used the dividers to separate the different topics. I really took pride in my revision notes and made them as thorough and effective as I could.

- Before I started the revision process, I found it helpful to plan out my history revision. I used the Edexcel specification given to me by my teacher as a guideline of which topics to revise and I ticked off each one as I covered it.

- I found it useful to revise in short, sharp bursts. I would set myself a target of revising one particular topic in an hour and a half. I would spend one hour taking revision notes and then half an hour testing myself with a short practice question or a facts test.

- I found it useful to always include some practice work in my revision. If I could get that work to my teacher to mark all the better, but just attempting questions to time helped me improve my technique.

- Sometimes I found it helpful to revise with a friend. We might spend 45 minutes revising by ourselves and then half an hour testing each other. Often we were able to sort out any problems between us and it was reassuring to see that someone else had the same worries and pressures at that time.

Refresh your memory

Revision Checklist

The following checklist provides the key points from each unit that you need to revise for your exam.

Unit 1: From East India Company to Raj

- Role of the East India Company in India to 1857
- Strengths and weaknesses of the Mughal Empire
- The 1857 Rebellion
- Establishing the British Raj

Unit 2: Snapshot 1900: living in the Raj

- Indian society: the importance of the caste system and of religion
- Ways in which India was used to serve British interests
- Way of life of the British in India: a separate caste?
- Attitudes of Indians towards the Raj

Unit 3: How was India governed in 1900?

- Extent of British rule in India
- Role of the Viceroy (exemplified by Curzon) and relationships with Whitehall
- Structure and work of the Indian Civil Service
- Involvement of Indians in running their own country

Unit 4: Change and continuity, 1900–19

- Nature and impact of the Morley–Minto Reforms, 1908
- Importance of the founding of the Indian National Congress
- Impact on India of the First World War
- The Montagu-Chelmsford Report, the Rowlatt Acts and the Government of India Act 1919

Unit 5: Flashpoint! The Amritsar Massacre

- Opposition to the Rowlatt Acts and reasons for unrest
- Roles of Brigadier-General Rex Dyer and Governor Michael O'Dwyer
- Differing British and Indian perceptions of the Amritsar Massacre
- Outcomes of the Amritsar Massacre

Unit 6: Gandhi, *swaraj* and the Congress Party

- Gandh's philosophy, including *satyragraha* and *swaraj*
- Gandhi as leader of Congress
- Effectiveness of the civil disobedience campaign of 1922
- Reactions of the Raj to Gandhi

Unit 7: Retrenchment in the 1920s

- Ways in which Congress consolidated its position
- The Simon Commission (1927) and its impact, including the Nehru Report (1928) and the Irwin Declaration (1929)
- Gandhi's salt *satyagraha* (1930) and the civil disobedience campaign
- Importance of the Gandhi–Irwin pact (1931)

Unit 8: Jinnah and the idea of separateness

- Underlying reasons for Hindu-Muslim clashes
- Significance of the founding of the Muslim League in 1906
- Significance of the rise and fall of the Khilafat Movement
- Problematic relationships with Congress

Unit 9: Consultation and conflict in the 1930s

- Importance of the Round Table Conferences
- Reasons for the passing of the Government of India Act 1935
- Impact on India of the Government of India Act
- Significance of the 1937 Indian elections

Unit 10: The impact of the early years of the Second World War

- Impact on India of the announcement that India was at war with Germany
- Internal and external threats to India
- The Cripps Mission and Gandhi's 'Quit India' campaign
- Ways in which the Muslim League and Congress negotiated with the Raj and consolidated their own positions

Unit 11: The ending of the Raj: dreams and nightmares

- Reasons why Britain was ready to grant Indian independence once the Second World War had ended
- Reasons for the failure of the Cabinet Mission
- Differences between Wavell and Mountbatten as Viceroys
- Reasons why independence led to Partition and violence

This revision checklist looks very knowledge-based. The exam, however, will test your source-based skills as well. So remember that when dealing with sources you must be able to:

- comprehend a source and break it down into key points
- interpret a source, drawing inferences and deductions from it rather than treating it as a source of information; this may involve considering the language and tone used as well
- cross-reference points of evidence between sources to reinforce and challenge
- evaluate the evidence by assessing its quality and its reliability in terms of how much weight it will bear and how secure are the

conclusions that can be drawn from it; this may include considering the provenance of the source

- deal with the sources as a set to build a body of evidence.

Result

You have spent a lot of time working on plans and constructing answers to the (a) and (b) questions. In Units 2, 5 and 10 you worked with (a) questions; in the other units you worked with (b) questions. So you now have a pretty good idea about how to plan an answer and write a response to the questions of the exam paper. But what are the examiners looking for? And what marks will you get?

What will the exam paper look like?

There will be three questions on the paper.

(a) Compulsory: everyone has to do this.

(b) (i) and (b) (ii) You will have a choice here and will only have to answer one (b) question.

There will be nine sources on the exam paper. But don't worry: you won't have to deal with them all! You'll only need to deal with six sources – three for each of the questions you will be answering. And here is the good news. So far, you have worked with very long sources, some of which were complicated. In the exam, because you will only have one hour and 20 minutes to answer the two questions, the sources will be much shorter. You'll probably be dealing with no more than around 550 words altogether.

Question (a)

What will you have to do and what marks will you get for doing it?

You will have to focus on reaching a judgement by analysis, cross-referencing and evaluation of source material. The maximum number of marks you can get is 20. You will be working at any one of four levels. Try to get as high up in the levels as you can.

Remember that the only knowledge, outside of that which you can find in the sources, is what examiners call 'contextual' knowledge. This means you can write enough to enable you to interpret the source, but no more. For example, if one of the three sources is by Jinnah, you should show the examiners that you know he was the leader of the Muslim League, which was pressing for separate representation for Muslims, but you should not describe various actions of the League and its relationship with Congress unless this information helps the understanding of a particular source.

Level 1
1–5 marks

- Have you shown that you understand the surface features of the sources?

- Have you shown that you have selected material relevant to the question?

- Does your response consist mainly of direct quotations from the sources?

Level 2
6–10 marks

- Have you identified points of similarity and difference in the sources in relation to the question asked?

- Have you made a least one developed comparison or a range of undeveloped ones?

- Have you summarised the information you have found in the sources?

- Have you noted the provenance of at least one of the sources?

Level 3
11–15 marks

- Have you cross-referenced between the sources, making detailed comparisons supported by evidence from the sources?

- Have you shown that you understand you have to weigh the evidence by looking at the nature, origins, purpose and audience of the sources?

- Have you shown you have thought about considering 'How far' by trying to use the sources as a set?

Level 4
16–20 marks

- Have you reached a judgement in relation to the issue posed by the question?

- Is this judgement supported by careful examination of the evidence of the sources?

- Have you cross-referenced between the sources and analysed the points of similarity and disagreement?

- Have you taken account of the different qualities of the sources in order to establish what weight the evidence will bear?

- Have you used the sources as a set when addressing 'How far' in the question?

Now try this (a) question:

- Study Sources A, B and C. How far do Sources A, B and C support the view that the people of the Raj operated like a separate caste?

Source A

We were looked after by Indian servants and we met a great many Indians, and some of us undoubtedly made a very close study of India and Indian customs. But once you stepped inside the home you were back in Cheltenham or Bath. We brought with us in our home lives almost exact replicas of the sort of life that upper-middle-class people lived in England at that time. Nearly everyone in official India sprang from precisely the same educational and cultural background. You went from bungalow to bungalow and you found the same sort of furniture, the same sort of dinner table set, the same kind of conversation. We read the same books, mostly imported by post from England, and I can't really say that we took an awful lot from India.

From Charles Allen, Plain Tales from the Raj, published in 1975: Vere Birdwood, is describing her life in India at the time of the Raj

Source B

I was influenced by the example of my parents who never went into any kind of society in which they were not treated as equals. I entertained no ambition whatever of hobnobbing with the English in India. As long as I lived in Calcutta I wore no article of English clothing and had none. In general, I disliked and despised the local English.

From Nirad Chaudhuri, *The Autobiography of an Unknown Indian*, published in 1951

Source C

You met the judges in court, and that was it. The very first time I made a breakthrough was when my wife's cousin got the Victoria Cross. He was the first Indian to win it, and I thought this was a good opportunity for me to exploit. So I threw a cocktail party and invited all the English judges to meet the first Indian winner of the Victoria Cross, and they all came. And then suddenly everything changed. Thereafter, if I invited them home, they came, and I was always treated with much greater courtesy, because that confirmed in their minds that I belonged to a family who were willing to fight on the side of the British with much enthusiasm.

From Khushwant Singh, an Indian barrister, recalling his experiences in the days of the Raj and how he established social contact with British judges in Zareer Masani, *Indian Tales of the Raj*, published in 1987

Now use the marking criteria to assess your response.

How did you do?

What could you have done to have achieved a better mark?

Question (b)

What will you have to do and what marks will you get for doing it?

You will have to analyse and evaluate a historical view or claim using two sources and your own knowledge. There are 40 marks for this question. You will get 24 marks for your own knowledge and

16 marks for your source evaluation. You can be working at any one of four levels. Try to get as high up in the levels as you can. The examiners will be marking your answer twice: once for knowledge and a second time for source evaluation.

This is what the examiners will be looking for as they mark the ways in which you have selected and used your knowledge to answer the question:

Level 1
1–6 marks

- Have you written in simple sentences without making any links between them?
- Have you provided only limited support for the points you are making?
- Have you written what you know separately from the sources?
- Is what you have written mostly generalised and not really directed at the focus of the question?
- Have you made a lot of spelling mistakes and is your answer disorganised?

Level 2
7–12 marks

- Have you produced a series of statements that are supported by mostly accurate and relevant factual material?
- Have you make some limited links between the statements you have written?
- Is your answer mainly 'telling the story' and not really analysing what happened?
- Have you kept your own knowledge and the sources separate?
- Have you made a judgement that isn't supported by facts?
- Is your answer a bit disorganised with some spelling and grammatical mistakes?

Level 3
13–18 marks

- Is your answer focused on the question?
- Have you shown that you understand the key issues involved?
- Have you included a lot of descriptive material along with your analysis of the issues?

- Is your material factually accurate but a bit lacking in depth and/or relevance?
- Have you begun to integrate your own knowledge with the source material?
- Have you made a few spelling and grammatical mistakes?
- Is your work mostly well organised?

Level 4
19–24 marks

- Does your answer relate well to the question focus?
- Have you shown that you understand the issues involved?
- Have you analysed the key issues?
- Is the material you have used relevant to the question and factually accurate?
- Have you begun to integrate what you know with the evidence you have gleaned from the source material?
- Is the material you have selected balanced?
- Is the way you have expressed your answer clear and coherent?
- Is your spelling and grammar mostly accurate?

This is what the examiners are looking for as they mark your source evaluation skills:

Level 1
1–4 marks

- Have you shown that you understand the sources?
- Is the material you have selected from them relevant to the question?
- Is your answer mostly direct quotations from the sources or rewrites of them in your own words?

Level 2
5–8 marks

- Have you shown that you understand the sources?
- Have you selected from them in order to support or challenge from the view given in the question?
- Have you used the sources mainly as sources of information?

Level 3
9–12 marks

- Have you analysed the sources, drawing from them points of challenge and/or support for the view contained in the question?
- Have you developed these points, using the source material?
- Have you shown that you realise you are dealing with just one viewpoint and that the sources point to other, perhaps equally valid ones?
- Have you reached a judgement?
- Have you supported that judgement with evidence from the sources?

Level 4
13–16 marks

- Have you analysed the sources, raising issues from them?
- Have you discussed the viewpoint in the question by relating it to the issues raised by your analysis of the source material?
- Have you weighed the evidence in order to reach a judgement?
- Is your judgement fully explained and supported by carefully selected evidence?

Now try this (b) question:

- Read Sources D, E and F, and use your own knowledge. Do you agree with the view, expressed in Source F, that Viceroy Mountbatten was to blame for Partition?

Source D

Now that Jinnah had rejected a move within the present Constitution based on parity, it is not clear what he would be prepared to accept short of Pakistan. Gandhi's final comment to me was that His Majesty's Government would have to decide sooner or later whether to come down on the side of Hindu or Muslim, of Congress or League, since they could never reconcile them. A discouraging comment, but true under present leadership.

From a letter written by Viceroy Wavell to Secretary of State, Leo Amery on 15 July 1945

Source E

Whereas it has become abundantly clear that the Muslims of India would not rest contented with anything less than the immediate establishment of an independent and fully sovereign state of Pakistan, the Council of the All-Indian Muslim League is convinced that now the time has come for the Muslim nation to resort to direct action to achieve Pakistan, to assert their just rights, to vindicate their honour and to get rid of the present British slavery and the contemplated future Caste-Hindu domination

From the Muslim League's call for direct action on 29 July 1946

Source F

The Prime Minister hoped that Mountbatten might, within fourteen months, bring Gandhi, Nehru and Jinnah round his viceregal table, teasing agreement from them to resolve their own problems. Britain could then withdraw its troops with dignity and take credit for leaving independent India unified. But Mountbatten was neither wise enough nor patient enough to accomplish what many older and more experienced British predecessors had failed to do. Nor did he have the humility or good sense to listen to India's two wisest political leaders, Gandhi and Jinnah, both of whom tried their frail best to warn him to stop the runaway juggernaut to Partition before it was too late.

From Stanley Wolpert, *Shameful Flight*, published in 2006

Now use the marking criteria to assess your response.

How did you do?

What could you have done to have achieved higher marks?

The examiners will not be nit-picking their way through your answer, ticking things off as they go. Rather, they will be looking to see which levels best fit the response you have written to the question, and you should do the same when assessing your own responses.

How will I time my responses?

You have 1 hour 20 minutes to answer two questions.

The (a) question is compulsory and you will have a choice of one from two (b) questions. Take time, say 5 minutes, to read through the paper and think about your choice of (b) question.

The (a) question is worth half the marks of the (b) question, so you should aim to spend twice the time on the (b) question. This means that, including planning time, you should spend about 25 minutes on the (a) question and about 50 minutes (again including planning) on the (b) question.

Practising questions

Each unit of this book finishes with an exam style question – either an (a) style (sources only) or a (b) style (sources and own knowledge). Use these to get plenty of practice.

You have now had a lot of practice in planning, writing and assessing your responses to the sort of questions you can expect to find on the exam paper. You are well prepared and you should be able to tackle the exam with confidence.

Good luck!

References

Many books have been written about the ending of the Raj and Indian independence. Some are general accounts and some deal with specific topics in depth. The references that are asterisked in the following list are particularly useful:

Books

Ashton, S., *The British in India: from Trade to Empire*, 1994 (Second edition; first published in 1987)

Besant, Annie, *How India Wrought for Freedom*, 1915

*Brown, Judith M., *Modern India: the Origins of an Asian Democracy*, 1994 (Second edition; first published in 1985)

*Chandra, B. *et al*, *India's struggle for Independence 1857–1947*, 1989

*Collins, L. and Lapierre, D., *Freedom at Midnight*, 1997

Colvin, Ian, *The Life of General Dyer*, 1929

*Copland, I., *India 1885–1947*, 2001

*Das, M.N., *India under Morley and Minto*, 1964

*Draper, Arthur, *The Amritsar Massacre*, 1985 (Second edition; first published in 1981)

Dyer, R.E.H., *Army Disturbances in the Punjab*, 1920

*Fay, P.W., *The Forgotten Army: India's Armed Struggle for Independence*, 1993

*French, Patrick, *Liberty or Death: India's Journey to Independence and Division*, 1997

*Furneaux, Rupert, *Massacre at Amritsar*, 1963

Gosh, P., *The Development of the Indian National Congress 1892–1909*, 1960

*Jalal, Ayesha, *Sole Spokesman: Jinnah, the Muslim League and the demand for Pakistan*, 1985

*James, Lawrence, *Raj: the Making and Unmaking of British India*, 1997

Judd, Denis, *Empire*, 1996

*Keay, John, *A History of India*, 2000

*Khan, Yasmin, *The Great Partition*, 2007

*Low, D.A. (editor), *Congress and the Raj: Facets of the Indian Struggle 1917–47*, 1977

*MacMillan, Margaret, *Women of the Raj*, 1988

Perkins, R., *The Kashmir Gate*, 1983

Reed, S., *The India I Knew*, 1952

Schlote, W., *British Overseas Trade from 1700 to the 1930s*, 1952

Smith, Adam, *The Wealth of Nations*, 1776

Spear, Percival, *A History of India*, 1965

*von Tunzelmann, Alex, *Indian Summer: the Secret History of the end of an Empire*, 2007

Watson, Francis. and Tennyson, Hallam., *Talking of Gandhi*, 1969

*Wolpert, Stanley, *A New History of India*, 1977

*Wolpert, Stanley, *Shameful Flight*, 2006

Memoirs, diaries and contemporary accounts

*Allen, Charles (editor), *Plain Tales from the Raj*, 1975

*Besant, Annie, *India Bond or Free? A World problem*, 1926

*Campbell-Johnson, A., *A Mission with Mountbatten*, 1951

Chaudhuri, Nirad, *The Autobiography of an Unknown Indian*, 1951

*Foss, Michael, *Out of India: a Raj Childhood*, 2007

Gandhi, M.K., *The Collected Works of Mahatma Gandhi*, 1960–94

Gandhi, M.K., 'Hind Swaraj', in R. Iyer (editor) *The Moral and Political Writings of Mahatma Gandhi Volume 1 Civilisation, Politics and Religion*, 1986

*Gandhi, Mahatma, *Essential Writings*, 2008

*Masani, Zareer, *Indian Tales of the Raj*, 1987

*Moon, Penderel (editor), *Wavell: the Viceroy's Journal*, 1973

*Moraes, Frank, *Witness to an Era*, 1973

*Mountbatten, Pamela, *India Remembered*, 2007

Nehra, Arvind, *Letters of a Indian Judge to an English Gentlewoman*, 1934

*Nehru, Jawaharlal, *An Autobiography*, 1942 (first published 1936)

*Nichols, Beverley, *Verdict on India*, 1944

*O'Dwyer, Michael, *India as I Knew it 1885–1925*, 1925

Collections of documents

*Bombay, Government of, *Sources for a History of the Freedom Movement in India*, 1958

*Chopra, P.N., *Quit India Movement: British Secret Documents*, 1986

*Hasan, Mushirul (editor), *India Partitioned: the Other Face of Freedom*, 1995

*Iyer, Raghavan (editor), *The Essential Writings of Mahatma Gandhi*, 1996

*Mansergh, N. and Lumby E.W.R., *The Transfer of Power 1942–47*, 1970

*Pandey, B.N., *The Indian Nationalist Movement 1885–1947*, 1979

*Phillips, C.H. *Select Documents on the Evolution of India and Pakistan, Volume 4*, 1962

Periodicals and newspapers

Jinnah, M.A., *Indian Quarterly Register*, 1929

Government documentation

India, *Statement of Policy of HMG,* cmd publication 6652, 1945

Glossary

Amir An independent ruler, commander or governor, particularly in Muslim countries.

Anglo-Indian Somebody of mixed Indian and British descent.

Anna Indian unit of currency.

Ashram A religious retreat or community gathered around a guru.

Ayah A children's Indian nanny or nurse employed by British families to look after their children while they were living in India.

Bagh A garden.

Babu A clerk; used by the British to describe western educated Indians.

Brahmin The highest Hindu caste, consisting originally of priests, then later including educators, law-makers and scholars preachers.

Bungalow A Hindi word meaning a single storey house.

Charka The spinning wheel became the symbol of the Congress Party. Gandhi believed that daily spinning would bring India's leaders into closer contact with peasant life and enhance the dignity of labour in the minds of India's intellectuals who had never had to do hard physical work.

Chitral A princely state, now part of north-west Pakistan.

Chokidar Watchman or caretaker.

Christian Christians believe in one supreme being: God. They believe that his only son was Jesus, whom God sent to live among men to show them the right way to live. They believe that God had Jesus sacrificed in order to show his love for mankind. They believe that, three days after his crucifixion, Jesus rose from the dead and ascended into heaven. They believe that there will be a day of judgement, after which sins will be forgiven and Christians will attain eternal life.

Commonwealth A loose federation of countries and states that once formed the old British Empire. After the Second World War, it became usual to refer to what had been the 'Empire' as the 'Commonwealth', the thinking being that in this way countries like Canada, which were largely self-governing, would have their status recognised and valued. To refer to them as 'colonies' was outdated and wrong, particularly when they had dominion status.

Dhoti Long, flowing piece of cloth worn by men, which could be hitched up to look like a loincloth.

Dominion status To be self-governing, but within the British Empire

Durbar In Mughal India, *durbars* were open ceremonial gatherings to receive subjects and visitors in audience, conduct official business and confer honours. The British Raj adopted the idea of a *durbar* and held great ceremonial events that they called durbars. Lord Lytton held a *durbar*, for example, when Queen Victoria was proclaimed Empress of India in 1876. The great Delhi *durbars* of 1903 and 1911 were staged to celebrate the coronations of the British kings Edward VII and George V. These were fantastic ceremonial displays, involving hundreds of *maharajahs*, bejewelled elephants, music and dancing.

Dyarchy Government by two independent authorities, in India this system divided power in the provinces between the Indians and the British from 1919 to 1935.

Factor An agent of a company, usually buying and selling on commission for that company.

Fast-unto-death This was a common Middle Eastern way of registering a deep personal protest. An individual would refuse all food until they died. Sometimes a person would refuse water as well and this hastened death. However, most people adopting this dramatic form of protest would accept water because it made the process of dying longer and so have more impact on their cause. Other examples of hunger strikers are the suffragettes and the IRA internees.

The authorities hate this form of protest because they believe it creates martyrs. Usually at a loss as to what to do, they have swung from one extreme to the other, from force feeding though to early release and then to simply ignoring the situation and removing the individual to hospital at the point of organ failure. The main objective has always been to prevent an individual dying in prison.

Federal   A form of government in which states or regions have a measure of self-government while giving certain powers, for example for foreign affairs, to a central government.

Guru   Teacher; religious mentor.

Hartal   A stoppage of work, usually occasioned by a lockout, and used as a protest.

Hajj   Pilgrimage to Makkah made by Muslims; one of the five pillars of Islam.

Hindu   Hindus believe that all existence comes from an eternal spiritual truth, *Brahman*. The purpose of life is to understand this truth and to understand one's eternal identity as the *atma*, or soul. The soul is eternal and lives many lifetimes in one human body or in many forms of life. The cycle of rebirth is called *samsara* and the soul moves upwards and downwards on the wheel of rebirth. When true understanding is reached, the soul will be released from the cycle of rebirth.

Hindu holy books   *Shrutis* are the books of authority. '*Shruti*' literally means 'that which is heard' because these scriptures were passed on by word of mouth. The main set of texts is called the *Vedas* and the parts of the *Vedas* that contain the philosophy of Hinduism are called the *Upanishads*. The *Bhagavad Gita* is a text that, although not part of the *Vedas*, is considered by most Hindus to be a text of authority. *Smritis* are scriptures of lesser authority. They consist of historic stories such as '*Ramayana*' and '*Mahabharata*', mythological stories called '*Puranas*' and law books like the '*Manusmriti*'.

Hookah   An Asian pipe for smoking tobacco or marijuana, consisting of a flexible tube with a mouthpiece attached to a container of water through which smoke is drawn and cooled.

Indian National Congress   Indian National Congress was founded in 1885 as an all-India, secular political party, but quickly became identified with the majority Hindus.

Inoculation programme   This was a systematic and well-organised programme aimed at protecting people from the killer diseases of cholera and smallpox. Those working on the programme inoculated thousands of men, women and children against cholera and vaccinated them against smallpox.

Gandhi regarded vaccination against smallpox as a manifestation of the evil that the British Raj had unleashed on India. Vaccination, he said, was a 'filthy process that is little short of eating beef.' He advised smallpox sufferers that they would be cured if they used enemas, made sure they had plenty of fresh air, wrapped themselves in a wet sheet at night and changed their diet.

Islam   The word 'Islam' means 'submission to God'.

Jat   Peasant farming caste in Hindu society

Jain   Jainism is an ancient branch of Hinduism. Jains reject the idea of a supreme being and advocate a deep respect for all living things. They are, therefore, strict vegetarians. Jains believe that an immortal and indestructible soul lies within every person and that the soul should seek liberation from the cycle of birth and death. Spiritual advancement will be achieved by following the five vows: non-violence, truthfulness, not stealing (including avoiding greed and exploitation), chastity (Jain monks and nuns are greatly respected) and detachment from the pleasures of the world.

Jihad   Struggle (or war) in defence of Islam. This is the definition of Lesser *Jihad*. Greater *Jihad* is the personal struggle for spiritual self-perfection.

Kaddar   Cotton cloth produced in India.

Karma   Karma is the sum total of a person's actions, including their intended actions, which determine the state into which they will be reincarnated.

Khilafat Movement   This movement was set up by Indian Muslims to support the Sultan of Turkey, who was regarded by many Muslims as their Caliph, or spiritual leader.

Kshatriya   Warrior caste in Hindu society.

Maharajah   An Indian prince: the ruler of a native state.

Mahasabha   This Hindu nationalist organisation was founded in 1915 to bring together diverse local Hindu movements in order to counter the Muslim League and the secular Indian National Congress. In the 1920s, it had branches in most parts of India. In 1948, a member of *Mahasabha* murdered Gandhi.

Mahatma   Usually translated as 'the Great Soul', in India this title is bestowed on someone who is deeply revered for wisdom and virtue.

Mansabdar   A person who holds a bureaucratic office in the Mughal Empire.

Maratha   A member of the princely and military classes of the kingdom of Maharashtra.

Masalchee   Kitchen boy.

Monopoly of trade   Only one company or organisation had the right to trade in a certain area or with a specific country or countries. In this case, the only British company allowed to trade in India was the East India Company.

Muslim   Muslims believe that there is one true God, Allah, and that Muhammad is his final prophet. There are five pillars of Islam: a declaration of faith in Allah and Muhammad; to pray (*Salah*) five times a day; to fast (*Sawm*) during Ramadan from dawn to sunset; to pay a welfare tax (*Zakah*) for distribution to the poor; and to make a pilgrimage (*Hajj*) to Makkah at least once in a lifetime.

Muslim League   The All-Indian Muslim League was founded at the annual Muhammadan Educational Conference held in Dhaka in December 1906. About 3000 delegates attended and supported *Nawab* Salim Ullah Khan's proposal that a political party be established to look after the interests of Muslims: the All-Indian Muslim League.

Nawab   A Muslim title; Muslim nobleman

Pakistan   The name Pakistan is an acronym of the names of the states that were to make up the new country: Punjab, Afghan Frontier, Kashmir, Sind and Baluchistan. Put together, the whole word meant 'Land of the Pure'.

Pamirs   A high plateau region in Central Asia, located mainly in modern Tajikstan.

Parsi   Parsis believe in a good and just God – Ahura Mazda – who created the world to be a battleground between himself and the evil spirit, Angra Mainyu, in which evil would be defeated. The role of mankind is to serve the creator and honour his seven creations: sky, water, earth, plant, animal, human and fire. Although Ahura Mazda is wise, he is vulnerable and humans must be his assistants in order to help restore harmony in a world stricken by evil.

Purna swaraj   Total independence.

Qur'an   Islamic scripture as revealed to Muhammad.

Raj   Rule, particularly British rule in India.

Rupee   Indian currency.

Salaam   A greeting accompanied by a low bow.

Salah   Performing ritual prayers in the proper way five times a day; one of the five pillars of Islam.

Satyagraha   A word made up by Gandhi to mean 'life-force' or 'soul-force' and which he and his followers applied to non-cooperation with the British authorities. It is important to note that Gandhi hated the term 'passive resistance' and never wanted it applied to his methods. Passive resistance means just that – resisting authority by doing nothing. So sitting down in the street or tying yourself to railings would probably, depending on the context, be classed as passive resistance. But removing your children from school and refusing to attend government parties would be an active way of resisting the Raj – by non-violent non-cooperation.

Satyagrahi   A person who follows Gandhi's teachings with regard to *satyagraha*.

Sawm   Fasting during the month of Ramadan; one of the five pillars of Islam.

Self-determination   The right of nations to determine their own future.

Sepoy   A soldier in the Indian army.

Shahadah   Reciting the Muslim profession of faith; one of the five pillars of Islam.

Shudra   Labouring and cultivating caste in Hindu society.

Sikh   Learner or disciple of the Guru. Sikhs believe that there is only one God, before whom everyone is equal and to whom everyone has direct access. Sikhs believe that human beings spend their time in a cycle of birth, life and rebirth, and the quality of each life depends on the law of karma and so is determined by behaviour in the previous life. Escape from the cycle is achieved by total knowledge of, and union with, God.

Swaraj   Self-rule.

Vaishya   Trading caste in Hindu society.

Verandah   A Hindi word referring to a porch, usually roofed, that runs along the outside wall of a building.

Viceroy   Literally, the deputy for the monarch; the title of the man who headed up the government in India.

Writer   A clerk, usually engaged in writing up invoices, checking payments, ordering goods and, in the days before photocopiers, a lot of copying out where duplicates were needed of anything.

Zakah   Giving alms to the poor and needy; one of the five pillars of Islam.

Index